The Way Home is a gripping account of the sojourn of one tired South African; tired of the savagery of grand and petty apartheid; and defiant of the degrading assaults on his humanity and psyche. Morley Nkosi's account of his exile life takes us on a meticulously detailed, painful, but ultimately triumphant journey from George Goch, trekking through several Southern, Eastern and Northern African countries; then onward to the UK, ending in the USA. After studying and working in the USA, he finally returns home personally transformed in both perceptible and imperceptible ways. While in exile, his country of birth had similarly been thrust into a metaphorical headspin.

It is a lonely and rough journey full of tribulations but equally infused with lessons about possibilities that could not have been imagined under the stifling conditions of apartheid South Africa. It is a story that captures, to varying degrees, the precariousness of exile life. Though unsettling, it is an experience that is full of affirmations. *The Way Home* adds a vital part of the literature on the lived experiences of formerly exiled South Africans; yet immensely valuable to those who waged the struggle on the home front as well. It is a must read for the old, young and, hopefully, those yet to be born.

- Dr Mokubung Nkomo
author of *Student Culture and Activism in
Black South African Universities: The Roots of Resistence*
(Praeger, 1984)

Also By Morley Nkosi

Black Workers, White Supervisors: The Origins of the Labor Structure in South Africa. (Trenton, New Jersey. Africa World Press. 2017)

The Way Home

Memories of a South African in Exile

Morley Z. Nkosi

UJ Press

The Way Home: Memories of a South African in Exile

Published by UJ Press
University of Johannesburg
Library
Auckland Park Kingsway Campus
PO Box 524
Auckland Park
2006
https://ujpress.uj.ac.za/

Compilation © Morley Z. Nkosi 2024
Chapters © Author(s) 2024
Published Edition © Morley Z. Nkosi 2024

First published 2024

https://doi.org/10.36615/9781776489732
978-1-7764897-2-5 (Paperback)
978-1-7764897-3-2 (PDF)
978-1-7764897-4-9 (EPUB)
978-1-7764897-5-6 (XML)

This publication had been submitted to a rigorous double-blind peer-review process prior to publication and all recommendations by the reviewers were considered and implemented before publication.

Language Editor: David Oldert
Cover design: Hester Roets, UJ Graphic Design Studio & Thenjiwe Niki Nkosi
Typeset in 9.5/13pt Merriweather Light

Contents

A Note on Sources i

Preface: Southampton, 1962 iii

Part One: South Africa 1

1   Dwelling of Honour 3

2   Ferreirasdorp 9

3   The School on Albert Street 15

4   Industriousness 25

5   George Goch 29

6   Emmarentia Hoërskool 37

7   Kilnerton 45

8   Religion 53

9   A Brush with the Pass Laws 61

10   The World of Work 69

11   Frederick Sage 81

12   Loss 91

13   The Pan Africanist Congress 101

14   Sharpeville 109

15   Hiding and Flight 119

Part Two: Stateless **135**

1 Across the African Continent 137
2 Another Continent 161

Part Three: America **179**

1   Arrival In New York 181
2   Lincoln University 185
3   Columbia University 199
4   Summer Visits to London 211
5   New York University 217
6   A Meeting and a Departure 235
7   Louis Berger 243
8   The Zulu and the Greek 249
9   Maine 259
10 Death and Birth 265
11 The New School for Social Research 271
12 Hoboken 277
13 A Changing Family 287
14 Hofstra 291
15 Manley 297
16 USA For Africa 303
17 Zimbabwe 313
18 The Way Home 319

Postscript 329
Acknowledgements 335

A Note on Sources

On Friday the 9th of September 1960 at the age of twenty-five, I escaped from South Africa, the country of my birth and my forbears for as many generations back as anyone knew. As part of the leadership of the Pan Africanist Congress (PAC), I had helped plan the campaign against the Pass Laws earlier that year, a campaign that had resulted in the Sharpeville massacre on the 21st of March. I'd spent the five months since that tragic day in hiding, in fear for my life, all the while continuing to organise the resistance. Once I crossed the border, I did not return to the country for thirty years.

This book is a record of the years of my exile, most of which were spent in the United States. It is also the story of my life until that forced departure. It chronicles the trials, joys, and hopes of a young man born and raised in colonial and apartheid South Africa. In these pages I look back at my upbringing, schooling, employment, and exposure to the Pan Africanist ideology that led to my political awakening and, ultimately, to my activism and exile. I hope hereby to contribute to the literature of apartheid-era exile, a literature I feel is thinner, in certain respects, than it ought to be, considering the complexity of the exile experience and the role those of us outside the country played in defeating the apartheid regime and the forces that supported and promoted it.

Looking back over more than eight decades is a challenging and risky task. During the earlier part of my life, that is, until I turned twenty-five, neither my parents nor I kept any written records chronicling our family history. Our family relied on oral historical narratives told by elders for tracing its genealogy and movements from one place to another. After escaping from South Africa, I was initially on the run to somewhere I would be safe from arrest. Where exactly this would be, I did not know. For years I was a stateless person, which was a difficult, humbling, instructive experience. All I owned were the clothes on my back and notebooks I kept safely stowed away in my pockets.

The Way Home

I had started keeping a diary in 1960 just before leaving the country. Subsequently, I began keeping notebooks for names and addresses I accumulated on my travels. When one is constantly on the move, crossing from one country to another, names and addresses add up and take on new meaning and value. These notebooks, when I returned to them, were skimpier than I remembered but useful in jogging my memory as I started to write this story. Even when I eventually settled in London, where I lived for just over a year, and then in New York City and Hoboken, New Jersey, where I spent over two decades, what papers I possessed were always complemented by notebooks containing addresses, phone numbers, reminders of errands I had to run, or events I was to attend or participate in. Consequently, a large portion of the story that follows is based on notebooks. Aside from that, I have also used articles and documents I saved, letters I received, scraps of paper that endured, as well as what I could recall from memory. To ensure that my memory was not in error, wherever necessary and possible I searched the internet for the people that I met in the countries where I sought refuge. Some of these were readily traceable online. This sometimes helped as a way of corroborating what I recalled. Many of my contemporaries, though, particularly those in South Africa, have passed away, most without leaving any testimonies behind. With those in the United States, I fared only a little better.

The loss of these people and their stories, both on the continent and in the United States, is tragic and has been an added motivation for me in the labour of writing this account. I am certain, too, that these people would have been able to add more detail to, or check the reliability of, some of my recollections. But as things now stand, as before in my life, I am mostly on my own. Any mistakes, therefore, though never intentional, are entirely my own.

Preface

Southampton, 1962

I arrived at the Port of Southampton on a mid-summer morning in the second week of August, 1962. This was my second time passing through the port. The first had been in January of the previous year, when I arrived in the UK from Egypt. That had been a cold, damp evening, though, and the escort sent to meet me, Jacob Maleka, a fellow Pan Africanist Congress cadre, had hurriedly dragged me from the port to the railway station and onto a train bound for London before I could see anything. This time I was alone and unhurried, it was warm, and I had the opportunity to look around. Everywhere were ships and boats, large and small, and a multitude of yachts, ferries, barges. Most of these vessels were moored and floating tranquilly while others, particularly the barges, rocked to and fro. The port was teeming with passengers and stevedores and other dock workers. It had several terminals and dry docks and vehicles, forklifts and trucks, cargo of all shapes and sizes, and warehouses lined up alongside the port terminals. To a curious twenty-seven-year-old, as I was, this was a wonderful sight, if all a little overwhelming.

One place that was relatively calm was the area where departing passengers assembled, and eventually I made my way over to join the people milling about there. There was only a small crowd of us waiting to board the ship, which we were told had sailed from Le Havre, a large commercial port in France. While we waited, I cast my eye at the others. Among them were many other young people. They seemed pleasantly tired, laughing and speaking amongst themselves. Later I learned that the ship was bringing back a lot of American students who had come to Europe for the summer.

It was not long before a port official came and led us to a waiting barge. He told us it would take us to our ship, a large ocean liner we could now see anchored in the dark water some distance from the dock. Apparently, this ship was not scheduled to dock at one of the terminals because its cargo and most of its passengers had been picked up in France, and Southampton was just a stop-over to collect the few remaining passengers going to the United States. That is where I was headed. Earlier that summer, the English summer of 1962 (I had been living for a year in Notting Hill), I had received a letter from an office in the US Department of State to say I had been granted a scholarship to study in Pennsylvania, and that my travel documents and schedule would soon follow in the mail. This was excellent news. After looking at the respective university programmes in the United States and Britain, I decided that the former would offer a more engaged and hands-on education. In due course, as promised, the documents arrived, and soon enough the day came for me to say farewell to those with whom I had stayed over the past year. Of these I was most sad to leave Martin Ennals, a key founding member of the anti-apartheid movement in England, who had become a dear friend. Martin was a friend of my colleague, Nana Mahomo, the PAC representative in the United Kingdom. Nana was out of the country then, and I asked Martin to inform him that I had left for the United States to further my education. It was Martin, wearing his usual tweed jacket and grey pants, who had accompanied me earlier that day to Charing Cross station, where I had boarded the train bound for Southampton.

The barge pulled up alongside the ship, its gangway lowered so we could climb up, one behind the other. It was then, while waiting my turn, that I noticed that everyone except me was carrying at least one large suitcase. Some were struggling with several large cases. I had only a small briefcase, which contained two items. One was an envelope with documents that I was told I had to present on landing at the Port of New York and New Jersey. This document was titled 'Special African Program No. P.I. 3016, Naturalization Service No. 11/22/55, File No. 314.6.300 E'. The other was a small bag containing a change of underwear, pyjamas, a toothbrush and toothpaste, and a comb. I decided to let everyone who was carrying luggage proceed up the stairway ahead of me. I noticed some passengers on the ship's top deck leaning over the railing and regarding me curiously. It later dawned on me that the reason they were puzzled was that I had no luggage for a journey across the Atlantic Ocean, which would take between a week and ten days. I did not even know it would take so long. Besides, even if I had known, I had no money to buy extra clothes or the luggage to hold them.

Fortunately, I had a cabin to myself on the deck below the upper deck. This was convenient not only because it allowed me to sleep peacefully but also because I could comfortably wash my underwear and shirt, hang these to dry overnight, and iron the shirt the next morning. My jacket, which I had bought in London, was charcoal grey in colour and so remained clean in appearance. The days on the ship had a repetitive but interesting routine. In between the meals – the breakfasts, lunches, and dinners that came round like clockwork – there were orientation sessions that had been organised by an office of the US Department of State. These sessions were for the African students who were, as I was, on their way to universities in the US for the first time. The sessions, which were held in a large room below deck, were led by African students who were already studying in the US. The organisers clearly thought it would be more effective to have other Africans advise the newcomers on what to expect and how to behave. These sessions were invariably followed by political discussions, which led to some testy debates focused on the different African countries where the participants came from. There were students from West and East Africa (I remember those who came from Guinea and Nigeria) and myself, from South Africa. Of great interest to me, I still recall, was the discussion on Guinea. There were two Guineans among us, and they told us in their own words how the French settlers had wrought havoc as they were leaving Guinea. Four years earlier, in 1958, the French government had collapsed, in large part because of its failures in dealing with its colonies, particularly Indochina and Algeria. The new government, the so-called Fifth Republic led by Charles de Gaulle, now gave France's colonies two choices: more autonomy in a new French Community led by France, or immediate independence. Of all the colonies, only Guinea chose independence. These students were now going to study in the US with the intention of returning to their country to help secure its independence. That I would not be able to return to my own country – or family – for the foreseeable future was a fact I did not allow myself to dwell on. I was moved by their story and curious about why they had travelled from Guinea to France before making their way to the United States. I did not ask them about this, though, because I was myself quite cagey about my travels from South Africa to Britain. Since I'd been involved in resistance politics, from my early days of organising and working underground in South Africa, I had realised that the way to survive was for people to know very little about me. This habit had only become more ingrained since I had gone into exile. So I evaded their questions and tried, through my silence, to subdue their interest in South Africa.

A few days into the voyage, I noticed a group of four white men, fellow passengers, regarding me with a little too much curiosity for my liking. I had noticed them watching me as I climbed the gangway. One afternoon while I was standing alone on deck, they approached me as a group and said they were curious to know where I was from. Their names, which for reasons that will become clear I still remember, were George, Norman, Hank, and Giuliano. At first, I felt slightly uncomfortable. I couldn't understand why they were so nosey, and I did not yet have a reason to trust them. They were persistent, though, and in time I decided they had no ill-intent; and once we started talking, I warmed up to these characters. George was a shortish guy with a nice round face and brown hair, older than the other three, and looked very respectable in his good sports jacket. Hank, on the other hand, was a scruffy, fidgety fellow, and you could tell he was radical because of the questions he asked. He was very inquisitive, a bit of a restless soul. He was also very useful in interpreting my English into Italian for Giuliano, a thin, soft-spoken young Italian. Norman was on the thinner side and the most curious of the four.

I told them I had been politically active in the movement that had resulted in the Sharpeville march and massacre. They knew about Sharpeville. I also spoke of my journeys as a refugee through several countries on the African continent. I had made my way through the Protectorate of Bechuanaland, Southern Rhodesia, the Protectorate of Nyasaland, Tanganyika (now Botswana, Zimbabwe, Malawi, and Tanzania respectively) as well as Kenya, Egypt, and, most recently, England. They listened attentively, interrupting only occasionally to ask well-informed questions. What I did not tell them, however – what I still could not speak about – was how in those months I had become conscious of what it was like to be destitute, to rely on the generosity of people I did not know, and, on several occasions, even to have to beg. It would be a long time before I could speak comfortably of those difficult, profoundly formative experiences. Their company did help me avoid going to the orientation sessions, which I'd started to find monotonous, and our discussions served a similar purpose. By asking them questions in turn, I got to know a little about the United States – and from people who turned out to be enlightened, progressive, and sympathetic to my political ideology and activities. Our conversations were quite deliberate and slow because Hank had to translate for Giuliano.

When I wasn't in the orientation sessions, ironing my shirt, or talking to George and the others, I stood at the railing and looked out over the water, thinking about where I was going and how it might be once I got there. I had only very sketchy notions of what America meant, based mainly on the music that we used to listen to in George Goch and the American magazines, such as *Ebony*, that we used to read. Over the past two years since I had left South Africa, I had quietly given up hope of ever going back home or of hearing from anybody again. My curiosity now was on what was going to happen the next day, which is something that developed during the years when I was in exile, because I never knew what each day would bring.

We had been at sea for a little over a week when word began to circulate that we would soon be within sight of land. I still recall standing excitedly, with many others, at the ship's railing, eager to catch my first glimpse of America. So many years have passed since that day, but I can still recall the first blurry outlines of the continent, coming closer all the time. The ship entered the mouth of the New York and New Jersey Bay and passed the Statue of Liberty. I remember gazing at it in wonder, even though I did not yet understand its significance. I can recall, too, being fascinated when I noticed the skeletal structures that were emerging from either side of the mouth of the Hudson River: these were the beginnings of what would become the Verrazano-Narrows Bridge. Then in front of me was the skyline, the famous skyline of a city of which I had seen pictures in magazines, but which, I realised in those moments, I knew nothing about.

Part One

South Africa

1

Dwelling of Honour

We come from a lineage of Africans who were enslaved, dispossessed of their lands, subjugated, corralled, and confined into labour-sourcing areas called 'locations'. This way, we were driven out of towns and cities, which were to be the preserve of whites. Our movements into and out of towns, cities, mines, and farms to provide labour were controlled by the state through the police. A pivotal instrument used for monitoring these daily movements was the pass system, by which black people coming into white areas had to carry documents, or passes, giving them permission to be in a particular white area for a given time. But more on that later. It was in one of these locations, Ethwathwa, an African township in Benoni[1] in the East Rand of the Witwatersrand (an Afrikaans word for 'White Waters Ridge'), that I was born, on the 3rd of May, 1935.

Baptised into the Dutch Reform Church in Ethwathwa, I was given the names Zebulon Phila Nkosi. The first name, Zebulon, came from the Old Testament. I grew up thinking that it meant 'the land of milk and honey', but in fact it is Hebrew for 'dwelling of honour'. Phila means 'to live' in Zulu. It seems my parents named me Phila because, before I was born, they lost a child who died in infancy. My parents hoped and prayed that I would live. Before these names took root, however, my elder brother Stanley saw the name Morley in the window of an Indian general dealer store in the neighbourhood and chose to call me by that name. I

---

1 Benoni goes back to 1881, when the then surveyor-general of the Transvaal Province, Johannes Rissik, named it after the Hebrew name that Rachel in the book of Genesis gave to her son after a difficult birth; it means 'Son of My Sorrow'. To Johann Rissik, the birth of Benoni was difficult because it consisted of unclaimed state land, called 'uitvalgrond', which was land that fell outside those areas already claimed by mining prospectors. This was Johannes Rissik's sorrow. It was not until 1887 that Benoni was found to be a gold-bearing area. It soon attracted all sorts of people from Europe, America, Australia, local whites, Africans, Indians, and Coloureds.

have no idea how my parents reacted to this renaming, but the name stuck and relegated the Biblical one to my middle name, while the Zulu one was eclipsed entirely. Later, when I began to question why I had an English name, I tried to salvage 'Phila'. I failed; somehow, it was too late. Later still, when I began to show an interest in the struggle for liberation, my father would occasionally call me Godide. At the time I had no idea who Godide was or what the name's significance was. I later found out that this was the name of Chief Godide kaNdlela Ntuli, who commanded one of the Zulu detachments that fought the British army in the Anglo-Zulu War of 1879.

My father, David Moses Nkosi, was an evangelist of the Dutch Reformed Church. He was born in 1892 on a farm owned by an Afrikaner family in eNgotshe, an area next to the town of Louwsberg in KwaZulu-Natal. Growing up on this farm in his teens, he had two options: one was to join the other black farm labourers; the other was to go for training as an evangelist in Stofberg in the Orange Free State. The Stofberg Seminary was the pre-eminent centre of theological instruction for the Mission Church, established and run by Afrikaner theologians of the Sending Kerk, the missionary part of the mother Nederduitse Gereformeerde Kerk (NGK). He chose to train as an evangelist and was ordained at Stofberg. The language spoken at this institution was Afrikaans, and he developed proficiency in Afrikaans. He was committed, dedicated, and passionate about his vocation and took very seriously the responsibilities that went with it. He was effective, too, and earned a lot of respect among his peers, the communities in which he served, and even from his white superiors. He was tall, of solid frame, walked straight, always sat upright, and had an impressive demeanour and presence. My father sported a thick and bushy but well-trimmed moustache which earned him the nickname 'Madevu' in IsiZulu and translates as 'Beard'. This nickname was used respectfully and quietly by adults only within the immediate and extended families.

One thing about him that puzzled me for years was that in a corner of his wardrobe – where he hung his three-piece black and grey suits and black attire, including the long tailcoats and matching pants worn by the clergy for church and other religious services – behind all these clothes, there was a collection of formidable knobkerries,[2] other thick fighting sticks, as well as a spear. It was a collection of weapons – the only thing missing was a shield – that belonged to a Zulu warrior. With his physical build, he would have been one, but he was now a man of peace who kept his weapons out of sight. When he converted to Christianity, my father had literally concealed parts of his Zulu upbringing, culture, and traditions, from which his family had been weaned. We were all baptised and inducted into the Christian faith. Unfortunately, it never occurred to me to ask him about his past. And as things turned out, I never got a chance.

One incident, though, which sheds some light on his hidden Zulu culture and traditions, occurred when I was in my early twenties taking my first steps in political resistance. I had organised a small meeting of what became the George Goch branch of the Africanists. I asked for my father's permission to hold a meeting in the old church building (a new church building had been built next to this one). A few people had been invited to meet with the leadership of the Africanists. He gave his consent on condition that there was no smoking in the church and that no one was to put his feet on the pews. I promised that neither would happen. I also informed him that the visitors had come to assist me and my close friend, Shadrack Mabuza, form a local branch of the Africanists. Five leading members of this group came. They were led by Robert Sobukwe, Potlako Leballo, and Selby Ngendane – three men who would soon form the key leadership of the Pan Africanist Congress. Several residents of the township came to listen to what they had to say.

After the meeting was over and everyone had left, my father wanted to know whether my elder brother was part of this group. I said he was not but asked, rather curious, why he had posed that question. He told me that in Zulu custom no two sons from one family were drafted into a single fighting unit; this was a precaution in case that unit was wiped out. Looking back, this conversation helps me to understand the conundrum of why this Zulu warrior's gear was tucked away in his wardrobe. Although

---

2 Clubs with solid rounded knobs on one end.

he was a clergyman in a European tradition, his connection to our ancestral philosophies and customs still ran deep. It also seems he had a premonition that I was getting involved in some kind of dangerous activity. And this is why he quietly nicknamed me Godide. He hoped or wished (and sometimes probably feared) that I would be like Godide, the warrior.

My mother was born Julia Buthelezi, also, like my father, in KwaZulu-Natal, in a town called Bergville on the 24th of December 1893. She came to Johannesburg to look for work. Her older brother, Johannes, was already in Johannesburg, working at the Turffontein Race Horse Club, where he was employed as a waiter and bartender for the exclusively white club members. When she got there, her brother found her a job as a washer woman, doing laundry for some of the members. In trying to reconstruct how she and my father met, I gathered that my father was introduced to my mother by Johannes during his usual evangelical rounds and visits to some of his congregants in the area. The racecourse was where people, including Africans, went to bet on horses and watch them race. In my father's book, and perhaps in the Bible as well, gamblers were lost souls who had to be saved. It appears that this is where my parents met. They got married and raised a family of four girls (two of whom were twins) and two boys. I was the last born and am now the only survivor.

My mother was both a homemaker and my father's partner in sharing the family's and parish's tasks and responsibilities. She was a very loving and generous person. This showed in how she treated her immediate and extended family members and the members of the church. She provided my father with insights and advice on family and church issues – discreetly, without us even noticing. She was a diligent, hard worker and in charge of how her home looked and functioned. As the leader of the women's church guild, she was effective because she was attentive to her colleagues' concerns and contributions and always consulted others before arriving at what would be a collective decision. This way of working with other people earned her their respect, friendship, and solidarity. Amongst her other impressive attributes, she had an infectious sense of humour. No matter how tough things got, she would invariably see a funny or amusing aspect to the situation. She also told some stories she remembered from growing up in rural Bergville in KwaZulu-Natal. Some of them, told at night after dinner and before the nightly prayer before bed, were quite scary.

Sundays in our house were very busy. Catechism classes started at ten in the morning. The regular morning church service began at eleven and went on until noon. One reason that the morning service started at eleven was to allow domestic workers who were employed in white suburbs time to travel to church. Between noon and three o'clock in the afternoon, some congregants went home for lunch; others visited families and friends. The main church service began at three and ended at four in the afternoon. Most of these church services were conducted by my father and sometimes by visiting clergy from within the district. Visiting clergy usually conducted afternoon services, and these were well attended. The women's guild met shortly thereafter until five or five-thirty. This was to allow the members who were domestic workers time to return to their backrooms on the premises of their white employers. This women's group met under the leadership of my mother. It also met on Thursdays in the early afternoons when most of its members had a day off from their jobs as domestic servants in the surrounding white suburbs. They would come to these meetings dressed in their church uniform, which consisted of a long black skirt and loose black jacket with long sleeves, a broad white collar, and a black hat.

The afternoon women's guild meetings on Sunday afternoons meant my mother would leave me in charge of completing the preparations for our Sunday family dinners. This was a test to see how much I had learned from her about preparing food and cooking it on the old coal stove, which could become red hot if it was over-stoked. I had to mind how much coal I fed into the stove and keep a careful eye on the pots, removing each one to the side once it was ready. My mother taught me how to cook, just as she taught me how to wash and iron the shirts and other clothes she took in from the white families who paid her to do their laundry. Generally speaking, all the household work I know I learned working alongside my mother. And it was a pleasant and instructive experience, even when I inadvertently overcooked or burned something. When that did happen – and it was not an unusual occurrence, especially when I was a very young boy – she would invariably dismiss the accident with a joke and a smile. How I wish I had spent more time with her.

2

Ferreirasdorp

Ferreirastown in the east of Johannesburg was named after Colonel Ignatius Phillip Ferreira, a Boer soldier and failed diamond digger born in Grahamstown (now Makhanda) in the 1840s. He left the Kimberley diamond diggings and went to Pilgrim's Rest in the Transvaal Province during the early days of the gold rush. From there he moved to Johannesburg where he established what was called Ferreira's Camp. This camp attracted other diggers to the site. He then formed the Ferreira Company Syndicate and the Ferreira Gold Mining Company, which began digging for gold in 1886. In Kevin Ritchie's article, 'Ferreirasdorp in the frontline of the firsts', Ritchie writes that Ferreirasdorp boasted the first proper building in the city, the Central Hotel, the first barber shop, the first circus, the first café, and the first school. But as Johannesburg developed and expanded Ferreirasdorp changed, and by the time my family moved there from Ethwathwa in 1930, when I was five years old, it was a poor, run-down neighbourhood.

The reason we moved was that my father's white superiors had recommended him for the position of leader of the Mission Church in Johannesburg, and he accepted the assignment. My father often reminded us that the premises on which both the church and our home stood – No. 1 Bezuidenhout Street – was a closed gold mine: the Ferreira gold mine. There were remnants of its headgear on the property. It turned out that the tunnels of this mine extended to Simmonds Street, where the old head offices of Standard Bank now stand. In the 1980s, when the foundations of the bank were being erected, the engineers intersected the underground tunnels of the defunct mine.

Our home stood in a cul-de-sac. There were two DRC Mission Churches on the same property. One was old and made entirely of corrugated iron, including its roof; the other was new and built with greyish bricks and a better-looking corrugated roof.

These two structures were separated by a wide walkway which led to the outdoor bucket toilets for men and women. On one side and to the right of the toilets was the entrance to the back of our home; our home was at the rear of the old church and attached to it. The old church was used for social functions like fund-raising concerts and other gatherings of church members. It also served as a dormitory for my parents' relatives who came from faraway places in KwaZulu-Natal and often needed a place to stay while visiting or looking for work in Johannesburg.

The new church was used for church services, communions, baptisms, funeral services, marriages, Sunday school and catechism classes, young adult groups, and meetings of the women's guild. Inside, it had a long aisle which stretched from the entrance up to a raised stage where the pulpit stood. On both sides of the aisle were rows of long, varnished wooden pews. On the left side (if one faced the altar) sat women, while on the right side sat men. Next to the pulpit were three short pews reserved for the deacons and my father who sat up front. On the other side of the pulpit were three other short pews reserved for the church choir, which essentially consisted of my four sisters, my elder brother, and a cousin of ours. In between these two sections but positioned a little ahead of both was the pulpit. Only my father and ordained, visiting clergy could use it. The protocols governing who could use the pulpit, conduct baptisms and communion services, and officiate at marriages, confirmations, and funerals, were strictly observed.

My father, for instance, who was an evangelist, could not conduct baptisms and communion services or officiate at marriages and confirmations. These roles were the responsibilities of his white superior, the dominee, who was in charge of the district in which the Mission Church was located. When this white dominee performed any of these functions, he spoke in Afrikaans and my father would translate into either Sesotho or IsiZulu, and often had one of his deacons help translate into another language. Services requiring this much translation ran for much longer. My father was permitted to use the pulpit and conduct funerals because white clergy did not want to be seen leading a black burial service. The foregoing example of what my father could and could not do is indicative of how the NGK dictated and sternly enforced rules and protocols similar to those decreed by the Council of the Reformed Church and given to Jan van Riebeeck by the Dutch East India Company (DEIC).

The building next to the two churches as you walked down Bezuidenhout Street, long before reaching its intersection with Marshall Street, was a single-storey, rectangular-shaped compound. It had small rooms like flats with most of their fronts facing a large open courtyard except for a few that faced the street (though their backs also faced the open courtyard). This courtyard was a common area, a kind of backyard for the flats which had water taps, garbage bins, and toilets located in the middle of it. This compound was the biggest shebeen in Johannesburg. It sold illicit liquor to Africans, Indians, and Coloureds and was the most notorious part of what was called 'Malay Camp'. The camp got its name from people of Malay origin who came from the Cape to Johannesburg looking for work when their jobs as transport drivers were made redundant by the introduction of the railway from the Cape to the Kimberley diamond mines and later to the Witwatersrand gold mines. These new arrivals from the Cape tended to gravitate towards the same neighbourhood, and hence the area was soon called 'Malay Camp'. Johannesburg grew and developed quite rapidly, but by the time my family moved there, this corner of Ferreirasdorp had become a slum. Malay Camp was run down, and its residents were predominantly Coloured and very poor.

The shebeen next to the church grounds was a very lively part of Ferreirasdorp. It was extremely busy during weekends and public holidays. Coloureds, Indians, Chinese, and Africans who lived in pockets of the neighbourhood around Malay Camp patronised this shebeen. Other patrons came from places like Vrededorp, Fordsburg, Pageview, Sophiatown, Newclare, and the Western Native Township. Saturdays, Sundays, Christmas, New Year's festivities and other major holidays were extraordinarily busy and noisy. These days tended to witness excessive spending on liquor of every kind and heavy drinking. Just about any kind of liquor was available, from highly priced bottled brands of liquor to cheaper ones in barrels to home-brewed concoctions.

Often some barrels of the home-brewed stock would find their way onto the church grounds where they would be hidden during police raids. The shebeen owners would sneak onto the church grounds without anyone noticing and hide their supplies just at the entrance of the brick church. They correctly guessed that Afrikaner policemen would not search for liquor on their venerated church's grounds. What was really surprising – and frustrating – was that my father and I, on discovering this stock, would keep a close watch, hoping to see who would collect it so that we could warn them that we would report them to the police. However, we never had the chance because, almost at the blink of an eye, the stuff would be gone! We gave up trying to catch the crooks. I now think I know how they eluded us. The veranda in front of the church's main entrance had two openings. One was closer to the main gate leading into the church, which we were watching. The other opening was on the opposite side, away from the gate and our view. They most likely used this opening to take their stock, even if it meant jumping over the fence and taking a longer route back to the shebeen.

At the corner of Marshall and Bezuidenhout Streets was a massive building complex that housed the Magistrates Courts. It was opened in 1941. It occupied a big block circumscribed by Marshall, West, Fox, and Bezuidenhout Streets. There is a book titled *From Jo'burg to Jozi* (2002) by Heidi Holland and Adam Roberts, which is a compilation of short pieces written by around 80 journalists and writers. In one piece, 'Malay Camp and the Drill Hall', Doc Bikitsha writes: 'Malay Camp fed and quenched thousands of people from the [nearby Magistrates] courts. Lawyers, cops, pimps, touts and thugs cracked bottles and broke bread together.' There were no class distinctions. What made this popular, big shebeen even more hectic was its proximity to the biggest police station in Johannesburg, called Marshall Square, which still occupies an entire city block.

Marshall Square was only three long street blocks up Marshall Street from the corner of Bezuidenhout Street, and the frequency with which the flying squad (police vans and cars) from Marshall Square descended on the Malay Camp shebeen was almost predictable. A large number of Africans, Indians, and

Coloureds were arrested and taken to Marshall Square where they were charged, fined, or locked up. Those who were arrested had to appear in the Magistrate Courts for a variety of liquor-related offences and/or violations of the pass laws. The shebeen owners, police, and the magistrates unwittingly kept each other very busy. Whatever fines were paid at the police station and sentences handed down by the courts, the shebeen kept feeding the system. Marshall Square and the Magistrate Courts were to a large extent staffed by Afrikaners who seemed to relish chasing, arresting, and sentencing black people for all sorts of petty infringements of the many laws designed to control them. The black policeman were subordinates and sidekicks who took instructions and commands from their white supervisors.

As a child growing up next to this shebeen, what I enjoyed most was watching the raids the police conducted on the shebeen. At this stage, I had not yet begun going to the bioscope (the cinema), but the flying squads would come tearing down Marshall Street and turn left into Bezuidenhout Street with white policemen jumping out of the moving vehicles, blowing their whistles, and swinging their batons high, ready to trounce anyone in their way. The flying squads would give me the same frightening thrill I would later know in the cinema. What would follow was a loud clatter of liquor bottles, cans, and drums of home-brewed liquor as the shebeen owners scrambled to hide their stock and figure out how to help their drunken customers avoid being arrested. It was mayhem and a comical spectacle to watch from outside the compound.

This drama was played out both in front of the compound and inside its courtyard. Most of it took place in the courtyard, but a good part often spilled out onto Bezuidenhout Street through the shebeen's only entrance and exit. The only other way to escape arrest was over a tall wall which separated the courtyard from the back side of our home, though no drunken patron ever scaled that wall or came tumbling into our backyard during the years we lived in Malay Camp. The proximity of the Malay Camp shebeen to the Marshall Square police station and the Magistrates Courts was toxic and ironic. Those who sold the alcohol were usually not arrested, but their customers were. One thus wondered to what extent the courts successfully intervened, mediated, or dispensed with justice in the contest between the vendors of illicit liquor, their daring clients, and the very enthusiastic police. It seemed to be an endless contest; no party could win.

Why the church was located in the city of Johannesburg was initially not a question that entered my mind. In Ethwathwa, the congregants came both from the African township and the outlying white suburbs. Those who came from the white suburbs were employed as domestic workers, nannies, gardeners, municipal and railway workers, and in a variety of other menial jobs. But in the case of Malay Camp, which was part of Johannesburg and much bigger than Benoni, the congregant population was much larger and more diverse. A new constituency had appeared here – the migrant mineworkers who came from other British colonies in the region, then called British Central and Southern Africa. They were drawn to join the church by my father and his colleagues who spread the gospel among blacks, not only in white suburbs but also in the mine compounds and hostels where migrant labourers lived. The mine owners encouraged the church to spread the Christian faith among its recruits. When these recruits started coming to church, they had to attend catechism classes first before they could be baptised and admitted as full members of the church. What surprised me most was watching grown men being baptised. Later, I learned that baptism was required no matter your age, if you wanted to be admitted as a full member. But until then I had only seen it performed on babies.

3

The School on Albert Street

The nearest school was the Albert Street Methodist Church Primary School. My brother Stanley, my sister Gladys (whom we called Nana), and our cousin Benina Alfred Kubheka were already attending this school, and now that I was six it was time for me to join them. The school was located east of Malay Camp. To get there, you had to walk a short distance down Bezuidenhout Street, turn right into Marshall Street, and then walk all the way down until you got to Kruis Street. You then turned right onto Kruis Street and walked until you got to Albert Street, just past the big Fire Station No. 1 on the right. Then turn left at Albert Street and just across from you would be the Albert Street Methodist Church. As you entered the gate of the parish, the church was on the left, and on the right was the house of the resident minister. (The directions that I have just recounted I learned on my first day at school out of sheer necessity.) Between these two buildings but straight ahead was a three-storey building. This was and still is the Albert Street Methodist Church Primary School. It was originally built in the city area designated for whites. However, as whites moved out and into the new suburbs, the school was turned over to the education of the workers' and labourers' children, who had to be converted into Christians and 'civilised'.

Nana walked me to school on my first day. Our mother told her to look after me and come back with me after school. This was a kindergarten class, I believe, and it started quite well, with most of the kids playing under the watchful eye of a lady called 'Mistress'. Lunch break came and went, and the first school day was short because we had nothing to play, write, or scribble with. Our class was let out quite early and most of the kids started to go home with people who had come to fetch them. I waited for a while and started to look for Sis Nana. She was nowhere to be found in the school building, and I got a little anxious because I wanted to go home. I then decided that I might just go home alone if I could retrace the route we had taken in the morning. I walked towards Kruis Street, turned right onto it, and walked up to the intersection with Marshall Street. I turned left onto Marshall Street and kept going slowly, trying to recognise the tall buildings I had seen in the morning. When I got to the Marshall Square Police Station, I knew that I could get home.

My mother was horrified to see me walk in alone. When asked about where my sister was, I said I didn't know and had looked for her everywhere at school. Nana arrived home quite late because she had been looking for me all afternoon. She was relieved when she saw me, but she could have strangled me out of anxiety and worry. What had happened was that she and the other older pupils who sang in the school's senior choir had gone to practise at the Bantu Men's Social Centre (BMSC), which was at the top end of Eloff Street, quite a distance from the school. When the choir returned before classes were officially over, they found that those of us in the lower classes had been let out early, and I was nowhere to be found. She panicked and was wracked with worry all the way home.

The next day we walked together to school and back home. But it was soon evident that I could go to school on my own and come home alone too, and as days passed I cultivated friendships of convenience with some horse-carriage drivers that were going my way up Marshall Street. I would hitch a ride on the flatbed of the carriage and jump off once it got close to Kruis Street, and from there I would walk to school. I enjoyed these occasional rides because they got me to school more quickly and earlier. This gave me time to play with the other kids before classes started. One of these rides turned out to be quite amusing. The carriage driver, a Coloured man, was sitting on the driver's bench holding the reins. To his left sat a hunched-up elderly white man who could have been the owner of the carriage or its passenger. The carriage had stopped at an intersection that had traffic lights which allowed pedestrians to cross. A white lady wearing a straw hat was crossing slowly in front of the carriage, and just as she came into the horse's view, in between its blinkers, the horse grabbed the straw hat and chewed up a good part of it. The white lady went ballistic. The Coloured driver was petrified because if the police had been around, he would have been blamed and would have had to account unless the white man sitting next to him had intervened. But this white man only laughed his head off at what happened. Neither of them apologised; instead, they found the incident hilarious. They joked about the smart horse that mistook the hat for forage. I chuckled discreetly and looked forward to telling the story to my classmates.

The Albert Street Methodist Church, like the Dutch Reformed Church in Ethwathwa, was a Mission Church established to serve the spiritual needs of black employees and their families who lived in the areas designated for Africans, Indians, Coloureds, and the many other migrant labourers who flocked to the Witwatersrand to work on the mines. This church was built in 1888. By 1890, it was the centre of the mission's strategy for evangelising on the Witwatersrand. Virtually all South Africa's white churches of different denominations chose to establish separate mission churches for their black congregants and separate schools for their children, who would be educated as wards of their denominations. Examples of this are the Methodist Church, which built and ran the Kilnerton High School and Teachers' Training College; the Dutch Reformed Church, which established Emmarentia Hoërskool and Stofberg Seminary for training African evangelists; the African Methodist Episcopal Church, which built Wilberforce Institute, consisting of four divisions (a high school, a training unit for teachers, an industrial training unit for masons, carpenters, tailors, agriculturists, and a home economics division for female students); and the Wright School of Religion. The Anglican Church had St Peter's high school, Marian Hill, and St Thomas, which was Roman Catholic.

The Albert Street Methodist Church received its first Black ordained minister, the Reverend Henry Ntsiko, in 1892. The church's stone was laid by Reverend George Weavind on 9 April 1893. In 1899, Reverend Michael Boweni was ordained at this church where the hymn, 'Nkosi Sikelel' iAfrika', what would become the opening verse of the post-apartheid national anthem, was sung for the first time in public. The church's stone was later re-laid on 31 December 1915 by General Louis Botha, the first Prime Minister of the Union of South Africa. This mission church conducted day and night school classes and was also the social centre for many mineworkers. A 'happy hour' was one of the ways in which it reached out to the lonely who were far from home. This was an afternoon social event which took place on certain days where people got to meet and have conversations about all sorts of experiences over tea, biscuits, and snacks. It was not a cocktail hour.

The Albert Street Methodist Primary mission school was at that time among the most prominent black primary schools in the city of Johannesburg. It was supported by a few social institutions such as the BMSC mentioned earlier. At the BMSC we could, with the permission of its manager who was an African man, play billiards, table tennis, darts, and tennis, take boxing lessons, and participate in other sports and games. All these activities took place only after school. There was a busy restaurant inside the building. It was managed by Oom Tuis (Uncle Tuis) who was a very congenial Coloured man. He always wore a spotless white apron with a dish cloth hung over one of his shoulders as he waited on the tables. He treated kids like any other adult customer as long as we behaved and paid for what we ate. We liked and respected him; that is why we called him 'uncle'.

Next to the BMSC was the Jan Hofmeyr School of Social Work for Africans, which was the first institution established to train social workers. Its namesake, Jan Hofmeyr, was Minister of Finance and Education in General Smuts's government in 1939. He was also president of a municipality that housed the Johannesburg City Council's Jubilee Social Centre. The school was funded with his help and that of the Young Men's Christian Association and established in 1941 under the leadership of Dr Ray Phillips, a Congregational Missionary. The school's mission was to train social workers to support black South African soldiers in North Africa during the Second World War. After the war ended, the school was converted into a college for training social workers in general, and some of the outstanding black social workers of that period were graduates of this institution. After the National Party (NP) came into power in 1948, the apartheid government stopped subsidising private education, and the Jan Hofmeyr School was forced to close in 1960.

Behind the BMSC and the Jan Hofmeyr School of Social Work, but some distance from them, was the Wemmer Barracks Hostel for black mineworkers, office building cleaners, and security personnel who were working in the city. What impressed me was the high standard of cleanliness that was maintained in this large hostel. The Wemmer Barracks Hostel grounds had two soccer pitches and a couple of netball courts located a few meters in front of its main entrance but on higher ground. Just inside, beyond the entrance, were neatly manicured lawns with flower beds on both sides of the walkway. A little further to the right was a big and well-kept swimming pool a short distance from the hostel buildings. But it was not used by the hostel dwellers. It was built for the staff that were in charge of the hostel, yet most of them did not use it either, because they did not know how to swim. Instead, the kids from the Albert Street School were often allowed to use it. The soccer fields and netball courts were also open for our school to use from Monday to Friday. On Saturdays this sports field was used for soccer matches, and on Sundays the pitches were used by mineworkers and cleaners who had organised themselves into dancing groups according to where they came from in the rural areas.

These groups usually practised their traditional dances and competed with one another on Sundays when they would be decked out in colourful 'beshus', headgear, plumes from a variety of big birds, other accoutrements, and of course cow shields and knobkerries. They did not carry spears, because they were considered dangerous and were not allowed in the hostel. From their build, deportment, and the manner in which they carried their shields and sticks, I imagined some of them could have been warriors in a Zulu detachment. They looked awesome. When they competed, what distinguished one group from another was how well its dancers were dressed and how meticulously their dancing was choreographed and performed. When they pounded the ground with their feet in unison, the entire field shook. To provide a cushion for their feet and also to look fashionable, they wore handmade sandals crafted out of discarded car tyres. These were called 'imbadadas'.

There were three restaurants closer to the school that served black patrons only. One was Mayibuye at the corner of Marshall and von Weilligh Streets. The other was the Blue Lagoon at the corner of von Weilligh and Melrose Streets, one block away from Mayibuye. Both were very close to the school. There was a third one whose name I cannot remember; it was on Delvers Street just off Marshall Street. This restaurant was frequented by political types, most of them ANC members and some members of the Unity Movement. School kids did not eat at any of these restaurants. They were places for adults where our teachers would send some of us to buy them lunches. School kids came with their lunch packs from their homes or bought fish and chips at a shop opposite Blue Lagoon. The fish and chips had a lot of salt, pepper, and vinegar and were always wrapped in old newsprint. We obviously ingested lots of printers' black ink as we ate these fish and chips, but perhaps that enhanced the taste.

When fish and chips got a little pricey, the other option was a 'chisanyama' ('burn-the-meat') shop around the corner from our school on Kruis Street. This place sold grilled and fried meat or liver with mealie pap (maize porridge). It was a sleazy joint. At any given time there would be more flies buzzing around than customers, so much so that its Jewish owner would often yell the order to the African cooks in the kitchen, adding the exclamation, 'Faka mpukane phakathi', meaning 'Put a fly in the order'. We avoided this place on Mondays in particular because you were invariably sold the previous Saturday's meat or liver leftovers. By Monday, this stuff had turned green, and some flies had died on or around it from feasting.

The teachers at Albert Street were very strict. They took their cue from the Standard 6 teacher, Mr Marawu, who was a taskmaster and strict disciplinarian. Discipline was enforced through corporal punishment. The instrument used was a bamboo cane, which Mr Marawu kept in his cupboard. Its appearance struck terror into most pupils. But there were a few who had somehow developed thick skins and were not afraid of it. Depending on the seriousness of the transgression, boys would have their pants pulled down, and the cane would lash their buttocks. This was done in full view of the entire class of boys and girls. Sitting on your hard desk after the thrashing was very painful. Girls were caned on the palms of their hands, also in full view of the entire class.

There are two caning incidents that I vividly recall. One involved Ernest 'Bula' Mzila – he often got into trouble for one thing or another. We were in the Standard 6 class, the last grade before secondary school. Something had gone awry, and Mr Marawu was furious. Bula was instructed to pull his pants down to just below his knees and to lie on his stomach on top of his desk. Bula was fat and his buttocks were quite big. The cane came down hard twice, and on the third stroke it disintegrated. We all thought that that was the end of the caning, but no, it was not. Bula was instructed to pull up his short pants, tuck his shirt in, tie his belt, and was given money to walk downtown to Vrededorp, close to Malay Camp, to buy a replacement. What went through Bula's mind as he walked all the way to buy a new cane only he knew. For we who witnessed this spectacle, it was torture. The class continued as if nothing had happened until Bula came back carrying a new cane. He was made to lie on his stomach again, his buttocks exposed and showing three welts, and another three lashes were administered. We were traumatised. When I recall this incident, I get upset and angry.

The second incident was also frightening. During choir practice for the upcoming eisteddfods (local music competitions) the music teacher, Mr Marawu again, would randomly select a soprano, an alto, a tenor, and a bass to sing a particular song or part of it. This exercise was meant to ensure that each singer knew his or her part and gave it his or her best. On this occasion, the boy who was to sing the tenor part of the chosen song was for some reason inaudible. The music teacher kept prompting him to sing a little louder but without success. Then the cane appeared, accompanied by frustrated gestures and ranting from Mr Marawu. It landed on the boy's back several times. The boy started to cry, and as the tears rolled down his cheeks, the music teacher told him to sing alone. He sang loud and clear and beautifully, with a quivering voice that enhanced the melody of the piece. We were all startled, and Mr Marawu kept saying, 'That's it my boy, that's it.' From then on, no one needed the cane to sing loudly and clearly and with a quivering voice. We sang our way to first place at the choral music eisteddfod and returned with a glittering silver trophy. Recalling this incident makes me laugh a little. It was amusing but still brutal.

The most memorable part of my early school days in Albert Street were the friends I made and kept for many years. Two of them lived on premises owned by the Chamber of Mines. These premises were used for receiving new recruits for the mines and billeting and processing them in order to distribute them to other Chamber mines. The Chamber of Mines had established the Witwatersrand Native Labour Association (WNLA), commonly called 'Wenela', in 1901 as a recruiting agency for the mining companies who were its members. The new recruits were migrant labourers sourced from British Central Africa. Wenela was a large organisation with depots at different labour collection points and buses and airplanes spread all over Southern Africa. The Chamber of Mines also formed the Native Recruitment Corporation (NRC) in 1912. It recruited migrant labourers from inside South Africa and the British Protectorates of Basutoland and Bechuanaland as well as Swaziland. Wenela was bigger than the NRC. These organisations did not compete with each other; in fact, they tended to complement one another in sourcing labour for most of the mines on the Witwatersrand.

Perhaps my closest friend at that time was Cyprian Mahlaba. Cyprian was smart and good at table tennis, tennis, and soccer. His father was a clerk at the WNLA centre located on Eloff Street Extension. My second favourite was Joan Tatane. She was the best netball centre forward of our girls' school team. She was also very smart, a powerful athlete, and fun to be around. Her family lived close to Cyprian's, and her father was also a mine clerk but for the NRC, whose functions were similar to those of the WNLA. The black mine clerks were employed by the two labour brokerage companies, WNLA and NRC, to perform the functions involved in receiving and processing the new recruits. They lived on the organisations' premises with their families, and all their children attended the Albert Street School. There was no other primary school for black children nearby.

Cyprian and I had a Sunday job at the Bantu Sports soccer stadium. Our employer was Mr Dan Twala, who was fondly referred to as 'Mr Sport'. Twala had been the manager of the Bantu Sports Club since 1935 and held that position for over two decades. We began working for him in the late 1940s when both of us were at the Albert Street School. Our job started round one o'clock every Sunday when soccer fans started arriving to watch the first soccer match. This was an opener that would be followed by the second match, which was the main game of the day. We sold ice cream to both the players and the fans. We carried the ice-cream packets in boxes containing dry ice and hung them around our necks so that they rested on our stomachs. We strolled around the field shouting 'Ice cream!' and it was fun to watch the teams play and their supporters root for them and deride them for making errors and losing a game. The high point of the afternoon for Cyprian and me was always watching the last minutes of the main game. Players from the winning side would be anxiously eyeing the main exit as they were playing, because the fans of the losing side would be getting ready to pelt them with all sorts of debris once the final whistle blew. It was hilarious to watch players running out of the stadium still in their soccer shorts, shirts, and boots, while carrying their regular clothes in their hands. It sometimes got a little rough, though no one was ever injured.

4

Industriousness

I grew up in a household in which there was always some work to be done during the day. This upbringing, with its emphasis on diligence and industriousness, instilled habits that have remained with me throughout my life. At home I learned to make my bed, collect the wood and coal, light the coal stove, clean, wax, and sometimes polish the floors, dust and polish the furniture, help my mother cook dinners in particular, watch over pots that were cooking (especially when the stove plates got red hot), and wash the family clothes as well as the laundry that she took in from white families. She would then iron the laundry and sew garments that needed stitching. Most of these tasks I learned working like a young apprentice alongside my mother. I had to help because I was the last born in the family of five older siblings who no longer stayed in the house. Being the last born meant that I spent a lot of time with both my parents. My father, for his part, taught me gardening, maintaining the parish grounds, dusting the church pews and pulpit, minding the chicken run, and milking the two cows that he kept, one a Friesland and the other a Jersey. The cows were kept because my parents preferred unpasteurised milk, some of which would be stored in what in Zulu is called 'igula', a calabash container shaped like a gourd, and allowed to become sour milk. The curdled part of this fermented milk looked like cottage cheese but was creamier, richer, and tastier. We would eat it with sorghum: ground, cooked, and cooled. This was a much-loved traditional Zulu dish that we relished. It was called 'amasi no phuthu'.

Our house had a flower garden and a sizable vegetable garden in which my dad grew maize, squash, string beans, tomatoes, and other seasonal vegetables. There were a few peach and apricot trees which I had to mind too, and I had other chores, including turning over the soil and preparing it for planting, adding fertiliser, which consisted mostly of cow dung that we collected from the cow shed, watering and weeding the garden, trimming fruit trees, and harvesting. Harvesting was determined by what my mother wanted to cook or give to visitors. I also mended fences and sheds and built small retainer walls and other things, and so learnt from an early age how to use tools like nails, hammers, saws, plyers, cutters, trowels, the level, and the tape measure. Little did I know that these and other skills I was learning in and around the house would prove very useful at the boarding schools I attended and later on when I was in exile. In the course of performing all these chores, a strong work ethic and discipline were instilled in me, values that would guide me for the rest of my life. Going to school was almost a respite from housework.

My father also inculcated a strong value system of honesty and accountability in whatever I did at home or away from home. Two stories illustrate how much my parents valued honesty. The first one had to do with tithes, which were collected on Sundays. These were kept in a bowl in the open on top of the sideboard with a piece of paper showing how much money was there. This money would be taken by my father later during the week to the dominee (his white superior in charge of the church district). If someone had for some reason borrowed a penny from the bowl, he or she had to make a note of how much was taken because it had to be returned. Of all the tithes my parents had collected over their lives in the different parishes to which they were assigned, I doubt whether they once pocketed a penny.

Perhaps a more telling incident will bear this out. We were living in George Goch next to the Eastern Native Township, and my father, riding his favourite Raleigh bicycle, had gone to City Deep to visit some of his congregants. On his way there or on his way back, he came across a neatly wrapped bundle of money and took it straight to the nearest police station and told them that someone had lost their money. The police could not believe what they were hearing and seeing from the venerable-looking old man. They gratefully took the money and commended my father for his honesty and being a good Christian. When he came back home and told us the story, no one said or thought that what he did was foolish or wrong; no one in our home would have kept that money. This story has been passed down the generations, and now

Industriousness

most young people in our extended family regret having inherited this kind of honesty, which, they say, with their tongues in their cheeks, has impoverished them.

Nevertheless, I learned from a young age that honesty did pay dividends, even if these dividends did not always come in the ways that I expected. This is illustrated in the following story about the cinema. Every day after school was a torture because I often wanted to go to the cinema with some of my friends, especially those who lived with their parents, who were domestic workers in the white suburbs. Those friends could go to the movies because there was very little housework waiting for them where they lived in the servants' quarters with their parents. One of the most testing chores I had was minding my father's two cows. My job every afternoon was to find these two cows somewhere on the perimeter of the township, herd them home, and milk them before sunset. But whenever the matinee show at the bioscope ran a little late, I would be in serious trouble. One day I was so late that my father had to find the cows and milk and feed them before locking them up in the cowshed. When I got home, he called me into the dining room and asked me to explain why I was late.

A son or daughter of a DRC clergy was not allowed or expected to go to the bioscope or dance hall. Such places were seen as ungodly or downright evil. This time I just felt tired of lying as I had in the past. Once I had entered the dining room, my father and I found ourselves standing and facing each other at opposite ends of the rectangular table. When I told him that I was late because I had gone to the bioscope, he made a dash for me. But the rectangular table was an obstacle, and he very quickly realised he could not get his big hands on me. He stopped, and I stopped too. Stanley, my brother, was discreetly peeking through the window pane from outside, watching the dramatic performance and standoff. I was terrified. Then came an unexpected question – in Zulu. My father wanted to know whether my brother also went to the bioscope. I quickly said yes for fear of lying again.

Stanley suddenly dropped out of view. I was then told to go and fetch him. I thought we were in for a serious hiding. When I found Stanley, he was livid at being implicated and scared of what might happen to him. We returned to the dining room and found ourselves standing and facing our father across the table. He told us in a firm tone and in no uncertain terms that the cows must be found, milked, fed, and put in their shed before sunset every afternoon. Going to the bioscope was not to interfere with this task. Surprisingly, however, he then said that which of us was to go to the bioscope and when, and who was to take care of the cows, was for us to decide. I couldn't believe it! What a relief that was. That night during evening prayers Stan and I recited the Lord's Prayer with gusto and went to bed smiling. I couldn't resist reminding my older brother that I was the one who got us permission to go to the bioscope. By telling the truth and incriminating my brother, I had achieved what had seemed to be impossible.

5

George Goch

Early in 1943, when I was eight years old, my parents decided to move to Clermont in Durban; they had bought a property there. My father's white superiors must have supported the move because there was another parish there awaiting him. I moved with my parents while Nana and Stanley remained in Johannesburg with relatives because they were still in school at the Albert Street School.

Unfortunately for my father, the damp and humid climate in Durban was bad for his health. He was asthmatic, and doctors recommended that he move to a drier climate like the 'platteland' he had just come from, 1 500 meters above sea level. So, we had to return to Johannesburg but not to Malay Camp because that post had already been occupied by another priest, Evangelist Dludlu.

However, there was fortunately a vacancy in a place called George Goch at No. 2, Vickers Road where another DRC mission church was located. I was happy that I would be able to return to Albert Street Methodist Church school! To get there, I had to catch a bus or a train, both of which were close to my new home. On the first day that I returned to my old school, just before classes began (Standard 3 now), Cyprian saw me and was over the moon. Before I could report to the principal that I had returned and find out which class I would be assigned to, Cyprian grabbed me by the hand and took me to the teacher who was teaching his class and told the teacher who I was and that I had always been in the same class as him and therefore must be in his class. The teacher acquiesced.

My new home was situated where Vickers Road split, curved a little to the right, and headed down towards City Deep. The other part of the road went straight down to the main gate of the Eastern Native Township (ENT). Here lay the neighbourhood of George Goch, which was named after a gold mining capitalist of the 1890s who later became the mayor of Johannesburg from 1904 to 1905. In 1923, the Native Urban Areas Act was promulgated as a measure to control the movements of blacks in urban and rural areas. This township was built in 1924 by the City Council of Johannesburg to house Africans who worked in the city and its surrounds, including Nourse and the City Deep gold mines. Other renters were Africans who worked in and on the mines, in factories, in workshops in industrial parks, at the railway stations and shunting yards, in office buildings in the city as cleaners, messengers, drivers, and clerks, and in other menial jobs that kept the city functioning.

George Goch was close to the city centre of Johannesburg. In fact, it was about a forty-five-minute walk from the east end of the city. When an African said that he or she was going to George Goch, more often than not what was meant was that he or she was going to the ENT. To get from the city to George Goch, one could catch a train at Park Station, Johannesburg's main railway station situated at the head of Eloff Street. Alternatively, one could catch a bus around the corner from the Jan Hofmeyr School of Social Work at the other end of Eloff Street. When I grew up, Eloff Street was the high street of Johannesburg. It ran from Park Station up to the BMSC, a glittering street with shops like Levisons, which sold fashionable men's clothes, Katz and Lourie, which sold expensive jewellery and watches, and Williams Hunt, which sold fancy cars.

At Park Station, before a train travelling to the east pulled out of the platform, a white train conductor would shout either 'All stations' or 'First stop Jeppe, then Germiston' and so forth. If one was going to George Goch, one would take the train that stopped at all the stations before it went to the end of the line, which was either Springs or Welgedacht. The conductor would then blow his whistle, signalling that the train was about to pull out of the platform. The train on the eastern line would first stop at Doornfontein, then Ellis Park, then Jeppe; George Goch would be the fourth stop. This train ride took no more than twenty minutes from Park Station. On the north side of the George Goch station lived whites only. These whites were mostly poor; it was evident in their houses, front yards, the watch dogs and pets they kept, and in the general state of the surroundings. Blacks lived on the south side of the railway but some distance from the station, and this is where the ENT was located. As in many South African towns, the railway tracks separated the white from the black neighbourhoods. The distance between the township and the station was a fairly long walk.

This electric train heading east had around eight coaches. Three at the front were for blacks and the following five were for whites. The three coaches for blacks were further sub-divided. The first coach was partitioned into three sections. The first section was where the white train driver sat alone. Behind this section was a space for freight. Then followed the third section, which was set aside for blacks who could afford to travel first or second class, though very few could. The second two coaches were third-class and for Africans. These were very crowded, especially during peak travel times in the mornings and afternoons. The remaining five coaches of the same train were for whites only. Looking in from outside as the train left the station's platform, we could see that the coaches reserved for white passengers were not crowded. All the passengers in these coaches were seated comfortably on cushioned seats. I don't recall seeing standing passengers in the coaches carrying whites, whereas standing passengers were the norm in all coaches carrying Coloureds, Indians, and Africans. Third-class was the worst: those who had seats sat on solid hard-wood, and those who were standing were packed like sardines.

The other way of getting to George Goch from the city was by bus. This bus company was called the Van Zyl Bus Service, though it later changed hands and became known as the Morosina Bus Service. Its terminal was at the top end of Eloff Street and the buses would go to George Goch and City Deep. On one end of Eloff Street, where it began, was Park Station, while at the other end, where it became an extension, was the terminal for buses going to George Goch and City Deep. These two places had mines and compounds that housed black mineworkers and residential accommodation for black mine staff. The ride from the bus terminal at the upper end of Eloff Street to George Goch took about half an hour to forty minutes depending on the traffic. Its main bus stop for passengers heading into the township was a few steps away and on the same side of our home, so from our home's kitchen window I could see who was getting off the bus. Across the street was the bus stop for those coming from City Deep and going into the city, so I could also see who was going into town.

~

The ENT was a small, very intimate, and close-knit community. It had many churches, the most prominent of which, in terms of size of building and congregation, were the Dutch Reformed Church, the Methodist Church, the Anglican Church, the Salvation Army, the African Methodist Episcopal Church, and the Bantu Methodist Church. Three of these churches, the Anglican, Methodist, and the Dutch Reformed churches, were situated one next to the other just outside the main gate to the township. Opposite this cluster of churches and across the street from them was another smaller church called The Broer en Suster (The Brother and Sister) whose congregants were Coloureds. Then followed the Zion Congregational and the Lutheran Churches which were located in the township. The latter held its services on Sundays in a house that from Monday to Saturday was a shebeen. There were other smaller churches whose names I did not know. Altogether there were eleven churches in the township.

The township was nestled between several mine dumps or slime dams that had hardened and became solid over time. Unknowingly, we as kids played on the flat tops of these mine dumps, raising dust particles that turned out to be toxic. We knew nothing about the dangers of this fine dust. When it was windy, the dust could be found in almost every house in the township. The entire perimeter of the township was enclosed by a wrought-iron fence approximately six feet high and made of vertical steel slats which were spaced in such a way that no matter how thin and wispy one was it was impossible to squeeze through. Within this enclosure were 625 houses, most of them two-roomed. Very few were three-roomed. All the houses had electricity. The township had two primary schools, six shops, and a population of around 5 000 people. The monthly rental for a two-roomed house, during the 1950s, was 17 shillings and 6 pence. The backyards of these houses had enough space for a garden or for a small shack and an outside bucket latrine.

There was one major entrance into the township through which people and vehicles of every kind entered and exited. These vehicles were regular motor cars, three-wheeled side-cars, motor bikes, horse and donkey-drawn carts, bicycles, and mule-drawn carts that collected night soil. All came and left the township through this main gate. It was always half shut so that every vehicle coming in or going out had to stop at the gate. A 'Black Jack', the township municipal policeman, who was dressed in a black uniform from head to toe, manned the gate and would cast a searching look at whoever was entering or leaving before opening the other half of the gate.

Next to the entrance for vehicles was a curved semi-circle gate for pedestrians. It was deliberately designed to slow down people entering and exiting so that the 'Black Jack' could observe and control movements in and out of the township. To the immediate left of this gate were the administration offices where the superintendent, township councillors, and clerks had offices. It seemed that the township councillors were appointed by the superintendent, who also hired the clerks on the recommendations of his councillors. Residents paid their monthly rents and rates and lodged whatever complaints they had about issues of service delivery or often disputes of one kind or another with neighbours. The township councillors were called 'izinduna' or 'izibonda' (Zulu words for head men or councillors). They were briefed by the clerks and usually met in one of the administration offices to discuss and resolve problems facing members of the community. They also acted as advisors to the superintendent of the township who was a white man. These councillors knew just about every family in the township including the children of those families. They were respected, feared, and regarded as the elders of the community. Most kids walked the straight line anyway because of the omnipresence of surrogate fathers, mothers, uncles, and aunts. All of them were respected and feared, even though they were not councillors. They were efficient informers.

Directly opposite the administration offices and the police station was the residence of the superintendent, Mr Swan. His home was at the corner of James Avenue and Plata Street, which was the first intersection after the entrance to the township.

This police station had several African policemen who patrolled the township on foot. They were complemented by a couple of 'amafokisi' (detectives) from the Civil Investigation Department (CID). The police and detectives worked very closely with the Black Jacks. The Black Jacks were recruited from the community and viewed as municipal police and not regular state police. The police station had a small jail comprising three holding cells, which were used as overnight facilities for men or women who had to be transferred to the bigger police stations or magistrate courts in Cleveland or Jeppe the following day.

The infrastructure serving the township was basic. The township itself was established in 1925. Its community hall and two tennis courts were built around 1929, and electricity was introduced around 1950. A water sewerage system came in around 1953, and the roads were tarred by 1958. Our home got electricity much earlier because it was located outside the township and in a neighbourhood with white-owned shops that served the community residents and black mineworkers who passed by on their way to and from the mines. For some time, the toilet bucket system with individual toilets built behind the houses was used for collecting night soil. These buckets were emptied every other night into large carts. Each cart was drawn by two mules and guided by two men who picked up the buckets, emptied them into the carts, and continued on their way along the passages behind the houses where all the outside toilets were located. This unpleasant job was carried out by tough Africans, the majority of whom were from the Eastern Cape. These men were called 'amabaca' because of the traditional scars on their faces, and were derogatively referred to as 'tshutshas', which translates as 'picker-uppers'. No one dared poke fun at them or their work, though. If you did, you would definitely wake up to your bucket of night soil having been spilled on your front door. It did happen from time to time but not to our home.

Living in George Goch did not hinder my friendship with my schoolmates who came from WNLA and the Robinson Deep mine compounds. I enjoyed the visits to the WNLA compound because of the recreation facilities that Cyprian had access to. We often played billiards, table tennis, darts, or tennis; we swam; and on certain nights we watched movies with mine workers and staff. These facilities were provided for the black clerical staff and their families but not for black mineworkers. Occasionally, we would also queue for the food that was served to mineworkers, especially the 'mbunyane', a solid brown loaf of bread which was fortified and touted as a health bread. The African clerical staff quarters were well appointed and, in most cases, better than the township houses in the locations. Mining companies who were members of WNLA and NRA made sure that their employees were comfortably housed and provided with proper recreation facilities. It was clear that the black clerks were an indispensable element of the mining industry.

During school holidays I found some temporary jobs to earn some money, and with this I often bought clothes. I worked from Monday to Friday. Saturday mornings I spent at the City Deep golf course as a caddy where I usually carried golf bags for white women because theirs tended to be lighter than those of white men. And women usually played only nine holes in the morning, unlike the men who played eighteen holes from mid-morning until late in the afternoon. The white men also treated the black caddies very badly. I have to admit that the white women were generally not as crude, cruel, nasty, or cheap as their male counterparts. The expression 'kaffir this' or 'kaffir that' was standard fare from the white men, and what they paid the caddies was peanuts. When I did not have a temporary job, I would ask my parents to lend me a few shillings with which to buy and sell oranges on the trains travelling between Johannesburg and George Goch. I would also sell these at the George Goch station. I often made a little profit on the trains and at the station and managed to pay back my parents.

On some Saturday afternoons and Sunday mornings before church, I played softball on the mine dump with my team called the Eastern Native Township Dodgers, one of the first in the townships of Johannesburg. I founded and captained this team. I had been following the fame of the Brooklyn Dodgers in the United States and adopted its name. Sunday mornings in and around the township were quiet, especially after the usual fun-filled Fridays and Saturdays when there were parties and jive sessions in the community hall. One of the regular Sunday sounds were the church bells, which rang almost at the same time – mid-morning at about 10:45 and mid-afternoon at about 14:45. These bells rang three times in the morning for the morning service and three times again for the afternoon services, at intervals of a couple of minutes.

In addition to these sounds, there was the Salvation Army music band that would march down Vickers Road which lead into the township. It consisted of a varied crew of army members marching in step to ditties played on a big brass trumpet, a small trumpet, a couple of drums, a trombone, cymbals, and one or two other instruments. In front of the band was its leader who was also the conductor. Then followed the Zion Congregational Church (ZCC) and Stokvel groups just before the other churches' afternoon services began. By the early afternoon, once all these marches had finished and the cacophony had stopped, the Sunday sounds were over. What followed was the usual serious preaching and singing of hymns in the different churches as services were being conducted.

My own involvement in the DRC was to a large extent a family affair. My father was the head of the parish and my mother led the women's church organisation. They were partners in the activities of the church. The core members of the church choir were essentially my four sisters, Beauty, Emily, Thoko, Nana, my older brother, Stanley, and myself. Beauty and Nana were the sopranos while Emily and Thoko were the altos. I sang the tenor part and Stanley sang the bass. In addition to being in the choir, I also attended the children's Sunday catechism classes, which met every Sunday morning from ten until a few minutes before eleven, when the first church service began. This was when I was much younger and had not yet started the softball team. I often had to ring the church bell as well, particularly in the morning. Thus my Sunday mornings were usually very busy ones.

6

Emmarentia Hoërskool

After I completed my primary school education at Albert Street Methodist School at the end of 1948, my parents enrolled me at the Emmarentia Hoërskool near Warmbaths (now called Bela-Bela). This was a high school located at a place called Buiskop just past Warmbaths when travelling north to Pietersburg (now called Polokwane). It was a boarding school run by the DRC for boys and girls, most of them from families who were members of the DRC in parts of South Africa, Southern Rhodesia (Zimbabwe), and South West Africa (Namibia). It was at this school that I met Jariretundu Fanuel Kozonguizi, the founder and leader of the South West African National Union (SWANU) of Namibia. Little did I know then that I would meet him years later in London, when both of us were exiled and SWANU was part of the South African United Front (SAUF).[3]

To reach Emmarentia Hoërskool I had to catch an overnight train to Pietersburg, which left Park Station in the late afternoon. This train was pulled by a steam-engined locomotive that stopped in Germiston, Pretoria, and Warmbaths. After Warmbaths, the train stopped at Buiskop. 'Buis' is the Afrikaans word for tube, pipe, canal, or duct, and 'kop' is the Afrikaans word for head. This place was in the middle of nowhere at the bottom of an ominous-looking hill. The journey from Park Station to Buiskop took around seven hours. The train stopped there in the middle of the night, and it was pitch dark when we got there. The only lights were at the front of the locomotive and the lights from the train coaches. There was not a single structure anywhere resembling a station.

---

3   This front was formed in May 1960 shortly after the Sharpeville massacre on 21 March 1960. SAUF consisted of the African National Congress (ANC), South African Indian Congress (SAIC), Pan Africanist Congress (PAC), and SWANU. But it was dissolved in March 1962 largely because of the wrangles between the PAC and the ANC. There were fundamental ideological and organisational differences that could not be reconciled and which went back to the formation of the PAC.

Only students going to Emmarentia High School disembarked here, and when the train stopped, we descended a couple of steps then jumped to the ground. Our luggage and food trucks were lowered to us by a few helpful students who were proceeding to another high school in Pietersburg called Pax High School. (It was a Catholic-run school, but some of its pupils, whom I knew, were thugs. Their behaviour on the train, particularly their treatment of newcomers, was horrible. I have never, before or since, seen such abusive hazing as that meted out by the boys of the Pax High School.)

As the train started pulling off, darkness gradually engulfed us. We could see some stars, but we couldn't make out where we were, let alone where we were going. The darkness was eerie, especially because I was accustomed to the city lights of George Goch and Johannesburg. Fortunately, on my arrival, we were met by returning seniors who had arrived a day or so earlier. One of them was my older brother, Stanley; it was because he had spent two years there that my parents decided to send me to the same high school. He and a couple of friends had come with flashlights and carried our luggage and led us to the school premises which were about a kilometre away, nestled on one side of the Great North Road heading to Pietersburg and eventually Beit Bridge, the border between South Africa and Zimbabwe.

The school was beautiful. It was situated on an expansive farmland in a valley below a range of lofty hills. Its old Dutch architecture and layout were striking, especially if you looked down at it from the mountains beside the Great North Road. The white buildings with their dark brown thatched roofs , the symmetrical layout of the complex, and the lush green foliage are etched in my mind. When the jacaranda trees were in bloom, it was a sight to behold. On the lowest part of the slope of the hill and located from a vantage point overlooking the entire campus at the bottom of the valley were the residences of the principal and his deputy, Meneers Engelbrecht and Wiid respectively. Just below these houses were the white male teachers' houses. A little lower down, but on one side, were the black teachers' quarters, which were not houses. Further downhill on the opposite side was a neatly maintained gravel road where there was a workshop where male pupils were taught basic skills such as woodworking.

Across the road and to the left of the workshop as you walked down the slope was the dining hall for both boys and girls. Further down and to the left of the dining hall were the girls' dormitories, while the boys' dormitories were in the opposite direction. Coming out of the dining hall were a few concrete steps leading to the classrooms, and these were laid out in the form of a horseshoe. The open court portion of this horseshoe was used for morning prayers and announcements every school day. When Meneer Engelbrecht was away, his deputy Meneer Wiid would preside. All these beautiful buildings were surrounded by lush green jacaranda trees and other indigenous species. These trees, lawns, and farmlands were kept neatly trimmed by labourers and boys (the boarders) during the manual labour periods at school. The diligent hard work by these little boys of the Protestant faith was evident.

I recall a couple of features that characterised Emmarentia. The mountains were home to many baboons and snakes. The snakes tended to avoid us but not the baboons. We did not know that we shared this lovely landscape with them until they descended on our dormitories when we were in class, in the dining hall, or in the fields doing manual work. They would ransack our dormitories for anything edible and rip open our trunks, which were tucked away beneath our beds and held our snacks. The mess they left made us very angry. They did not raid the girls' dormitories because these were too far from their usual routes.

One day a few of us decided enough was enough and one afternoon when they came down on their rampage, we laid in ambush armed with stones and sticks. When they saw us, they started running back up the mountain. The females and offspring were in front while the males held the rear. We kept chasing them up the hill while shouting all sorts of obscenities at them as if they could understand us. When they crossed the Great North Road at the top of the hill, we continued to pursue them. Sometime during this chase, the big males suddenly stopped, stood their ground, and began breaking branches from the trees. We did not have to tell one another what was coming. We turned around and ran like hell as the male baboons chased us. They stopped chasing us only after we had crossed back over the road and were on our school's side. They earned our grudging respect, and there was a truce for a little while.

There was another incident that was rather daring and foolish, which took place late on a Sunday morning. A friend from Pretoria, Stephen Moloto, and I decided that we would not attend the church service. Instead, we decided to round up a cow and tie it to a tree and milk it. We took some matches and a little bowl with us and went into the corn field to harvest a few good corn cobs, which we roasted over a fire. We had just finished munching the roasted cobs and were lying on our backs quite content and pleased with our adventure when out of nowhere there appeared Mr Engelbrecht. I could have died. All he said in Afrikaans was that we should untie the cow, put out the fire, and return to the dormitory. We knew that that evening during study time, he would open the door, stick his head into our classroom, call out our names, and tell us to come to his office. Whenever this happened, everyone in the class knew someone was going to be walloped for some transgression. It was very embarrassing for whoever was summoned to the office.

That evening during study time, Steve and I could not concentrate on studying and doing our homework because of our anxiety about being called out. Then, indeed, the door opened, and there was Mr Engelbrecht. He looked like he had had a nice dinner with some strong stuff to drink and called us to his office. Our classroom was close enough to his office that you could hear and count the lashes that every truant received. In some cases, you could even hear the cries and screams following the lashes. He used a sjambok (a whip made out of a hippo's hide) on the buttocks of all male recalcitrants. This whip was stronger and more durable than the cane Mr Marawu used at the Albert Street Methodist School.

Meneer Engelbrecht was a tall hulk of a man. He had piercing, menacing blue eyes, a tough-looking head, and a thick neck that rested on broad, strong shoulders. He looked more like a rugby player than a teacher. When he walked, he looked like he was leaning forward, almost ready to fall or run. He wore short-sleeved shirts and short pants no matter the season, his socks were always pulled knee-high and turned over at the top, and his shoes were the usual farmer's veldskoene (beige leather shoes worn in the field). His regular dress was casual except on Sundays.

Once we were inside his office, there was no talking about what we had done and why. We were ordered to take off our pants. For some reason, Steve had worn two pairs of pants in order to cushion the impact of the lashes, but how he thought he could get away with this escapes me to this day. He was told to take one pair off. We got a good hiding. We tried very hard not to scream or cry because we did not want our classmates from the bush to poke fun at us. We had to keep up the reputation of being city boys who did not cry. On returning to our classroom, we both could not sit at our desks it hurt so much. Some of our classmates, especially those who came from rural parts of the country and South West Africa, laughed at us, the city slickers from Johannesburg and Pretoria who had gotten their just desserts. The pain and subsequent swelling were such that I vowed I would never again do anything to incur such punishment and humiliation.

For many Sundays following the spanking, Steve and I never missed a single church service, and the school's cows and corn were left alone. To ensure that our attendance was always noticed we sat right up front. On Wednesday afternoons during manual work time, boys were assigned the jobs of weeding or harvesting the maize corn, groundnuts, squash, sunflowers, and other agricultural produce. We diligently delivered what we harvested in wheelbarrows to the school's produce storage shed. Not a single corn cob or groundnut went missing.

There was another incident at Emmarentia that was hilarious. 'Landboukunde' or agricultural science classes were held in the afternoons shortly after lunch. Lunch usually consisted of a generous serving of maize porridge, some meat and gravy, and vegetables sourced from the school's produce shed. The meat was bought from a large butchery in the town of Warmbaths. Summers in that part of the northern Transvaal (now called Limpopo) could get quite hot. Attending an afternoon class on a stomach full of maize porridge, meat, and vegetables was torture, and having to be taught in Afrikaans made things worse because some students were not fluent in Afrikaans. The heat, full stomachs, and limited understanding of the instructor's speech made some of us slowly fall asleep.

The classroom was rectangular in shape in order to accommodate a long table, which was also rectangular. We, the learners, sat on the longer sides of the table facing each other while the instructor, Meneer Brink, stood at the head of the table. Behind him was the chalk board. One day, Franz Dube, a pupil who had come from Bulawayo in Southern Rhodesia and who had difficulty understanding Afrikaans, was struggling to stay awake. I sat opposite him and could tell that he was bored. Meneer Brink was lecturing about pests, one of which was 'muise' (mice). Frank raised his hand and wanted to know from Meneer Brink what 'muise' was. Meneer Brink was a little man with a neatly cut moustache and was very sure of himself. He was a graduate of one of the Afrikaans universities and determined to educate us. In answering Frank's question, Meneer Brink began to chuckle with a wry smile and laughed at Frank for not knowing what 'muise' were. 'Mouses' he exclaimed! The entire class woke up and broke out in laughter. Meneer Brink thought he had really scored a win. He continued to address Frank by saying 'see Frank, the whole class is laughing at you!' Frank was also cracking up while softly muttering that the plural of louse must then be louses. Meneer Brink was really entertaining with his poor grasp of English. But then we had to remember that the medium of instruction in the school was mostly Afrikaans, except for subjects like English and Mathematics. No IsiZulu and Sesotho were taught. I later found out that Meneer Brink was a member of the Afrikaner Broederbond (Afrikaner Brotherhood League). His name appears in Appendix 1 of the Broederbond Membership List on page A13 in a book written by Ivor Wilkins and Hans Strydom titled *The Super Afrikaners Inside the Afrikaner Broederbond* (2015 edition). He is identified as Brink C T, 43, P/A Emmarentia Geldenhuysskool Warmbad, Onderhoof (Deputy Principal), 1965.

After spending three years at Emmarentia, I completed my first high school diploma, called the Junior Certificate. I then asked my parents to allow me to go to Kilnerton High School for Matric. Kilnerton High School was a boarding school but nearer home. They agreed, so I applied and was accepted. I was by then a seasoned boarder. There had been a few sports and debating competitions between Emmarentia and Kilnerton which gave me opportunities to familiarise myself with Kilnerton while I was at Emmarentia. I also met some of my friends from Johannesburg who were already there. I had often been on the Emmarentia Afrikaans debating team when we visited Kilnerton. What I spoke then was proudly referred to as 'suiwer Afrikaans', meaning pure Afrikaans, as spoken by the educated Afrikaner elite, and because of this, we beat our Kilnerton adversaries in debates conducted in Afrikaans, though they trounced us in English. They had been schooled by the Methodist Church mission, which was English, while we were the wards of the Dutch Reformed Church mission, which was Afrikaner.

7

Kilnerton

Kilnerton opened in 1885 as one of the major missionary schools that the Methodist Church established to educate Africans. The land on which it was built was granted by Paul Kruger, the president of the Boer Transvaal Republic. It was a co-educational institution that had a teacher training college called Kilnerton Normal College and a high school referred to simply as Kilnerton High School. Kilnerton as a whole was attractive but not as lush and scenic as Emmarentia. Fortunately, its grounds had many jacarandas and other trees, which softened the harsh appearance of the solid brick buildings with their corrugated iron roofs.

Most of Kilnerton's pupils came from primary schools run by the Methodist Church or from families that were members of the Methodist Church. On my first day at Kilnerton, I was welcomed by a good number of former classmates who had come from the Albert Street Primary School and others who had come from other schools in the townships of Johannesburg like Orlando, Western Native Township, and Alexandra. Most of the kids at Kilnerton came from urban environments. I was very happy to be reunited with my mates from the Albert Street School in Johannesburg after spending three years at Emmarentia.

Somehow, in my first year at Kilnerton, I was elected to be the prefect responsible for the junior dining hall, which catered to the first-, second-, and third-year high-school male pupils. This is where they had breakfast, lunch, and dinner. Being in charge of the dining hall meant having access to better pieces of meat, bread, and other food items at all times. Food at a boarding school is an important commodity, and as a prefect, I had the keys to the pantries where the food supplies were stored. All prefects at Kilnerton at this time were called 'G Men'. This term came from the American slang for 'Government Man'. In the United States, it was used when referring to the staff of organisations such as the Federal Bureau of Investigations (FBI) and was often heard in movies. Its use at Kilnerton had a psychological impact on the 'G Men' and their wards too. The latter were very respectful of and deferential to the former, to the point of being in awe of them.

I recall that I needed two assistants to help me supervise the dining hall because of the large number of junior pupils. The search for the two assistants resulted in fierce competition among the few friends I had. I chose one of my roommates in Room 13, whom I thought was a nice chap. This was Washington Mposula who was training as a teacher at the institution's teachers' college. I did not know that Washington loved food so much. Whatever food he could not finish eating in the dining hall he would take to our room and store in his food trunk, which he would secure with a padlock and tuck under his bed. It was as if he thought a famine might start at any moment. He did not trust any of his roommates, including me, with his food trunk. I later realised that helping me amounted to helping himself, so that he could hoard the food he liked, and his hoarding, I remember, upset me quite a bit. I preferred my second assistant, who was a real trooper. I don't know what influenced him to be the principled and caring person he was. He had a pleasant demeanour and recognised the responsibilities we had in ensuring that all the junior students under our care were well fed and taken care of. We were accountable to our superiors for how we looked after our fellow boarders. The 'G Men' always had the best cuts of meat, which were served at our high table after all our wards had eaten, and invariably, we were the last to sit down to eat. I really liked working with this assistant; I wish I could remember his name. I could rely on his custodianship even when I had gone missing over some of the weekends because I had returned home.

~

Kilnerton, unlike Emmarentia, was close to home. This made it possible for me to sneak away on a Friday afternoon and return on Sunday in the early evening. All I had to do was catch a local train from the railway station, which was next to the campus, to the Pretoria main railway station. There, I would catch an electric train bound for Park Station in Johannesburg, but before it got to Johannesburg, I would transfer to a different train at the Germiston station so that I could get off at the George Goch railway station and walk home. When I first showed up at home unexpectedly, I had to convince my parents that I had not absconded. I said that I had permission to visit, though that wasn't true. Thereafter, I did not have to explain my unexpected visits, but my conscience did bother me because I was lying.

I had also persuaded my roommates to be accomplices to this scheme. For a prefect and the son of a clergyman, I was behaving like a crook. When I was away, just before the lights were turned off at night round ten over the weekends, my roommates would construct a dummy in my bed, so that it would appear as if I were lying there asleep. This would deceive the African teacher who usually came round at night before the lights were turned off to make sure that we were all accounted for. The dummy in my bed consisted of two pillows lined up to resemble my body, covered by the sheet and blanket. The head would be a night cap stuffed with a towel and positioned to face in the opposite direction to the door, so that when the teacher making the rounds opened the door and counted all the bodies in the beds without checking the faces, no one would be found missing. Fortunately, this ruse always worked.

But there was a small price I had to pay for this cover-up. Every time I went home, I was expected to come back with a small container full of home-baked cookies, some snacks, biltong (dried and salted strips of meat), fresh meat, and anything that confirmed that I had indeed gone home. Returning with these provisions (bribes) was a little expensive. Nonetheless, I enjoyed being the centre of attention when I returned. I would dole out the goodies like I was Father Christmas. Being updated about the Junior Dining Hall was the first order of business before the next Monday morning. Then, I would be briefed about other important events or incidents that had taken place in my short absence, as well as less important bits and pieces of information. This briefing occurred as we were munching on the goodies I had brought back.

Room 13, where I was a boarder, had a reputation of having good students both at the teachers' college and high school.

Individually, we excelled in our studies, choral music, tennis, soccer, debating, and other extramural activities. We were also dapper dressers. Our only competitors when it came to our attire were the crew in Room 20 who called themselves the 'McGregor Boys' because most of the clothes they wore were made in the United States and had the McGregor label on them. It so happened that a good number of them came from a notorious place called Alexandra. They were smart, not thugs.

Kilnerton was a great experience for me in a number of ways. It offered me a good education in a very vibrant and stimulating environment. Mr Charles Jackson, the principal of the high school, whom we fondly and secretly called 'Jackie', was a tough taskmaster, though very different from Meneer Engelbrecht at Emmarentia. To begin with, Jackie was English and Engelbrecht was an Afrikaner. Their physical and cultural traits and their demeanours were strikingly different. Jackson was respected by students while Engelbrecht was feared. Jackie was lanky, had an upright posture, and carried himself like a British officer. He wore glasses, shirts with ties, well-pressed grey pants, blazers, and often regular tweed jackets and polished shiny shoes. During the summer he would wear short khaki shorts, short sleeved shirts, and field shoes.

Assembly was held in the middle of a courtyard that had three sides and resembled a horse shoe in shape, with all the classroom entrances facing the inside of the courtyard – a design similar to that of Emmarentia. Jackie conducted these assemblies from the middle of the shorter side of the horse shoe but a couple of stairs higher than us. From that vantage point, he had a commanding view of his wards who stood in rows facing him, with boys to his left and girls to his right. Jackie always began by saying 'Good morning' and followed it with a short prayer and announcements before we dispersed to our classrooms. These were to the left and right sides of the courtyard.

The teachers' college was on the same campus but with separate administration buildings and other facilities. Its principal was Mr Kenneth Hartshorne, another English taskmaster and strict disciplinarian. Both Mr Jackson and Mr Hartshorne were effective teachers and efficient administrators, and the teaching staff at both the high school and the teachers' training college was very good. We liked them and held them in high esteem. At the high school we were amused by our mathematics and science teacher who was German. I don't recall his name, but I have vivid memories of this exuberant man, big and tall, with a round face and a big, slightly bald head cropped by white shaggy hair. He dressed casually like an absent-minded professor. We called him 'Zeeman' because he could not pronounce the word 'the'. Wherever there was a 'the', he invariably said 'zee'. He was very passionate about science and mathematics and keen on teaching us. We learned a lot from him. His science experiments were the high points of his classes. Of all the subjects I took, I excelled in Afrikaans, Botany, English, and Zulu, but with Science and Mathematics I merely got by.

Extramural activities that I enjoyed were singing in the school choir, debating in the school's debating team (in English and in Afrikaans), and playing table tennis, regular tennis, and some soccer. Our school's choir was ranked very highly in the eisteddfod circles in the Transvaal Province – we were one of the best. Our conductor, Osborne 'Brian' Ferdinand, was a trainee in the teachers' college. He had an excellent understanding of choral music and a wonderful, inspiring voice. His temperament was admirable and even. One could not help but want to sing and behave like him. Our school's tennis team had two brilliant and outstanding players, Timothy Mahlaba (my friend Cyprian's elder brother) and Billy Chikane, who was a distant relative of mine. Timothy had also come from the Albert Street Methodist School. Billy was a graduate of the Orlando High School located in Orlando East. Kilnerton's arch-rival in sports activities and intellectual competitions like debates was St Peter's Anglican School in Rosenttenville, Johannesburg. There was an undeclared war between the Methodists (Kilnerton) and Anglicans (St Peter's). Each won a battle or two, but no one ever won the war.

The most fundamental influence my two boarding schools had on me, apart from teaching me to read and write in both Afrikaans and English, was to think critically about my experience as a black boarder. Being in the care of white principals and some of their white staff, who had varying political attitudes and varying reactions to black people, began to open my eyes. I slowly began to understand some of the conditions affecting me, my family, my community, and black people in general in an environment dominated by white people. Being at boarding school for five years also helped me grow and develop some independence, confidence, and self-reliance, qualities which were to manifest themselves later in my travels and trials in exile.

Another influence that Emmarentia Hoërskool had on me was that it deepened the work ethos and discipline instilled in me by my parents at home. This deep-seated, pervasive ethos was strengthened at the boarding school – in the classrooms, wood working classes, and through the manual labour on the school's farm. It was here that I learned what farm work was really about. Working around the house with my father had prepared me to some extent, but on the Emmarentia Hoërskool farm, the manual labour was much harder because the farm was massive. This was no small garden. It was hard work preparing the soil for planting, spreading the fertiliser (which consisted mostly of the manure collected from the school's cowsheds), and planting corn, squash, groundnuts, sunflowers, and the other vegetables that were used in preparing our meals. Tending the fields, weeding, and harvesting was back-breaking work. On days when we had manual work, evening study periods were punishing because we were tired. And the study period began shortly after dinner, which often consisted of porridge, some vegetables, and meat – heavy stuff! Doing homework and studying after such a meal was difficult. Dozing off was easy. But on the whole, I performed quite well in my studies for the Junior Certificate diploma at Emmarentia.

Kilnerton helped me build and improve on what I had learned at Emmarentia. The language of instruction and general communication was English. This made me fluent in both English and Afrikaans, and my proficiency in both languages helped me to survive in the world of work and to organise political resistance, especially between 21 March and 9 September 1960, when I left home and went into exile. The course content and pedagogy at both Emmarentia and Kilnerton were rigorous, demanding, and of a very high standard. Obtaining Junior and Matriculation certificates was hard work, but the results were gratifying – until 1953. In that year the National Party government introduced what they termed 'Bantu Education'. It saw no use in providing good education to a people who were to remain servile to the white population. Consequently, the government systematically went around the country closing down all mission schools like Emmarentia and Kilnerton. This policy of degrading education for black people at all levels has had a lasting and crippling intergenerational effect on the black population of our country.

8

Religion

My father was an evangelist in the Mission part of the Dutch Reformed Church for his entire adult life, and I myself grew up in four of its parishes until I was 25 years old. The DRC therefore played a significant role in the early part of my life, as it did in the early lives of my siblings. Having studied the origins of the church has helped me better understand how it influenced my parents, my four elder sisters, my older brother, myself, and our upbringing, and at this point in the story I feel it may be important to share some of that history, as well as the history of my own relationship to its doctrines.

The church's introduction in South Africa can be traced back to the decision by the Dutch East India Company (DEIC) in 1651 to establish a station at Table Bay, halfway between the Netherlands and Southeast Asia.[4] This decision was taken during the Netherlands' Golden Age, which followed eighty years of war with Spain. Having won this war, the Netherlands emerged as a sea power with extensive trading ports and colonies in the Americas and Asia.

The war with Spain had been, to a large extent, a struggle for religious liberty, and the resulting combination of Dutch patriotism and religious fervour meant that church and state became closely connected. The duty of the state was, among other things, to promote and propagate the true Reformed Faith. Thus the DEIC was also obligated by its charter to establish the

---

4 The DEIC itself was then the world's largest commercial enterprise and operated under the charter granted by the Dutch States-General to which it was nominally sub-ordinate. In reality, it was a sovereign organisation of merchant capitalists who were totally independent from the Dutch state. They had organised and operated a monopoly for their own benefit. Buying cheap and selling dear to make a profit was the primary goal. Brute force was used to protect its monopoly, and this and the profit motive were strong religious dogmas imposed on all trading ports, settlements, and colonies in which the organisation conducted its business.

Reformed Religion among the natives in the distant East where it operated and at the Cape of Good Hope station.

In 1652, Jan van Riebeeck arrived at the Cape to establish a victualling, repair, and rest station for the company's ships and crews sailing between the Netherlands and Batavia (now part of Indonesia), which was by then the largest and most prosperous settlement in the company's trading empire. One of the instructions that the Gentlemen XVII, the directors of the DEIC, gave him was to build a Reformed Church that would provide his garrison and small settler community with the necessary pastoral care and spiritual nourishment. Thus, when van Riebeeck landed at the Cape, he was the custodian of both the religious doctrine espoused by his employers and the rulers in the Netherlands and their collective economic, political, and social interests and institutions. Van Riebeeck was a medical doctor and surgeon and came from a family of means. His grandfather had been the mayor of Culembourg, which, it is said, was the centre of social and political activity in the community and its surrounds. His upper-class upbringing meant that he was familiar with the teachings laid down by the Dutch Reformed Church, including its values, rituals, and symbols. He could be trusted and was well equipped to inculcate these values, rituals, and symbols in his motley crew.

It is recorded that van Riebeeck's crew of 125 men were recruited from the rabble of Dutch society. The crew consisted of day-labourers, vagrants, the unemployed, and thieves. Their individual and collective understanding of the religious wars, politics, and economics of their country – of everything, in other words, that had deposited them in the Cape – would have been scanty, to say the least. Van Riebeeck's first recorded count of his garrison, taken in December 1652, lists one individual in the group as a sick-comforter (siektrooster), whose duty was to comfort those who were ill or bereaved, read sermons on Sundays (but not preach), and instruct children of the company's employees in their religion. He was not mandated to offer communion, conduct marriages, or perform baptisms. These functions were the responsibilities of the Commander (van Riebeeck) or an ordained minister on a company ship which happened to call at the station on its way to Batavia or the Netherlands.

Religion

It was three years later, in 1655, when a resident minister was appointed and dispatched to the Cape. This appointment was made by the Church Council of the Reformed Church in the Netherlands, but the DEIC paid his salary. The early settlers believed that black people were the descendants of Ham, the cursed son of Noah, whose children were to be the hewers of wood and drawers of water for the descendants of Shem. In the book of Genesis, Noah said, 'Cursed be Canaan [son of Ham]; a servant of servants shall he be unto his brethren' (*Gen.* 9:25).

The idea that black people were servants or slaves was based on this interpretation of the Old Testament story; this was the racist theology that underpinned slavery. But this servile class was to be infused with the Protestant work ethic, the idea that constant hard work, diligence, and frugality are signs of grace, and the idea that good works bring salvation. Slaves and black people were to be driven to work hard for their masters, however salvation was not for them.

The settler community was strongly opposed to converting slaves to Christianity because they would then have to release them from bondage and treat them a little more considerately. When a deliberate effort was made to evangelise among the slaves, there was strong resistance from the colonists. Reluctant evangelising continued under the close supervision of the Nederduitse Gereformeerde Kerk (NGK) which was for white people only. It was much later in the mid-1700s that a separate church for black people – black people who were converted to Christianity – was built. This church struggled to gain acceptance, survive, and grow. Among the most important psychological, political, social, and economic reasons for proselytising among indigenous people was the need to pacify them, especially after forcibly taking their lands and livestock, and compel them to become labourers on what used to be their own lands. There was also an altruistic and paternalistic motive, which was to save the lives and souls of the damned.

This Church doctrine became an important instrument for appeasing both the slave and native populations that the DEIC and the white settlers were subjugating. Using selected parts of the Bible, they reinforced the notion that they were superior to all people who were not white. Whites were Christians and blacks were heathens. White supremacy and racism were planted very deeply in the religious dogma of the day. Consequently, the Netherlands Reformed Church contributed significantly to the religious and secular foundations of white supremacy and racism, and ensured their ability to reproduce over numerous generations.

~

When I look back at my own relationship with Christianity, I see an unfolding history of childish diligence, of occasional enlightenment, of boredom, of music, and eventually of creeping doubts. As a young child, going to church was routine, and listening attentively to a sermon was something I did without effort. When I started going to high school, however, particularly Kilnerton, the church services at home became increasingly monotonous. The DRC staple of 'brimstone and fire for all ye sinners unless ye repent', which struck terror in the minds and hearts of poor and uneducated black believers in townships, sometimes began to feel downright boring.

The approach at Kilnerton was different. Listening to the Governor of the Kilnerton Institution, Reverend Storey, conduct a service was enlightening. His sermons dealt with social issues that many of us could relate to, even though they were delivered using Biblical interpretations and references. Accompanying these sermons were well-chosen and uplifting Methodist hymns, which we sung with great fervour. Reverend Storey was more intellectual and sophisticated in his sermons than Meneer Engelbrecht, who was a strict Calvinist and stuck dutifully to the Biblical text. Consequently, Reverend Storey had a strong and lasting influence on many of us at both the high school and the teachers' college.

The little education I got at Kilnerton had also prompted me to start asking some basic questions about the heavy dose of religious doctrine I was exposed to at home, where praying was a constant. Every meal was preceded by a short blessing. Mornings began with another short prayer meant to guide us through the difficulties we would encounter during the day. In the evenings before dinner, a short blessing and dinner was followed by a longer prayer essentially thanking the good Lord and praising Him for having protected us from all the evils which we could have encountered during the day. I often struggled with evening prayers because they happened at the end of a long day and, having just had dinner, my stomach was full and I was tired. I usually ended up sitting cross-legged under the kitchen table when these prayers were said. This spot was sleep-inducing. Often, someone would give me a little kick because my voice could not be heard when it was time for all of us to say the Lord's Prayer.

As I grew up and went to high school, I began to have some difficulty in trying to reconcile my personal circumstances and experiences with the Christian teachings I was taught and believed. What the Good Book said did not tally with what I saw happening. Perhaps I took what was written in the Bible literally; I did not know how else to take it. One nagging question I had, I remember, concerned Beatitudes. There are eight blessings in the Sermon on the Mount in the Gospel of Matthew. Being able to read the Bible in both Afrikaans and English, these blessings were crystal clear to me. I read and thought about them and interpreted them literally. I could not reconcile them with the terrible conditions that black people lived under across the country. This conundrum engendered doubts in me about religion. But I kept these to myself until the 29th of May 1948, which, I recall, was a Sunday.

I remember the date because this was the first Sunday after Ascension Day, when the National Party and its smaller partner, the Afrikaner Party led by Dr D. F. Malan, a prominent dominee of the NGK, won the general election. For some reason my father was summoned to meet the dominee in charge of the George Goch DRC district after the service in the NGK in Jeppestown on that Sunday. The NGK was the mother church for white people only; it had established the DRC to serve black people. My father decided to take me with him. When we got to the church, we were the only two black people in attendance – something very unusual.

We were seated alone on the last row of pews close to the entrance to the church. It turned out that this was a victory service for the ardent members of the NP who were also members of the

NGK in the area. They had gathered to celebrate the victory of Afrikaners over the English, who were viewed as supporters of the United Party led by General J. C. Smuts. The joy of having defeated Smuts's United Party was visible in the faces of those who came to worship. Their collective elation at being victorious over the English-speaking party was almost palpable. They had come to give thanks to the Lord for having delivered them from the English. This was confirmed by the passage selected for reading in the Bible. The presiding dominee chose to read from *Exodus*, Chapter 14. This chapter is about Moses leading his people from Egypt to the promised land. To me, it seemed that Moses was Dr Malan and his people were the Afrikaners. I could not visualise the Promised Land but had an idea of what lay in store for black people in that land.

My father and I sat there quietly digesting what was being said and sensing that tough times were ahead for us as black people. Once the service was over, my father went outside to the back of the church to meet the dominee who had summoned him. I waited some distance away from all the beaming faces and grimacing white people who would occasionally glance at me as if to ask, what the hell are you doing here? When my father was done with his meeting, we left for home on his Raleigh bicycle with me sitting behind him on the carrier. Not a word was spoken between us about what we had seen, heard, and experienced – not even at home. The National Party was the governing party of South Africa from 1948 until 1994. During this period, its reign improved and elevated the lot of Afrikaners immensely and that of most white people at the expense of black people. God seems to have listened to the pleas of white people much more than to those of black folks, who are still praying faithfully.

Another event that added to my alienation took place during a Sunday afternoon service in my father's church. He had announced a couple of weeks ahead that on a particular Sunday everyone should try to attend that afternoon's service because the dominee in charge of our parish's region would be conducting it. Sunday arrived. I can still see it clearly in my mind's eye, the more so because it really galled me. The church was packed. My father, his deacons, my mom, the women's church group, and the rest of the congregation were in their Sunday best for the occasion. So was the church choir in which my four sisters, my brother, and I sang. The songs that heralded the commencement of the service were well chosen and sung with vigour. Then followed the reading of the scripture on which the sermon would be based. I do not remember what the dominee read from the Bible. What I vividly recall is that once he had finished reading the text in Afrikaans, it was read in both isiZulu and Sesotho. He then pulled out a big drawing wrapped in brown paper that he had brought with him; it was about a metre square in size. He placed it against the side of the pulpit where he was standing as he conducted the service.

Suddenly, like Houdini, he revealed what was on the drawing board: it was a painstaking drawing of a human heart. This heart was divided into four equal quadrants. In the first compartment, at its top left-hand corner, was a devil painted black, with horns and a long tail. The dominee went straight to the point: our hearts were populated by the likes of the devil in his drawing. This devil moved from one quadrant to another each day as we sinned. And the only way of exorcising this evil monster was through prayer, repentance, and asking God for forgiveness. To be saved from going to Hell, we had to confess our sins both actual and imagined and submit to the will of God. This was essentially the message he had come to deliver. I reacted with pent-up anger watching this little white man terrorising poor gullible black people who already felt damned in many ways given the miserable circumstances of their daily life. From the moment he stepped up to the pulpit, we were all damned and on our way to Hell. Had he come to save us? What in Hell's name had we done wrong? I also wonder what he thought was in *his* heart when he drew this damning picture.

The final straw was an incident that occurred on a rainy Monday morning in Brixton at the house of the dominee overseeing the George Goch DRC. I had again accompanied my father who, this time, had to deliver the previous day's church collection and report on some church matters. As usual, we entered through the front gate but had to go around to the back of the house to wait at the bottom of the stairs leading onto the veranda until our presence was acknowledged. It was pouring with rain; we had no umbrellas. My father and I stood in the rain for several minutes until the dominee slowly came out of the house and stood on the veranda, and deliberately greeted us before summoning us to come up the stairs. As if surprised, he said in Afrikaans, 'No man, David, don't stand in the rain. Come on up the stairs onto the veranda.' By this time we were of course drenched. What hurt was being nonchalantly left to stand in the rain by a very young man who went on to address my father as if he was his peer. This was done in front of me. The humiliation my father had to suffer was sickening. I again questioned how God could be so merciless towards black people, who were oppressed, and be so benevolent to the white oppressors.

The dull and monotonous sermons of my father's deacons exacerbated my gradual alienation from the church. Each time one of them conducted a service two excerpts of the scriptures would be read. These might be somewhat related or might purport to carry the same message. The choir would sing in between the readings, and the preaching would follow. Invariably, an interpreter would be required. If the person conducting the service spoke in isiZulu, the interpreter would repeat what was said in Sesotho; and vice versa. What would follow would be incoherent interpretations and repetitive incantations of what was read but in a dramatic style, in loud and high-pitched voices which were meant to emphasise the passages read and hopefully instil the fear of the Lord into those who weren't dozing. On numerous occasions I would catch my father sitting behind whoever was preaching, dozing off despite the loud repetitions. I began to doubt the whole story about believing and being redeemed.

9

A Brush with the Pass Laws

It was around nine-thirty in the morning on Market Street when I was stopped by a policeman dressed in civilian clothes. He had a gun in his holster, which was hidden by the jacket he was wearing. I was eighteen years old and in my last year of high school. The policeman asked me for my identification paper – this was before the introduction of the 'dompas' or 'dumb pass' booklet. I was carrying this piece of identification paper, which had been issued by the Pass Office in Johannesburg, but it had expired the previous day, and I was on my way to renew it just across Market Street when he stopped me. I handed him the piece of paper and explained that it had expired the previous day and that I was on my way to renew it just across the street. From where we stood, we could both see the entrance of the Pass Office.

I was hoping he would understand and let me go and renew my pass. But no, he said he was arresting me for not carrying a valid pass. I was his first catch of the day. He handcuffed me and bundled me into the back of a police truck which Africans called a 'khwelakhwela'. 'Khwela' is a Zulu word for 'climb into' or 'get on board'. When repeated rapidly, the word conveys being hurriedly pushed and shoved into a big police vehicle. This vehicle was basically a huge truck with a high canopy made of wrought-iron and covered with a metal sheet, a strong door, and, of course, a massive lock to secure its human and other cargo. African women who brewed illicit beer and their clients feared the sight of a khwelakhwela. It was always associated with the prospect of being arrested for any one of the innumerable rules black people invariably ran afoul of.

Once in the khwelakhwela, I sat uncomfortably opposite two huge barrels which were used to brew 'skokiaan' (an illicit African alcoholic concoction). They still had some skokiaan left in them. These barrels were originally used to carry oil or some other chemicals, but after they were 'cleaned', they were used to store large amounts of home-made African beer, which was brewed and sold by black women to black men mostly in African townships or other African neighbourhoods. These two barrels facing me had obviously been confiscated in a raid in some African neighbourhood, but the owners seemed to have eluded arrest. They most probably ran away or hid when the raid took place. But this zealous policeman was not deterred. He had confiscated the two barrels of beer anyway. And now he was on the prowl for more black people to arrest around Fiestas and Malay Camp. As he drove around with me in his cage, he collected a few more victims who had been arrested and handcuffed by other policemen on their beat and were ready to be picked up and delivered to the nearest police station. They had a method of hand-cuffing a catch of two or more blacks. When a policeman caught two blacks, he would handcuff the one's wrist to the other's so that it would be difficult for them to run away without tripping. A few such pairs of transgressors were thrown into the khwelakhwela.

After capturing more people during this search-and-arrest mission, our khwelakhwela headed for the nearest police station. It turned out to be the dreaded Marshall Square Police Station where we were off-loaded and hustled passed the regular charge desk. It was at this desk that anyone who was arrested was asked for personal particulars, interrogated, and booked, fined, or locked up. We were not taken to this charge desk or asked why we were arrested. Instead, we were herded past the charge desk behind which several white policemen were seated and simply looking at us as we were rushed up a flight of stairs. Their black subordinates stood quietly by at some distance from the charge desk and, like spectators, also watched us being rushed up the stairway into what turned out to be a holding pen for transient human cargo. Once inside this big room, all the handcuffs were taken off and the iron door leading into this room was slammed shut. Babel broke loose. Everyone was anxiously ventilating to the person standing next to him about why and where he had been picked up. We were still venting our fears and anxieties when the iron door swung open. A white detective and his African interpreter, who looked more like a clerk, walked in and shut the door behind them. They had come to tell us how they could help us solve our pass problems very easily and quickly.

The white policeman spoke in Afrikaans, and this was translated by the African clerk into both isiZulu and Sesotho. The translation was in a botched colloquial Zulu and Sesotho spoken in Johannesburg, but fortunately, it was understandable. Having grown up in the DRC and been schooled at Emmarentia, I understood Afrikaans very well and got a better understanding of what the proposition was all about. The offer we were being made was that we should go and work on some farm for a few months, after which we would be returned to Johannesburg and our identification papers would be fixed by the police administration. This offer was punted strongly and coupled with the threat that if we did not take it, we would have a rough time trying to fix our identification papers, let alone live in Johannesburg. This document featured your name, surname, ethnicity, employment, whether you had permission to be in the area, and so forth. We were given the 'lunch hour' to seriously consider this offer. No questions were asked by the arrested, and it was clear that none would be entertained by the two making the offer. Nothing was said about the kind of work we would be doing. Terms and conditions of employment did not exist; it was a take-it-or-leave-it threat. Both left and bolted the iron door behind them.

A few minutes later the same door opened, and two large dirty hessian bags filled with coarse brown bread were literally thrown into this holding pen and an old-fashioned dairy steel milk can full of black chicory coffee was dragged in and left next to the bread bags. Some old steel army mugs were also thrown in for us to use to drink the coffee. These mugs were dirty and had bread crusts that had accumulated over time around their lips, a reminder of the many mouthfuls of bread and chicory coffee they had served without being cleaned. Many of my fellow-prisoners took the bread and coffee because they were hungry. No one knew where and when the next morsel of food would come from. I did not touch the bread nor did I drink the coffee. The look of the bag containing the bread, the bread itself, and the coffee mug turned me off. I did not feel like eating or drinking anything. In fact, I did not feel hungry. As people were munching away at the bread and gobbling down mugs full of chicory coffee, there were animated exchanges about whether to take the offer or refuse it. The big question was, what would be the consequences of not taking it?

During this desperate search for the right decision, I spoke to an older man whose appearance was that of someone who had had a rough time. He was about twice my age and looked weathered. He looked at me with sad eyes and advised me not to take the offer to work on the farm and that the promise that my pass would be fixed after I had finished my stint and returned to Johannesburg was a blatant lie. He then showed me his hands. They were callused and, when his palms faced down, I saw that he had no fingernails. He had lost them working on a farm digging out potatoes with his bare hands. He had returned from the farm because the police had reneged on fixing his pass but had been arrested again and had now resigned himself to returning to whatever farm he would be sent to. He was caught in a vicious and unbreakable cycle. I was terrified. I knew there and then that I was not going to take the offer. There were two other youngsters my age in this group. I went to tell them what I had learnt and tried to persuade them to reject the offer and wait to see what would happen next. A few other cellmates overheard our conversation and said they just wanted to get out of this holding pen. They were going to take the offer, and somewhere between leaving Marshall Square and being carted to wherever the farm was located they would jump off and escape.

I suddenly remembered that I had often seen trucks on Marshall Street carrying African men and boys seated on the open deck of a truck – but not in prison uniforms. At the two corners of the rear of the truck would be two armed white men guarding them. The two white men were not policemen: they looked more like farmers, and the trucks were regular trucks without steel canopies like the dreaded khwelakhwelas. It quickly dawned on me that this was what was going to happen. I then told those around me what I knew from having grown up walking up and down Marshall Street for years when going to Albert Street Methodist Church Mission School. A couple of older but quite fit-looking men said they would take the chance because there were numerous traffic lights on the streets and the truck would have to stop at some of these traffic lights. That's when they would jump, they figured. But I said that that's when they might be shot. This risk did not deter them.

It wasn't long before the lunch hour was over, and the door swung open again. This time, the white detective who had made the offer walked in with a farmer who was wearing a khaki shirt and shorts, a wide-brimmed farmer's hat, and veldskoene (shoes worn in the fields) with socks that reached to the knees like Meneer Engelbrecht's. The detective wasted no time. He was agitated and impatient and instructed us to form two lines. One consisted of those who had accepted the offer and the other of those who had rejected it. A long line formed of those who had accepted the offer; only two of us turned it down. He abruptly handed the farmer a piece of paper and told those who had accepted the offer to follow the farmer down the flight of stairs. Once all of them had left the cell, the two recalcitrants, myself and the young man who was about my age, remained locked up. I then ran to the barricaded window in the hope of catching a glimpse of how our former cellmates were being transported. Voila! Just as I had suspected: they were being hurried into the back of the truck and seated. And they were handcuffed! Two armed white farmers were positioned at each rear corner of the truck. My prison-mate and I looked at each other as if to say, 'we told them so'. The truck drove off with its human cargo – forced and unpaid labour. The complicity between the police and the farmers was evident.

Now there were just two of us left. The deceitful persuasion continued. A different African clerk came alone without his white superior to offer us another 'opportunity'. This was another job, also on a farm, but this time we were told that we would be engaged in milking cows and performing other tasks related to cattle farming. This offer was presented rather half-heartedly by the clerk who didn't seem to care whether we took the offer or not, unlike the white detective who was eager and determined to get rid of us by means of the first offer. This time we were not given any time to think about the offer; the African messenger wanted our response immediately. We both rejected it. The clerk took his pencil and notepad and left us locked up in the holding pen.

65

The Way Home

It was now getting dark outside, and we had no clue how this adventure would end or when. Again, the door swung open. Another white policeman in civilian clothes walked in and had us handcuffed to each other and commanded us to walk down the stairs and out the same door that our cellmates had used. But this time the two of us were thrown into a police van and driven somewhere. The drive was not long. When we got out of the van, I realised that we were in a police station somewhere in Fordsburg. This was not far from the Braamfontein Railway Station but a little further from Park Station. I then figured out how I could escape even before being taken inside the police charge office and perhaps being locked up for the night.

Now that we were in the police precinct yard, the handcuffs were removed. We were told to walk up a flight of stairs into a big office with a big desk at the other end. No one was sitting behind the desk. We were told to sit on the floor next to the door and wait for the station commander to arrive. While waiting, another African detective entered the room. He stood in front of us for a short while looking at us carefully, as if inspecting us. He then asked whether I did physical training and boxing. I was a little surprised because I did neither, but without hesitating I said I did both. He then quickly turned his attention to my companion and, like a bully, instructed him to get up and follow him.

My fellow prisoner was ordered to sweep the entire yard of the police station. It was big. He swept it very quickly and came back sweating and quite angry. I realised that he was anxious about being separated from me. We continued sitting as we waited for the commander of the police station to arrive, and it wasn't long before a big burly Afrikaner dressed in civilian clothes walked in and went straight to the big desk where he sat down and started rummaging through some papers. He called my name. I jumped up and went to the desk and stood at attention waiting for my sentence to be pronounced. He told me that I had to pay ten shillings for not being in possession of a valid pass. I had more than twenty shillings on me, so I paid the fine and got a receipt. But I also asked him for a letter stating that I had been arrested and detained for a whole day and that on the following day I should be allowed to go and revalidate my pass. He wrote the letter in Afrikaans and gave it to me. The commander was done with me; next was my companion.

He too was fined ten shillings but didn't have any money. I lent him ten shillings and also gave him his bus fare to get home to Alexandra. In my desperation to get home, I hardly asked for his address so that I could recoup my ten shillings. He also did not ask where to find me in order to pay me back. Both of us just wanted to get home after having survived potentially disappearing into some potato farm without our families' knowing. I could not believe that I had lost twenty shillings in an attempt to avoid being jailed or dispatched to some obscure farm. I had not eaten or drunk anything since I had left home early that morning. We both walked towards Park Station because he had to catch a PUTCO bus going to Alexandra. This bus stop was on Noord Street, which was near to Park Station, where I could also catch a train to George Goch. When I got home, my parents were worried because it had taken me a whole day to renew my pass. I told them the story. In the evening prayer, my father thanked the good Lord for saving me. The next day I fixed my pass. The law and I did not cross paths again until 1958, when I became a political activist resisting these very same pass laws. This second brush with the law would be more severe and had much graver consequences.

10

The World of Work

Like the parents of many of my classmates, my parents could not afford to send me to university. The expense of sending us to boarding school and helping us through high school was as much as they could manage. While I was at boarding school, I worked during the school holidays as a caddy and at a toy factory located on the poor whites' side of the railway tracks of George Goch station. There were times during these short school breaks when I bought oranges at the Portuguese produce market located on the whites' side and sold them at a profit at the entrance to the George Goch station on the blacks' side of the station. The experience of navigating the taunting racial slurs of poor whites when I went to buy these oranges proved to be useful in other jobs I found. This was in 1953; I was 18 years old.

Truck and Car

I landed my first proper job at Truck and Car, a used car dealership that faced Eloff Street and backed onto Joubert Street. Its owner was a Mr Hamburger, a Jewish immigrant from Frankfurt, Germany. His young, pleasant secretary told me that when Mr Hamburger arrived in South Africa, all he had was the suitcase carrying his belongings. (Little did I know that I too would soon find myself in the same situation.) Mr Hamburger's company advertised itself using a catchy slogan, which was 'They Come from Afar to Truck and Car.' And indeed, some did come from faraway places, but most came from Johannesburg and its surrounds. They came to sell their vehicles or exchange them for better-looking or newer models. The better-looking cars had their exteriors, interiors, and engines cleaned fairly nicely. When I was not making tea or being sent out to deliver mail, I was one of the cleaners. These cars were better-looking, but whether they were better-performing was in doubt. Truck and Car sold used cars but did not repair or service them. It did not have an in-house mechanic employed to do any repairs or conduct any checks on the cars it sold. You bought what you saw and found attractive, looked at what was under the bonnet, paid, got the keys, started the car, and drove out the exit, which was on Joubert Street. No guarantee or warranty was given; only a receipt for the purchase.

It was interesting to see a white person drive a beaten-up old car into the shop from the Eloff Street side, park it in the shop, and get out. The floor salesperson would be waiting to welcome the unsuspecting and eager prospect who invariably wanted to sell his car and buy a better one. The better one was always the one that had been cleaned, looked nicer, and was, in some cases, a later model. Unfortunately, this nicer-looking car often stalled shortly after it had left the shop because it had not been checked, serviced, or certified as roadworthy. The acrimonious exchanges that ensued between the buyer and the salesperson, who always took the position that the car left the shop in good and running order, were often comical. I had helped to clean the car and knew that few checks, if any, had been conducted and no repairs had been done. Mr Hamburger always came out ahead. He lived in the leafy suburb of Orange Grove and drove a car imported from Britain. Every day he wore a dark suit, white shirt, and tie, and on his jacket's lapel he always pinned a fresh rose. To complete the appearance of an esquire, he donned a black Homburg. In short, he looked like he was making good money selling used cars.

When I was not cleaning the cars, I made tea for the young secretary, the manager of the shop, and Mr Hamburger himself. And when doing neither, I was out picking up mail at the Post Office on Jeppe Street or delivering mail in the inner city of Johannesburg. I liked going out to collect and deliver mail because it gave me the opportunity to search for a better job. Indeed, on one of my errands, I found a job at an insurance company on Loveday Street between Main and Fox Streets, and I gave Mr Hamburger my notice. This company was called the Yorkshire Insurance Company. I was moving up in the world of work – or so I thought.

The World of Work

Yorkshire Insurance Company

The Yorkshire Insurance Company was housed in a tall building on the north side of Loveday Street between Fox and Main Streets. The building was No. 26, Loveday Street and still stands but is now empty and boarded up. Its managing director was a Mr Svidsson, a Swede. The company insured homes, businesses, automobiles, boats, and individuals against fire, accidents, theft, and disasters. Contracts were entered into and signed between the insurers and the insurance company, and each party walked away with his or her copy of the policy. At Truck and Car, you bought your car and paid for it in cash or by cheque and drove it out of the shop. The papers you walked away with were a small receipt and another paper showing that you were the new owner of the vehicle. Insuring it was your responsibility.

At the Yorkshire Insurance Company I had to look presentable, unlike at Truck and Car where the dress code was quite informal. This meant that I had to wear a nice shirt, tie, neat pants, a jacket, and had to polish my shoes every day. Once in the office, I had to take off my jacket and hang it neatly in the addresso-multigraph operating room where I worked and put on a clean khaki dust coat. The daily routine began with going to the front counter which was near the main entrance to the offices. This counter was where every client who walked into the company stopped to ask for assistance. Behind this counter stood Samuel Makhubo, the most senior black employee, Jacob Sibiya, who was next in line in the hierarchy, and me, ready to open the morning's mail that was delivered by Mangena, who was responsible for collecting it at the main Post Office on Jeppe Street. We opened the mail and sorted it into piles for the different departments it had to be directed to.

In front of this counter was the main entrance. We were expected to greet every white person who walked in with a pleasant smile and say, 'good morning, sir' or 'good morning, madam'. The greetings were sometimes acknowledged; some were grudgingly responded to. After we finished opening the mail and sorting it every morning, Monday through Friday, the three of us would then go to the filing room where all the paper files were properly kept by the remaining black staff of about six young African men. Our task in the filing room was to ensure that the filing of documents, representing all the individual contracts the firm had entered into, were correctly filed and up-to-date before the white staff came and asked for specific files in order to deal with whatever inquiries they had to respond to.

Once we had finished opening and sorting the mail and checking the paper filing room, the three of us headed for the addressograph/multigraph plate embossing room where we spent the remaining part of the day cutting and typing metal plates, on which we captured names, addresses, types of insurance policies taken out, premiums to be paid by the insured, and when the payments were due. These metal plates captured the critical and essential information gleaned from the paper files which were in the filing room. The plates were also filed appropriately and updated depending on the changed circumstances of the insured and used for sending out renewal notices and reminders to clients so that they could pay their premiums. These metal files also served as a backup for the paper policies kept in the filing room.

What was interesting about working in this noisy room was that because Sam, our leader, was thought to be Coloured, Jacob and I tended to be treated as if we too were Coloured. The fact that both Jacob and I had a little education also made quite a difference. I tried to dress like Sam but could not afford to; I earned less than either Sam or Jacob. But what I earned was much better than what I was paid at Truck and Car. The other interesting point about our work was that we were very efficient in calculating the premiums that had to be paid for any policy. Often young Afrikaner men who were new employees were sent to us to be taught how to calculate premiums for different policies. We found this a little amusing but also galling because we would soon watch them being promoted and posted as area managers. This always reminded us that being educated and clever was fine, but being black was an insurmountable handicap.

The monotonous 'good mornings', opening and sorting of mail, inspecting of the filing department, and being confined to a very noisy room for a good part of the day finally got to me. The tipping point was the pay; I had to find a better paying job, so I visited the Jan Hofmeyer School of Social Work to find out what social work was all about. I was interested in training as a building inspector, but I was told I had to first go back to school and qualify as a social worker. I would not be earning any income while studying, and the pay after graduating was not much. I needed a different plan. My brother at this time was a school teacher. Between what he and I earned, we bought a navy-blue, second-hand Buick sedan for the family. I immediately got a driver's licence, as having a driver's licence opened up the possibility of getting a better-paying job. I had spent a year at the Yorkshire Insurance Company when I went looking for a job as a driver. And I found one – at Perkins Peterborough Engines (Pty) Limited, which was walking distance from home.

Perkins Peterborough Engines

This firm was the South African subsidiary of the Perkins Peterborough Engines located in England. F. Perkins Limited was incorporated on June 7, 1932 in Peterborough, England, and it produced the world's first high-speed diesel engine, a Perkins four-cylinder Vixen which made its debut also in 1932. In October 1935, Perkins became the first company to claim six world diesel speed records for a variety of distances set at the Brooklands race track in Surrey, England. Its South African branch was situated on Main Road near the George Goch railway station.

I was hired to chauffer the Managing Director, act as an assistant to the stores' manager, drive a small delivery van which was used to collect mail at the Jeppe Street Post Office, deliver or pick up spare parts and other parcels, and help construct big wooden crates for used engines that would be packed for shipping to Peterborough in England for reconditioning or repair. Building wooden crates and packing big engines was the toughest of these jobs. This is where I learned to use a moving crane in order to position a huge engine onto a platform that I had built and then secure the engine with iron brackets so that it would not move as it was transported by truck to the port of Durban, whence it would be shipped to England. After this was done, I would then construct the sides of the crate and its lid. What my father taught me in handling tools, and what I learned at Emmarentia working with wood, were helpful. I learned a lot and became quite adept at using a movable crane, different sizes of saws, and a variety of nails and hammers to build large crates to carry different sizes of engines.

The store manager, Harty, who was a white man, was often absent, and during these absences I would act as assistant store manager. The store manager was often away managing South African boxing champion, Willie Toweel. My diligence was a source of conflict between the store manager and me because I often found discrepancies between the items that were in the bins and the inventory cards. When I found these errors, I would correct them. And when the manager of the branch would himself fetch an item in a bin and discover that I had properly reconciled it with what Harty had written on the inventory card, he would curse out softly, sometimes in my presence. When Harty returned, he would be told by the manager of the branch to pay more attention to the stores than to his boxing business. Harty hated me for reconciling stock with the inventory cards. He made my life miserable by demeaning and taunting me and even came close to calling me a kaffir. It hurt so much that I decided to leave without giving notice. On the morning that I walked out, the managing director had not yet arrived.

On that same day, late in the afternoon, I was at home contemplating my next move in my job search when I heard the sound of the Humber Super Snipe roaring to a standstill at our house gate. This was a big car made in England and a favourite among top business men and other professional classes. The Managing Director was tall and burly with scruffy hair and had the face of one who loved his whisky even during lunch. He had come to fetch me, he said, and I drove back to work with him. A big mistake! The next day Harty's hounding and taunting continued and was even more aggressive this time. An Englishman who was visiting from the head office in England was surprised to see me back. He called me into the board room where he was camping out. He did not mince his words. He told me that I should not have come back no matter what I was promised. His reasoning was that the odds were heavily weighed against me. He felt sorry for me because I, as a black person, was dispensable and Harty, being white, was not. The message was loud and clear. I left that afternoon and came back at the end of the week to collect what pay I was owed. This was at the end of 1955. I informed a friend, Roy Matlare, who lived in the township that there was an opening at Perkins and asked whether he was interested. He took the job and somehow survived – and for a long time. I, on the other hand, having a driver's licence and some experience, went looking for another job as a driver, and being a full-time driver did fetch me a better wage.

Dr Henry Gluckman

There was a big timber company also on the Main Reef Road past Perkins Peterborough Engines going east towards Denver, the next station after George Goch. I forget the name of this firm. I had heard from someone that this company was looking for a chauffeur for one of its directors, so I went for an interview, and because I already had some experience driving and knew the city and its surrounds very well, I was hired on the spot. The next morning I was handed a white dustcoat, a pair of white gloves, and a black cap of the kind usually worn by chauffeurs.

My passenger was a short, elderly, distinguished-looking white gentleman who was always very neatly and finely dressed. He had an expensive wardrobe. His name was Dr Henry Gluckman, and whenever he got into and out of the car, I had to stop the car, turn off the engine, and get out to open and close the door for him. Wherever we went, I had to wait for him until he finished whatever business he was conducting. Sometimes we would be out during the early evenings. He lived in one of the upmarket flats in the city centre and also had a beautiful family compound past Uncle Charlies, which is beyond what is now Southgate. It was not long before I came to know who this Dr Gluckman really was.

He was the last Minister of Health and Housing in General Smuts's United Party Government. I also found out that he was the first Jew to hold a cabinet position in South Africa. He was an active public figure in numerous and diverse organisations. At one stage, he was the President of the Timber Trade Federation as well as Chairman of the South African Wood Foundation. While researching this book, I discovered that there was a government report named after him, the *Gluckman Report*, which was released in 1944. This report came out at the same time as the *Beveridge Report*, which gave birth to the National Health Service in the United Kingdom. Henry Gluckman's vision for South Africa was a countrywide national health service funded through taxation and delivered to 'all sections of the people of this country according to their needs and not according to their means.' With the defeat of the United Party by the National Party in 1948, what was a promising and progressive policy died. I wonder whether our ANC comrades have looked at Gluckman's report to see how it could help to inform the development of their National Health Insurance Scheme.

Being a chauffeur was monotonous and quite boring, and dressing up as I had to made me feel like a real minion. That I was driving someone who was a former Minister of Health in Jan Smuts's United Party did not console me. I realised that I had reached a dead end in being a chauffeur or driving a regular motor car. I had spent less than a year driving Dr Gluckman around, and I needed to move up the ranks among drivers by trying to obtain a licence that would permit me to drive trucks or buses. This kind of licence was called a public service licence. The wages paid to public service licence holders were much higher than those paid to regular drivers, including chauffeurs. The challenge I faced was that I needed money to pay for lessons on how to drive a truck or bus. This was going to be an expensive venture, so I came up with an alternative plan. I had a friend, Nana, who was already employed as a truck driver and asked whether he could take me along on his rounds unofficially and teach me how to drive the truck he was driving. Nana was a nice, soft-spoken, and likeable person; he lived two streets down as you entered the township.

Stork Nappies

Nana was a few years older than me. He drove one of Stork Nappies' medium-sized vans, which collected soiled linen diapers in the white suburbs of Johannesburg and took them to the factory where they were cleaned. He would then load the van with a clean batch and return them to the owners. He did these rounds daily from Monday to Friday driving, picking up, delivering, and making notes of what he had collected and returned. We decided to divide these tasks. I would do most of the driving in and around the suburbs while he did the rest. Having me accompany him was helpful in that it reduced the hectic pace required to execute all the tasks of his job singlehandedly. I also benefitted immensely from spending time learning how to drive a bigger vehicle. This arrangement suited both of us quite well, even though it was very risky because it was unauthorised.

It was not difficult to learn how to drive a big van. The experience I had gained as a chauffeur was useful, but the greatest advantage was that during the better part of the day, there was very little traffic on the streets in the white suburbs. When we stopped to pick up or drop off nappies, we saw madams and their black nannies and occasionally black gardeners. Our contact was usually with black domestics, with whom we exchanged the parcels of dirty or clean diapers. It seemed that all the white men had gone to work.

Challenging aspects of the driving were going up or down steep hills when I had to change gears to accelerate or slow down the vehicle. Automatic gears and power steering had not yet been introduced. But I learned quickly because I was determined to pass the driver's test and avoid disappointing Nana, especially given the risk he had taken in helping me learn how to drive a large vehicle. If his employers had found out, he would have lost his job and I would have been arrested.

Once I had gained enough confidence in handling the van and Nana also felt I was ready, I went and hired a bus from a driving school and headed for Langlaagte Drivers' Testing Station. On the testing day, I was scared and very anxious. The bus looked huge because I was small and only in my early twenties. At the testing station offices, I filled in some forms and paid the fee. A hulk of an Afrikaner was assigned to test me. The first test was to park the bus in the testing yard's premises. Buses of that period, like the vans, had no power steering or automatic gears. One had to manage the hard clutch and gear lever to change gears and the tough brake pedals to stop. I performed well in parking and was then told to drive out of the yard and go into the city.

I don't remember how I made it into downtown Johannesburg around midday during the week as I drove around observing traffic rules, lights, and pedestrians while also being instructed to turn left or right or go straight. All I remember is that when the official who was testing my driving said we should drive back to Langlaagte, it seemed as if we had been driving around the city for a very long time. I was exhausted from being careful, anxious, and nervous. I only wanted to know whether I had passed the test or not. Failure was not on my mind because I thought that I had handled the monster-bus well. And indeed, I did pass and was immediately issued my public service driver's licence. In my mind, I had just joined the elite class of drivers who earned good wages from driving buses and big trucks. I was over the moon. Walking down Main Reef Road to the city was like walking in the clouds and floating home to tell my parents and brother the good news.

On my way to Park Station to catch a train back home, on the corner of Jeppe and Harrison Streets, I heard what sounded like a gun shot. I saw people running in all directions away from where the sound came. My curiosity got the better of me, and I had to see what had happened. When I got to the scene, I saw a tall black man wearing khaki pants and a khaki shirt with folded sleeves. He was propped up against a shopfront window with his legs stretched out and bleeding from his right thigh. Apparently there had been a sharp altercation between him and a white man over a parking space. Evidently, the black man was trying to reverse in order to park his truck and offload some shop fitting materials while the white man was eyeing the same space for his car. The black man had gotten to the space ahead of the white man, and a confrontation had developed.

The conflict escalated because the black man, who was already reversing into the empty spot, would not give it up or defer to the white man. Strong and emotive language ensued, and in the heat of this exchange the white man pulled out his gun and shot the 'native' in the thigh. Someone had helped to move the black man from the sidewalk and propped him up against a shopfront window. The white man had walked away and left the scene. On the doors of the truck that the wounded African had been driving was the name of the company he worked for: Frederick Sage & Company. I immediately realised that this wounded man would not be able to drive that truck for some time. Perhaps this was an opportunity to pursue. I finally got home with the good news about the public service licence and the bad news of having seen someone who had been shot. I also shared my idea of going to Frederick Sage & Company first thing the next morning and inquiring whether the firm needed a driver given that one of their drivers had been shot the previous day.

11

Frederick Sage

Frederick Sage was born to a village carpenter in Freston, a small village in England in the mid-1800s. Early in his life, he understood the implications of the economic revolution taking place around him. Radical changes in business organisation and business policy of that period saw buildings erected that were bigger than ever before. These buildings came with highly specialised stores and display windows. Three factors influenced this development: first, the expansion of display spaces; second, the use of new materials; third, the intensification of sales techniques driven by the rapid pace of the modern era. There was also, of course, the growing class of capitalists whose demands had to be met. Picture-frame window shopfronts were revolutionary when they were introduced by the House of Sage. The use of metal mouldings, plate glass, and glass joints for the deep vestibules required elaborate planning. Such plans enhanced the lighting and dressing of shop interiors as backgrounds for items displayed even on short frontages. An observation is made that it is not surprising that a people whom Napoleon nicknamed a nation of shopkeepers should build the first business to concentrate on the needs of shops as a specialised industry. This was the achievement of the House of Sage.[5]

In South Africa, Frederick Sage established its first branch in Cape Town round the turn of the twentieth century. In 1915, the company and factory moved to Johannesburg and was located on

---

5   Among its high points was the House of Harrods, which became the finest establishment in London. From 1900 to 1905, the House of Sage devoted almost all its resources to Harrods, thereby consolidating its reputation. Around the same time, the House of Sage received the honour of being appointed as Showcase Makers to His Majesty King Edward VII. Later in 1924, the company was further honoured by being awarded the warrant as Case Makers to Her Majesty Queen Mary. Another of Sage's most striking accomplishments was the Principal Floor Plan and other sections of the House of Commons, which was opened by King George VI on October 26, 1950.

the corner of President and Von Weilligh Streets. Fourteen years later, it moved to Heidelberg Road at the south end of Von Weilligh Street. It was from this large factory that the Anstey's Store, John Orr & Company, the Colosseum, the Twentieth Century Cinema, and other prominent buildings in Johannesburg and Pretoria were outfitted. Frederick Sage also provided shopfront fittings and related products to smaller towns outside major cities.

The Frederick Sage & Company that I went to the day after its driver had been shot was located on Heidelberg Road. At its main entrance was an elderly black man, his crop of white hair sprinkled with tufts of black, wearing a plaid sports jacket, brownish pants, white shirt, and a tie. He controlled access to the firm's workshops. Most importantly, he made sure that everyone, black and white, punched the clock when arriving in the morning and again when leaving the premises in the afternoon. This elderly man was indeed the gate-keeper. However, management, staff, and draughtsmen did not have to come and go through this gate; they entered and left through the front entrance of the building facing the main road.

I explained my opportunistic initiative in coming to apply for a job as a truck driver and cushioned this by assuring the gatekeeper that as soon as the wounded driver had recovered, I would relinquish his job and leave. Evidently, this thoughtful approach and candour impressed him. He told me to wait at the gate while he walked up the driveway to consult another African, a younger man, who turned out to be the foreman of all the black workers in the factory. They talked for a few minutes out of sight. When they appeared, the younger man was walking very briskly in front, befitting his position in the firm, with the elder gentleman in tow. The younger man's surname was Sibiya.

Sibiya was the same height as the older man. He was dressed in matching khaki long pants and a short-sleeved khaki shirt. He sported a crop of thick curly black hair, which he parted in the middle. His moustache stood out: it was black, small, and rolled out and up at the edges somewhat like Salvador Dali's. He was alert, clever, and a fast talker and walker. Evidently, he had been adequately briefed by the older man, as he went straight to the point, rattling off questions: What was my name? Where did I live? What did my parents do for a living? What were my educational qualifications? Did I have a truck driver's licence? Is it true that if I were hired, I would relinquish the job once the injured driver recovered and returned to work? I answered all these questions and confirmed the last one. He told me to follow him. I figured I was hired.

As Sibiya and I were walking up the driveway, I saw the truck I had seen the previous day when I came across the injured driver. There were two other smaller trucks standing idle, one alongside it and the other in front of it. Two older African men, the truck drivers of these two trucks, stood on the loading platform next to the trucks. I presumed they had more experience driving trucks than I did. And from the way they were looking at me, it was clear that neither wanted to drive the big truck. Nor were they keen on giving me, the little kid, a break by letting me drive a smaller vehicle. They went on to tell me that I was hired to drive the big truck, and I was given the keys and left to take the truck out for a test drive. The driveway in which the trucks stood was between two buildings. One was an iron shop, in which steel, bronze, and aluminium frames and structures were built. The other was a joinery shop, in which wooden display furniture and ancillary parts were made and painted. The three trucks owned by the firm were parked and ready to load any structure from either building. What was loaded had to be delivered to a work site where the company had been contracted to work. The width of the driveway could accommodate two trucks parked alongside each other. On the side of the woodwork building was a loading platform where most of the shopfront fittings were loaded and off loaded. The big truck was standing next to this platform, ready to be used.

Sibiya, the two other drivers, and a few other black and white employees stood around to see how this youngster would manage to drive a big truck that was usually driven by a big tall man. I got into the driver's seat only to discover that my feet could not reach the brake and clutch pedals and that the back of the seat was also too far back. The driver's seats of that period were not adjustable. A howl of laughter came from the onlookers. I was hopping mad at being laughed at. My brain instantly shot into overdrive. I got out of the truck and my eye caught two twenty-five-pound, empty, brown reinforced bags. Not far from them was a pile of unused rags, and in no time I grabbed two of the brown bags and stuffed them full of rags, then returned to the truck where I used one bag as a seat and slipped the other behind my back. Voila! I could easily reach both the brake and clutch pedals. I must have cut an interesting figure and looked like a small boy sitting high in the driver's seat of a monster truck. I started the vehicle, shifted into reverse, and slowly but deftly drove down the driveway onto the street. I left the laughing crowd bewildered. I don't think they had ever seen such a performance. When I returned from familiarising myself with the truck's quirks, Sibiya was waiting to congratulate me with gusto. He was so pleased that he called me a *tsotsi*, a clever crook.

On the first day at work, I earned myself the position of senior truck driver by driving the biggest truck the firm had. All the large loads of shopfront fittings that had to be delivered near and far were passed on to me. I had an excellent partner who was called 'Shorty' because he was short – no more than five feet tall and of medium build. I never got to know his real name, but I knew he came from the Northern Transvaal (now called Limpopo). His responsibility was to supervise every job that was loaded, ensure that it was fastened properly, and also supervise the off-loading of the consignment. He had the strength of almost two bigger men; and it did not matter what we had to load and deliver, sections of steel or bronze frames, huge plate glass pieces, solid and heavy doorstops, or small bornite letters and the black boards that went with them – whatever it was, Shorty knew where and how to pack any item and fasten it so that nothing fell off when we drove to our destination. On arriving there, he would supervise whoever helped to offload, telling them how each piece should be handled. Shorty and I never had a single piece of broken or damaged cargo. He was very respected for his expertise in packing, just as I was for driving both short and long distances. We were a great team!

One afternoon, Shorty and I were returning to the factory from somewhere in the West Rand when we noticed an oncoming car that looked like one belonging to the senior manager. Indeed, it was his car, and from a distance he flagged us to stop, so we did. He came to the driver's window so that I did not have to get out and asked me to come to the office the next morning because he wanted to discuss moving me from driving to assisting in managing the stores. I was shocked! So was Shorty. An elderly white man was going to be laid off as an assistant stores manager and replaced by a young black man. In a big factory where the racial divide was palpable, this was almost unbelievable. How would the white workers react? There were close to two hundred of them. And would I survive? I suspected that I could rely on the tacit solidarity and muted support of my fellow African workers. And they too were many.

The following morning, I was called to the managing director's office, Mr. C. A. Robinson, where he and his deputy, the one I had talked to the previous day, were waiting for me. They offered me the job of assistant stores manager, just as I had been told the previous day. The pay was more than I was earning as a truck driver. Again, I had a sense that I was moving up in the world of work. My immediate senior would be Laurie (I forget his surname). He was a young Afrikaner who seemed comfortable with working with the English. But working with a black man? I suppose he had no choice; it was not his decision to make. Still, when I was being interviewed for this new job, I raised the question of how I would be protected from the reactions of white artisans and craftsmen who might not tolerate seeing a black man take what they perceived to be a white man's job. Management said they would instruct the heads of the different shops that I should be treated with respect like anyone else who was white. Very interesting, I thought.

The big workshops in the firm were those for iron, steel, bronze and aluminium, and woodwork and joinery. The glass and paint workshops were smaller. The inventories for all these workshops were my and Laurie's responsibility. These were in the store and would be drawn down against named and numbered job sheets signed off by architects and draughtsmen who had calculated the required quantities of different materials needed for each job. Each job had a name, the shop it came from, the date on which it was sent to the store, what material was being ordered and in what quantities, and by whom. Laurie and I released whatever was requisitioned only if the job sheet had all the foregoing details. Whatever was left over on any job was credited to the drawn down quantities for that job. Such surpluses were used in other smaller jobs or treated as scrap if too small to be used for a job.

All the white workmen were instructed to send their 'boys', their black helpers, to fetch material needed for specific jobs from the store. Management had instituted the system of sending 'boys' in order to keep the white workmen busy and productive at their work benches, instead of having them go to and fro to fetch small items such as a round or flat head screw 'that long' – they used their fingers to indicate the length. Some workmen, especially the Portuguese ones, were usually those who constantly ran down to the stores because they had difficulty expressing themselves clearly in English. Oftentimes they could not explain what they wanted their boys to fetch. Invariably, they would then accompany the 'boys' to the stores themselves to point out what it was they were looking for. Sometimes it was funny, particularly when the 'boys' knew exactly what was needed but would not say.

Laurie and I worked together quite well. He had a competent and eager assistant who worked more smartly and diligently than the previous elderly white man. The job was very demanding and quite hectic. We started working at eight in the morning and stopped at five in the afternoon. Lunch break was from twelve to twelve thirty – just thirty minutes. All the white staff and workers had their lunch prepared and served in the cafeteria reserved for whites only. Coffee and tea were also served during short breaks, one in the morning and another in the afternoon. These were also for whites only. Thus I had a problem. The nearest restaurant at which I liked to eat was some distance away on Von Weilligh Street. It was the Blue Lagoon where I used to collect my teachers' lunches when I was at Albert Street School. Black workers at Frederick Sage went either to a 'chisanyama' ('burn the meat' in IsiZulu), also along Von Weilligh Street, or to the municipal beer hall opposite the Bantu Sports Ground, which was much closer to the firm. For me, these two places were unsuitable because they weren't healthy.

At Frederick Sage, white supremacy and the racial division of labour were clearly visible. White men were the artisans, craftsmen, professional draughtsmen, and management; these were the aristocrats of white labour who directed and supervised black labour. Black men were handymen and helpers who performed the heavy, dirty, and dangerous tasks, especially in the metal and glass workshops. Whenever something went wrong because of a black worker, the explosive expletive 'you bloody kaffir' was heard loud and clear. Other derogatory expressions like 'you monkey' hurled by whites were also standard. There were also instances when the 'kaffir' at the receiving end of such vicious torrent of insults would react very threateningly. In a few cases, this often resulted in the black worker menacingly wielding a hammer or hurling a piece of metal into the face or over the head of the white man involved. The effect was both terrifying and salutary.

The habit and culture of using the 'k' word was standard practice. It was not used in the stores where Laurie and I presided because it was known that I would react by leaving the job and that whoever had used the word would put his job on the line. Management had let that be known. There were three Africans who worked with me and Laurie in the stores who were also spared this abuse because of the edict protecting me. They were referred to as 'delivery boys'. When not running errands or stealing leftover cuts of bronze sections to sell to scrap-dealers, or tapping into industrial spirits for tots which they mixed with Coca-Cola, they would assist in measuring sections of metal required for particular jobs, help take stock from the floors, shelves, and bins, and keep the stores clean. Some of the white men who chafed at not being able to use the 'k' word at me and the 'boys' in the stores substituted the 'k' word with the expression 'my black friend'. This euphemism did not escape us. We knew what they really wanted to say: the tones and facial expressions that accompanied the two words 'black friend' were provocative and intended to hurt and humiliate.

There was a Mr Mullen (an Afrikaner) who was the deputy of Mr Dickson (an English man) in the metal shop and who relished coming to the store for little items which he could easily have told one of his black underlings to come and get. Coming himself gave him the opportunity to taunt us – and to taunt me, in particular. It hurt me so much that one day in the presence of my superior, Laurie, I looked Mullen in the eye and told him that he was heartless. I went on to say that he obviously did not have any children because if he did, they would likely be the same age as I was, and he might be more sensitive towards my feelings. His whole face turned red. In a split second, he stormed out and walked up a short flight of stairs. He forgot whatever he had come to fetch. Laurie, with his glasses perched just above his nose, was standing over his desk pretending to be checking some paper, a job sheet or invoice, but had evidently been listening to the confrontation. He had never seen me so angry nor heard me express myself so strongly. Peering over the top of his glasses, and in a soft and measured voice, he told me that the Mullens did not have any children. I felt good and vindicated.

I learned a lot about what goes into shopfront fittings in different buildings simply from managing the stores. I began to think it would be good if I were promoted to the drafting office upstairs and started as an apprentice. The idea of being a draftsman was exciting. I decided to broach this idea with Mr Robinson, the managing director, my promoter and protector. It took a single meeting between us. After telling him that I thought I had done very well in helping run the stores and now felt that I needed to move on to a more challenging job in the company, he asked me where I thought I would like to be moved to, so I told him that I wanted to be apprenticed as a draughtsman. He looked stunned. I was puzzled. His response was immediate: he asked whether I knew that there were many white draughtsmen employed in the firm who would all walk out if I were to join them. He told me that he could not risk a walkout. I then gracefully tendered my resignation. I walked out of his office and left him looking lost and in a bit of a bind because he did not want me to leave. He could tell that I was determined to leave if I wasn't promoted. But he could not think of where else I could move to in the firm. So I left after working there for two years, from 1956 to 1958. This time I decided it would be better to be self-employed.

I would then carry a passbook indicating that I was my own boss. This would mean fewer hassles with the police.

12

Loss

The experiences of working at Truck and Car, Yorkshire Insurance Company, Perkins Peterborough Engines, of driving Dr Henry Gluckman and driving a truck at Frederick Sage & Company, and later of working as an assistant stores manager slowly and quite unconsciously alienated me from working for any white firm. What helped me develop my political consciousness was the exposure to the uncompromising racial divide and the hierarchy by which whites dominated blacks in all workplaces. The menial status and positions that I was being consigned to as a black person, in churches, schools, the workplace, and in society at large, made me aware of the resistance being waged by various organisations against racial discrimination and apartheid. This led me to reading some of the pamphlets distributed by a group called the 'Africanists'. It was not long thereafter that I became interested in reading a few books on Pan-Africanism and the writings of prominent Africanists like W. E. B. Du Bois, George Padmore, and Kwame Nkrumah, the Prime Minister and President of Ghana. Ghana's independence meant a lot to me and other Africans, I'm sure. I was ready to join the ranks of Africanists in the Witwatersrand. Their catchy slogan 'Izwe Lethu' meaning 'Our Country or Our Land' was emotive, more strident and more appealing than the ANC's 'Mayibuye iAfrika', which meant 'Let Africa Come Back'. In 1958, my best friend, Shadrack Mabuza, and I invited Robert Sobukwe, Potlako Leballo, Sidney Ngendane, and Peter Raboroko to help us establish a branch of the Africanists in the Eastern Native Township. And they did.

It was during this period of political conscientisation, while I was still working at Frederick Sage, that I returned home one evening to the news from my siblings that my mother had fallen ill during the day and had been taken to hospital. This was on the 5th of September, 1957. I was shocked and, like the others, felt helpless that all we could do was wait for news. The shock became total several hours later when we got word from my father that she had passed away. The doctors said she had died from the complications of a blood clot. When I recall how my mother passed away so suddenly, I'm left with great sadness and a wish that I had known her more. She was only sixty-four years old. I was twenty-two.

The shock I felt was compounded because I had been told months earlier by a sangoma (soothsayer) from Limpopo that she would fall ill and die soon thereafter. The man who made the prediction was a construction worker by day on a building site just off Nugget Street as it crosses over a bridge connecting downtown End Street with the bottom of Hillbrow. At night, he doubled as a watchman guarding the site. He lived in a small one-room shack made of corrugated iron. What had drawn my attention to him were the few people I would notice waiting outside his shack in the early evenings. Most of them were black. There were whites too, though very few. One evening out of curiosity, when no one was around, I went to ask him about the people I'd seen waiting outside his place. He invited me in.

Inside his shack, along one of its corrugated walls, was a skimpy mat on which he slept. On the mat were some blankets and a few basic items for preparing and dishing out food. The room was lit by a single electric bulb hanging from the centre of the corrugated roof. This shack did not have a ceiling. Directly below the light bulb, but on the ground was a brazier with a sieve on top of it. On this sieve was a very small piece of fat that had been cut off some meat that was no longer there. I asked why this piece of fat was on the sieve and dripping oil onto the red coals. He pointed to a tripod on the side of this brazier in which he had cooked some maize porridge. He explained that because he could not afford meat, when he took a mouthful of porridge from the tripod and put it into his mouth, the smell of the burning fat served as a substitute for meat on his tongue and in his mind. I have not forgotten this scene nor the power of imagination.

In answer to my question about why there was a line of people at his door in the evenings, he told me that they came to consult him. During the day he was a construction labourer;

at night, he said, he was an 'iSangoma'. His evening clients paid him well and made up for the meagre wages he earned as a construction worker. I believed the money part of his answer but not the 'iSangoma' business. When he noticed that I was sceptical about his ability to see into the future, he offered me a free consultation, and I jumped at it. He turned off the only light bulb and pulled out a bag containing all sorts of small bones, which he rubbed with his hands. These were coated in phosphorescence that made the bones glow and magnified their varied forms, especially in the dark. He also had a small baton that glowed. He used this baton to spread the glowing bones and interpret their formations and the meaning of each. I still cannot figure out how the bones told him where I lived, what parts of its surroundings I was afraid of at night, or how he seemed to have a pretty clear view of my home.

Of all the correct things he told me, I thought he had lost it when he told me that my mother would fall sick and we would think it was just a passing illness but she would die soon afterwards. I politely thanked him and left. I was baptised as a Christian and my parents were believers; bones and soothsayers were for lost souls.

I never told anyone at home about this prediction until the afternoon that we were leaving the Croesus Cemetery, having buried my mother. It was only then that I remembered and hesitantly told my father about what had happened. I also said that I was very sorry that I had not mentioned it earlier. Calmly, my father said he understood why I had not told him, then looked away and said no more on the matter that day – or ever again. The sangoma's prediction was simply never talked about. And as I record it here, I am still flabbergasted by how that man knew what he knew.

That was the passing of my mother, Julia. Her influence, as I have recorded, lives on in me in many ways. I am deeply indebted to her and grateful for all she taught me. My ability to navigate difficult times with my own life partner, and my ability to laugh at myself, I learned from her. I still miss her. She was a great storyteller and had an infectious sense of humour.

Bereavement weighed heavily on my father. It weighed heavily on all of us. Life had to continue, though, and I watched my father recommit himself to his work in the parish. With heavy hearts, my siblings and I continued with our lives as well. It was some months later that I left Frederick Sage & Company. In the process of trying to think of what kind of work or business I would like to be engaged in next, I came across a few newspaper articles reporting on the buying power of the natives in the city of Johannesburg. These news reports said that black people were spending around one million guineas (a guinea being one sterling pound and one shilling) daily in Johannesburg, except on Sundays when they were confined to the townships.[6] When these reports came out, I was already attracted to Africanist publications and gatherings. I had begun attending discussions organised by Africanists. It was at one of these meetings that I met Edwin Makoti, a bookkeeper with some knowledge of business. We both saw an opportunity to form an advertising company that would enable white businesses to showcase their products. But our problem was that we knew nothing about advertising, let alone selling advertising space.

Preparing to start this little enterprise took several months and was a little scary because I was unemployed and living off my savings, which were dwindling rapidly. Fortunately, I would not run afoul of the pass laws because the passbook I carried said I was self-employed. I went browsing at the Central News Agency (CNA) bookstore at the corner of Commissioner and Loveday Streets looking for books on how to sell. I found two books by Dale Carnegie, *How to Win Friends and Influence People*, and another the title of which I can't recall. I bought both. I walked out of CNA and turned left onto Loveday Street and walked towards Fox and Main Streets. I was about to pass the entrance to the Yorkshire Insurance Company when I heard someone call my name from across the street. It was Mr Robinson, my former employer at Frederick Sage & Company. He wanted to talk to me. I crossed the street to meet him. We exchanged pleasant greetings and his

---

[6] From 1910 until 1961, the currency of the Union of South Africa was tied to the British pound until the rand replaced it, at an exchange rate of two rands to one British pound.

first question was, what was I doing? I told him that I was in the process of starting up an advertising business with a friend but that it was proving difficult. He acknowledged that and said that if it did not work out, I should come and see him at Frederick Sage. I had no idea what he had in mind, but I knew that I would not go back there. I had learned my lesson before when I was persuaded to return to Perkins Peterborough Engines after I had resigned. That was a horrible experience which I did not intend to repeat.

Dale Carnegie's books helped me a great deal. Once the mock-up of the magazine was ready, Edwin and I hit the road selling advertising space to merchants in the city. We had prowled around and researched how to price the advertising spaces in our magazine. It took a lot of courage to walk into a white-owned shop and ask a white secretary to tell one of her bosses that a Mr Nkosi or a Mr Makoti wished to speak to him about advertising. On many occasions we were confronted by white men who were perplexed but interested in buying advertising space with a new company that had latched on to the bright and promising idea of advertising them to the African market. It was hard for these men to believe their eyes and ears, seeing and hearing a sales pitch from one or two young black men talking very confidently about how advertising in their magazine would increase their sales revenue. But our proposition was irresistible. The news that black people were spending around one million guineas a day in the city was an opportunity they could not ignore.[7] Selling advertising space quickly became easy. Apart from being dressed like business types, we both spoke good English and Afrikaans. Having attended Emmarentia Hoërskool and Kilnerton High School was paying off.

---

7   Fortuitously, some years earlier in 1960, shortly after Edwin and I had started our company, which we called African Advertising, J. Walter Thompson and Company, an American advertising firm, came out with a publication titled 'The South African Market'. This company was founded in the early 1950s and conducted research and analysis of markets in the United States, Canada, Latin America, Western Europe, Japan, Philippines, Hawaii, Australia, and India. It also did the same work in South Africa but much later. The wealth of information, experience, and expertise shown in its analysis of the South African market, which it dissected in several ways, was very encouraging for our venture. The analysis included the industrial sectors of the economy, distribution and consumption patterns and investments, the classification of racial groups, and their incomes and standards of living.

Nkosi Family circa 1942. Taken on steps of church portico, Ferreirasdorp, Johannesburg. Seated on ground: Cousin Benina Kubheka, Morley and brother Stanely. Middle Row: Gogo Sibulelo Nkosi holding great grandchild, Reverend David Nkosi and Mama Julia Buthulezi Nkosi. Rear Row: Four sisters – Thoko, Beauty, Emily and Nana.

Side view of Reverend Nkosi's mission church in Ferreirasdorp, Johannesburg. Taken in 1991.

Benina Kubheka, Morley and Stanley in school uniforms for Albert Street Methodist School, circa 1942.

Entrance to Albert Street Methodist School, building is at the rear. Building in the foreground was the home of the resident clergyman. Taken in late 1990's.

Main entrance of Albert Street Methodist Church. Taken in late 1990's.

PAC group led by Robert Sobukwe marching to the Orlando Police Station on 21 March 1960. Morley is second from the left in the second row. Taken by Peter Magubane 21 March 1960.

"An identity document, commonly known as a "chitupa," issued in Johannesburg in September 1960 to Morley with the pseudonym 'Johannes Ndaone' for travel through Botswana and Zimbabwe to Malawi.

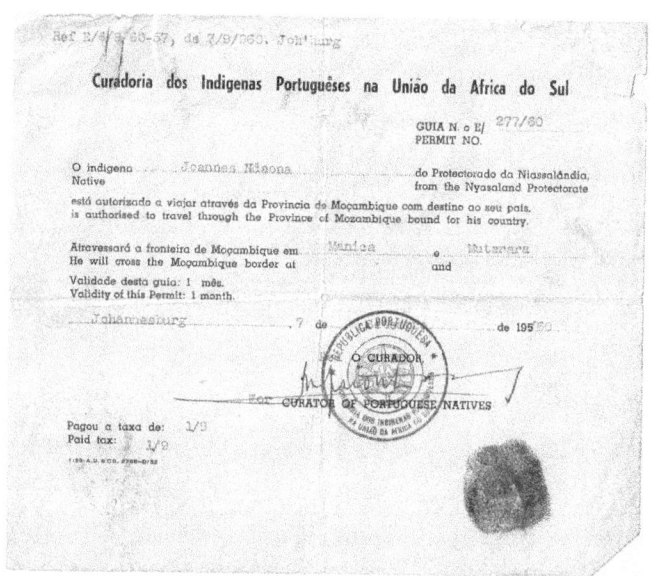

Backup "chitupa" issued in Johannesburg to Morley for passage via Mozambique in case the route to Malawi had to be shifted. Also September 1960.

13

The Pan Africanist Congress

While the advertising business was gaining momentum, I was engaged in earnest political activity with a group of like-minded Africanists. In mid-1958, Ntsu Mokhehle the leader of the Basutoland Congress Party (BCP) had advised Robert Sobukwe, Potlako Leballo, and Josiah Madzunya to form a new political party of Africanists which would be supported by the All African People's Congress (AACP) in Ghana. (This information came to my attention later.) My introduction to the Africanists was via a close friend, Shadrack Mabuza, who worked as a clerk for Jack Berman, a lawyer. He had the opportunity of meeting some of the young literate blacks like him who would often discuss the oppressive conditions under which black people lived. He met some of the early members of Africanists both in and outside of the ANC. He would talk about these encounters with me, Vela Mabuza, Sonny Boy Bhengu, and others, who would hang out together on weekends simply to talk and have some drinks. I was one of those Africans who had been given permission by a white magistrate to buy a limited number of spirits and not be arrested, and these weekend gatherings introduced me to the activities of the ANC and the Africanists. I was attracted to the militancy of the Africanists, given my exposure to the practices of apartheid at my junior high school, work places, the Dutch Reformed Church, and the state.

Before the launch of the PAC on the 4th of April 1959 and the beginning of the Pass Campaign in March 1960, a couple of political turns shaped the future of my political activism. Firstly and most importantly, in the meetings of the national leadership of the PAC leading up to its launch my name came up as a candidate for the National Executive Committee. Sobukwe felt that I was too young for the position. And indeed, I was, especially considering some of the older and more experienced national leaders like Potlako Leballo, Selby Ngendane, Peter Raboroko, Zephaniah Mothoping, Peter Molotsi, Nana Mahomo, Jacob

Nyaose, Josias Madzunya, J. B. Ngcobo, and Howard Ngcobo. These men were much more experienced in the politics of liberation. So, it was then proposed that I serve on the Witwatersrand Regional Executive Committee. This is one turn in my life that I cannot forget. I was soon thereafter elected and served on the first Regional Executive Committee of the PAC of the Witwatersrand Region. A few months later, this Regional Committee was called to account by a special congress of the organisation because of its dismal overall performance. At this special congress, I was the only member re-elected to the second Regional Executive Committee because I had been seen visiting and organising at existing branches and establishing new ones. This time I was elected Vice President of the region with George Siwisa as President. I was a little uncomfortable about being chosen for the position of Vice President, which I thought should have been filled by the veteran militant from Alexandra, Josiah Madzunya, who was an older man and more experienced.

The first three weeks of March 1960 leading up to the 21st, the day of the Sharpeville massacre, were very hectic and quite dangerous. I organised several committed and passionate Africanists into a unit (and financed it) that would address African passengers in trains leaving Park Station and going home to the townships in the East and West Rand almost every working day in the late afternoon. We had to travel to these townships after leaving work. On these train missions, we would engage in political agitation and announce where and when we were going to hold meetings in the townships that we had chosen to visit. On arriving at a chosen township, we would get off the train and walk to the venue for the pre-arranged meeting, then catch another train back to Park Station and disperse to our respective homes. We often got back very late at night just before the curfew for blacks began at 11 p.m. It did not take long before we overheard some people in the trains saying they had seen us the previous day. People were beginning to talk about us. This was exciting and very encouraging because the 21st was imminent.

There was no sense of foreboding. In the second week of March 1960 I was in Durban and Pinetown selling advertising space for our business. In Pinetown, I signed up the Frame Textile

Company for a full-page advertisement. This firm was best known for the colourful blankets it manufactured and sold in African markets throughout the country, and signing it on as a client was a great achievement. I boarded a train from Durban on Friday the 18th of March bound for Johannesburg, where I arrived the next day round 12 p.m. When I disembarked, Nobuntu Msila was waiting for me. She was a senior clerk at Ellis & Company, a large furniture shop in the city which was patronised mostly by Africans. Nobuntu was also a trusted courier of the PAC's national executive. She had been sent by the president of the PAC to meet me and bring me with her to Mylur House where a press conference was to take place at around 2 p.m.

Nobuntu and I arrived at Mylur House and found several national leaders of the PAC already there. Sobukwe was his usual calm, composed, and articulate self as he briefed a few members of the press about what was going to happen on Monday the 21st of March. The objective of the pass campaign was to overwhelm the entire prison system with Africans who were no longer willing to carry passes. It was calculated that this would render the pass laws unfeasible. Sobukwe was briefing the reporters in the hope that the next day's newspapers would help publicise this event. However, the press briefing did not generate the excitement some of us had expected, and very few members of the press were in attendance. Earlier, on the 16th of March 1960, Sobukwe had sent a letter to the Commissioner of Police, Major General Rademeyer, informing him that the PAC would be embarking on a five-day, non-violent, disciplined, and sustained protest campaign against the pass laws, beginning on Monday the 21st of March.

I left Mylur House and headed straight for home in George Goch where I quickly unpacked and visited an upmarket modern printing shop that was situated across from my home on Vickers Road. I sought out a couple of friends in the printing shop in whom I confided that the PAC had planned a pass campaign for Monday and I needed leaflets to be printed announcing this. I told them that I intended to distribute these from Springs in the East Rand to Randfontein in the West Rand overnight. The distribution had to be carried out on that Saturday and completed the next day on Sunday the 20th. They agreed to stay late on that Saturday afternoon until I had all the leaflets I had asked for. They did this at no cost to me but in solidarity with the organisation that was challenging the apartheid state. This was done, of course, without the knowledge of their white bosses, who were not there. My friends ran the risk of being fired and then arrested if found out. I organised this risky initiative after being told at the Mylur House press briefing that a certain Mr Jordan Ngubane, who was a member of the Liberal Party based in Cape Town and a supporter of the All Africa Convention held in Accra, Ghana, had promised that he would produce the leaflets announcing the campaign but had not done so. I then decided to use my contacts at the print shop. They frantically produced hundreds of leaflets, enough to distribute in strategic townships across the Witwatersrand where the PAC had branches and supporters.

To this end Shadrack Mabuza, who was chairman of the George Goch PAC branch, and I, the secretary general of the same branch, recruited Vela Mabuza, a close friend of ours who lived in Sophiatown, to help and accompany us. His father was a prominent member of the Liberal Party, but his son Vela had Africanist leanings. Vela was also helpful because he had a car. It was a navy blue two-door Citroen. We picked up the printed leaflets from the printing shop late Saturday afternoon and left the first batch at the George Goch branch. For the three of us, this was a daring and exciting mission. Vela's car made it possible to undertake the distribution of the leaflets throughout the night. We drove to Springs in the East Rand, stopping at every township on the way. There we turned around and headed for Randfontein on the West Rand, stopping at targeted locations along the way. We finished distributing the leaflets in Randfontein around ten the next morning. After our last drop-off in Randfontein, we went into a general dealer's store to buy something to eat and get an English newspaper to see how Monday's happening was being reported. There was no report in the newspapers. Perhaps we missed it because we found out later that there was something in both the English and Afrikaans newspapers, the *Rand Daily Mail* and *Die Volksblaad*. We were looking for front page bold headlines, but they were not there. Somewhat disappointed, we drove back to George Goch, content that we had done our best.

I left George Goch for Orlando on the afternoon of Sunday the 20th March in order to meet with other PAC leaders and members of the Witwatersrand Region in the evening. We were preparing for Monday morning's march to the Orlando Police Station where we were planning to incite arrest for deciding not to carry passes any longer. That evening, a group of us walked around mobilising other PAC members along the way to converge at Sobukwe's house in Orlando West before marching to the Orlando Police Station in Orlando East. A good number of us, regular members as well as regional and national leaders, converged at Sobukwe's house until the early hours of Monday the 21st of March. It was still dark when we all left Sobukwe's house and marched to the Orlando East Police Station.

Unbeknownst to me, that Sunday night my brother, Stanley, who was a Zulu broadcaster in the Rediffusion Department of the South African Broadcasting Corporation (SABC) called Radio Bantu, had done something daring when he closed the station around 11 p.m. In the township, Radio Bantu was called 'Umsakazo', meaning 'the broadcast' in isiZulu. This service began broadcasting to the 'Bantus' (Africans) of Orlando township on the 1st of August, 1952. It broadcast in three languages, Zulu, Sesotho, and Xhosa. All its programmes were selected, vetted, and produced by the SABC head office's white staff on Commissioner Street who then sent it to the Rediffusion black staff on Fox Street to translate into the three languages before broadcasting. The music to be played was left to the black staff to choose. Some houses in Orlando were fitted with a little brown box measuring about thirty centimetres square with a relatively large hole in its middle where the speaker was located. There was only one button on this funny box, the on and off button which was also used for adjusting the volume. This box was usually stuck high up in the corner of the walls in the living room of the house. On the nights leading up to his closing the station before the much-anticipated Monday march, Stanley played songs such as 'Vukani mawethu ni manyane', meaning 'Wake up compatriots and unite'. This was a hidden but stirring reminder to those who knew what the PAC had planned for the next day.

He left the radio station and took a train to his home in White City, Orlando West. When he left the train station close to his house, he was assaulted by a bunch of men. I don't know how he got himself to hospital. What I remember was that when I saw him on Tuesday the 22nd of March, his whole head was bandaged. Only his eyes and nose were visible. When he turned up at work on the morning of Monday the 21st of March, after having gone to the hospital, the officials of the SABC who were in control of Radio Bantu called him in and fired him on the spot for the previous night's transgression. That was the beginning of his endless trials and tribulations with the South African state security system. He was later arrested for his political affiliation with the PAC and served two years in a Pretoria prison. On his release, the Special Branch made sure that he could not be employed on the Witwatersrand. So, he moved to Swaziland (now Eswatini) with his family where he was employed as a sales representative at a car dealership.

In Swaziland, Stanley continued his engagement in PAC political activities with other comrades and supporters. While there, he harboured a number of PAC and ANC refugees as well as, albeit unknowingly, agents of the South African state security system. Clandestine arrangements had been made by the PAC leadership to relocate Stanley to Dar es Salaam in Tanzania where he was to set up a PAC radio station. This information evidently reached the South African Special Branch officials, and they conspired with Stanley's employer in Swaziland, who sent him to Ermelo in the Transvaal under the pretext of going to repossess a car from someone who had defaulted on his payment obligations.

When Stanley got to Ermelo, the Special Branch police, to his surprise, were waiting for him. He produced a Swazi passport, but the police would not accept it. A minister in the Swaziland cabinet was sent to Ermelo to secure his release and testify that Stanley Nkosi was indeed a Swazi citizen. The Minister went to the rescue but failed. Stanley told me later that one of the Afrikaner security men simply said 'Stanley, jy weet jy is nie 'n Swazi nie! Kom jong!' ('Stanley, you know you're not a Swazi! Come man!') He was re-arrested and again spent some time in jail in South Africa. On his release, he was again employed, now by Radio

Zulu, a division of Radio Bantu based in Durban. From then on, he had a much more difficult time with the state security system. Sometime later, he was hired as a sales representative for the record label EMI and, later still, for Gallo Records.

I doubt that my brother was aware of the power of the SABC when he dared to use its channel to disseminate a subversive message. This is not to suggest that, had he known, he would not have done what he did. For the Afrikaner Broederbond, the SABC was the most effective instrument for promoting its ideas and recruiting more members. It had a monopoly on all radio and television broadcasts from its inception until the late 1980s. In the preface to 2012 edition of *The Super-Afrikaners*, Max du Preez writes that 'the board and management of the SABC were completely dominated by Broeders during this time [1960–1972] and Afrikaner channels were used unashamedly to promote and bolster Afrikaner Nationalism and the National Party. Black channels put a shiny veneer on apartheid and heavily promoted Bantustans – *Radio Bantu*, as it was called, was for a long time a special Broederbond project.'

14

Sharpeville

A Monday morning in late summer. The date: 21st March 1960. The day started early in the morning for me, at the Sobukwes' home in Mofolo. A few of us had gathered there to prepare for the march to the Orlando Police Station. We left Sobukwe's house round 06h30 and walked through Dube, Phefeni, and part of Orlando West where we were joined by other members. Along the way, we collected some other PAC members. One such member we tried to collect was Andrew Tshetlane. On our way to his house, Potlako Leballo, the PAC's National Secretary General predicted that Andrew would be hiding when we got there. And indeed, when we got to his house, his wife was waiting for us. She was in her night robe, leaning over a windowsill. She said that Andrew was not home, despite his knowing that he was to join us on our way to the police station. Leballo's response to Mrs Tshehlane was that she should tell her husband that we knew he was hiding under the bed. This was said in Sesotho. We all had a great laugh and continued our journey to Orlando East without Andrew. He did not join us.

After a 12-kilometre march, we arrived at the Soweto main police station in Orlando East at around 08h30. Along the way, it was evident that many people were simply going about their day. In fact, most of them looked surprised at us marching and singing our liberation songs. The closer we got to the police station, the more determined we were to test the enforcement of the pass laws and institutions that enforced these laws. Yet when we arrived at the police station, it looked like we were unexpected. The black policemen standing outside the station looked quite bewildered. The policemen's demeanour, posture, and facial expressions showed that they were really puzzled. Firstly, why had we come to the police station to court arrest for not carrying our passes? Secondly, what was the end game anyway? It was strange that the Station Commander and a complement of white detectives who were hanging around did not seem to be expecting us, despite Sobukwe having sent a letter to the Commissioner of Police, Colonel Rademeyer, the previous Friday informing him about the anti-pass campaign and then holding a press briefing the following day about the planned campaign.

We stood outside the police station for some minutes waiting to be charged and arrested. Then the officer in charge of the station, Captain J. J. de Wet Steyn, came out of his office and hurriedly separated us into two groups: one group consisted of members of the National Executive Committee and other known leading political activists; the other group consisted of members of the Regional Executive Committee and other branch members. The first group was taken individually and driven by white security officers to their respective homes where searches were conducted for subversive documents. These searches proved to be futile because the materials had already been hidden. Once the national leadership had been taken on this wild goose chase, the Commander came out of his office and instructed the second group that was left standing outside the police station to form two lines.

Logically, the leaders of this group were up front, and I, as vice president of the region, was one of the first, together with another regional leader standing next to me. (It was not George Siwisa, the president of the region: he had been taken with the first group.) The Commander then called me into his office. What struck me as I walked in was the smell of the black ink used on the Gestetner cyclostyling machine when producing duplicated sheets of paper. A pile of them was stacked up on one side of his desk. When he sat down, there was already a form in front of him. I stood in front of the desk waiting to be interrogated. A flood of thoughts was racing through my mind, mingled with anxiety and fear.

A torrent of questions followed from him in Afrikaans: What was my first name? Surname? Birthday? Where was I born? Where did I work? Who was my employer? and other questions, the answers to which would have appeared in my pass, which I was not, however, carrying. My answers being satisfactory, he quickly posed the major question which I was anxiously waiting for, 'Waar is jou pas, jong?' ('Where is your pass, man?') I replied curtly that I did not have it and was no longer willing to carry it. He retorted by saying that I had to pay a fine or alternatively be jailed for a week. And if in two weeks I did not produce my pass, the fine and jail time would double. I responded by repeating a little more emphatically what I had just said, which was that I was not going to pay a fine or carry a pass.

At the back of my mind as I was responding were our slogans, 'Service, Sacrifice, Suffering' and 'No bail, no defence, no fine'. The Commander was frustrated and furious. He abruptly dismissed me and told me to go to the Braamfontein police station and pay a fine of twenty shillings (one pound) and said that if I failed to do so, I would be jailed for a week. I responded by telling him that I was not going to go to Braamfontein for anything. My point was that I was not prepared to carry a pass and wanted to be arrested there and then. He told me to get out of his office and that I was courting serious trouble. What was interesting is that the entire exchange between us was conducted in Afrikaans. I walked out very confused.

Once out of his office, I quickly walked to my comrades who, seeing me come out of the Commander's office, were anxious to hear what had happened. I briefed them hurriedly because I could see that the Commander had followed me to call the next law breaker. The last thing I said to my colleagues was that anyone who was not locked up should wait behind any of the many big gum trees close to the police station until I returned round midday. I wanted to go and find out what arrangements had been made to provide relief for the families whose breadwinners had been arrested. My first stop was Richard Maponya's general dealer store in Dube. Arrangements had been made that Maponya was to receive basic supplies of maize meal, sugar, condensed milk, and other food items which would be picked up by affected families. He was also a member of the Relief Committee that had been set up for that purpose while I had been in Durban and Pinetown selling advertising space.

The Way Home

As soon as I was done visiting Maponya's shop, I returned to the Orlando Police Station as I had promised. It was round midday. As I entered the treed section in front of the police station where I expected to find some of my colleagues who had been let go, like me, there was not a soul in sight. I got an eerie feeling of being alone in this forest of tall gum trees, its canopy covering the sky but allowing streaks of sunshine to come through its branches and leaves. Nothing was moving. I stopped and stood still while scanning the huge tree trunks, hoping to see someone pop out because he was waiting for me. No one did. As I started walking slowly, cautiously, and hesitantly towards the police station, someone popped out from behind a tree. It was Nobuntu Msila, the trusted and indefatigable courier of the PAC. This was the same person who had met me at Park Station on the previous Friday and accompanied me to Mylur House for the press briefing. But this time, she had a much more urgent and serious message for me. After I had been mistakenly allowed to leave the police station, she said, everyone had been arrested, and she instructed me to avoid arrest at all costs. This message came from our national leader, Robert Sobukwe. Apparently, when the Special Branch detectives who had driven off with each of the National Executive Members returned to the police station, they and the station Commander decided that everyone should be arrested. But I had already left. And that is how I got away.

When the news arrived that 69 of the many people who had gone to the police station in Sharpeville, also to protest against the pass laws, had been shot dead and more had been injured when the police opened fire, the unexpected had happened. What was planned as a peaceful protest against carrying passes suddenly degenerated into a bloody massacre in Sharpeville. Other reports that came through looked very ominous, including one from Cape Town where three police stations were overwhelmed by 30 000 protesters who were marching to Parliament led by Philip Kgosana, the regional secretary of the PAC in the Western Cape.

Following up on Sharpeville, I immediately contacted a few individuals who I trusted and asked them to please get the details of the affected families, convey the organisation's sincere condolences, inform the local clergy, and ask them to help with the burials. I myself could not go to Sharpeville because I was now a wanted person. Whatever I could do to solicit help for the bereaved in Sharpeville, I did clandestinely. On the day the funerals took place, I did not attend.

The period from that day, the 21st of March until the 9th of September 1960, when I left the country, was the most difficult time in my short, active political life at home. It was not easy to avoid being stopped by the police, both black and white, who would demand that I produce my pass book. I was on the move every day, desperately trying to reconnect and resuscitate what pieces of the PAC were left in the Witwatersrand, the Western Cape, and other smaller areas. This initiative included reaching out to the ANC and the Unity Movement and motivating the need to work together in the face of the brutal massacre we had witnessed.

In notes that I prepared in Cairo on the 17th of September 1961, the first entry mentions the PAC office in Mylur House being run by a person called Monde for exactly seven days, that is, from the 21st to the 28th of March. During this week, the office handled messages, mail, and telephone calls from branches and regions as far as the Western Cape, particularly about the march to Parliament on the 30th of March by the 30 000 protesters. This was the largest turnout against the pass laws and one of the largest anti-apartheid demonstrations to take place in Cape Town. The ANC Anti-Pass Day was set for the 31st of March. On the 25th of March, the Commissioner of the Police, Rademeyer, issued a startling press statement saying that no Bantu man or woman would be jailed because he or she was not carrying a pass. The pass laws had been suspended! It was on that day that Chief Albert Luthuli, the president of the ANC, was photographed burning his passbook. The ANC called for a Day of Mourning which was also a stay-away from work on Monday the 28th of March. This protest was the biggest in South Africa's history to date. Whites in general were greatly alarmed and frightened. Three days later, on the 30th of March, the National Party government responded by declaring a State of Emergency in most parts of the country.

I spent the months of April and May on the effort to re-organise. In addition to the re-organisation, the relief effort needed attention because it was also not functioning well. Edwin Makoti and I were the only two regional leaders who had evaded arrest on the Witwatersrand. I do not remember how Edwin evaded arrest. It was round this time that he and I got wind of a Ghanaian emissary who was in Maseru, Lesotho, meeting with the senior leadership of the Basutoland Congress Party (BCP), Ntsu Mokhehle and Makalo Khaketla. The Ghanaian seemed to have come because of what had happened in Sharpeville. Ntsu Mokhehle was a member of the All Africa Peoples' Convention (AAPC) formed in Accra, Ghana in 1958 and a member of its Steering Committee as well. He was the best contact for the emissary to get a briefing from about the Sharpeville massacre.

Edwin and I quickly commandeered a Volkswagen combi from one of our supporters and drove from Johannesburg to Maseru in Lesotho. We arrived there on Tuesday the 24th of May, 1960 and went straight to the BCP offices where we met Ntsu and Khaketla. They were surprised to see us because they had been told the day before, by Ellen Molapo and Andrew Tshetlane (the fellow who hid when we walked, gathering comrades on our way, to the Orlando Police Station), two former ANC youth leaguers turned PAC members, that all the leaders of the PAC had been arrested and were in jail. They said that they were the only senior members still at large. Mokhehle and Khaketla then told them that a Mr A. K. Barden had come with some financial support for the PAC from the President of Ghana, Kwame Nkrumah. The financial support he had brought was quite large, a five-digit sum of sterling pounds. Ellen Molapo and Andrew Tshehlane were entrusted with the money.

This emissary from Ghana, Mr A. K. Barden, turned out to be a very important person and highly placed in the Nkrumah administration. He had succeeded the late George Padmore in the office which advised President Nkrumah on African affairs and helped shape Ghana's foreign policy in the African continent. When Barden took over the office, he changed the office by radicalising it and making it more effective. It was named the Bureau of African Affairs (BAC). There is a study in the University of Leiden's Repository authored by Matteo Grilli titled 'African Liberation and Unity in Nkrumah's Ghana: A Study of the Role of "Pan-African Institutions" in the making of Ghana's foreign Policy, 1957–1966'. Part 3.10 of this study focuses on Sharpeville, the Question of Refugees, and the South African United Front (between the ANC and PAC). The entire section chronicles Barden's travels in Africa on behalf of the African Affairs Committee (AAC) and later as the head of the BAC which reported directly to President Nkrumah. Maseru was but one stop he made on his journey. The visit was intended to develop agents for a radical Pan-Africanism in the liberation movements.

The money was given to Ellen and Andrew, who immediately left for the hills of Quitting. I still remember how the four of us, Ntsu, Khaketla, Edwin, and I, stood facing each other with puzzlement and anger over the deception perpetrated by Ellen and Andrew. Both Ntsu and Khaketla had met me several times when passing through Johannesburg on political missions in South Africa and beyond. They knew I accepted Edwin's *bona fides* as the treasurer of the Witwatersrand region. A messenger was instantly sent to fetch Ellen and Andrew for an urgent meeting at the BCP offices the next morning. No mention was made of anyone from Johannesburg being at this meeting.

The next morning Ellen and Andrew arrived at the BCP offices. When they were led into the room where Edwin and I were seated, they nearly fell over. Ntsu went straight to the point. All he wanted to know is, did they know who we were? Yes, they said. The next question was, what positions did we hold in the PAC? They said that I was vice president of the Witwatersrand Regional Executive Council (REC) and that Edwin was the treasurer of the REC. 'So, you lied yesterday' – Ntsu was livid. He demanded that they hand over the money. They said that they had left it where they were staying and promised to bring it to us in Johannesburg. They never did. Once back in Johannesburg, Edwin and I were informed that Ellen had hosted a lavish party at her house where she and Andrew had invited their friends. My informant was a smart Mozambican networker, Chester Lazarus. He attended this party and was curious about where the money spent on this party had come from. He knew that the PAC was struggling to raise funds and resources for the relief efforts. I thanked him for the information and his concern about the PAC's financial plight.

It was around the same time that Edwin and I travelled to Maseru that another member of the National Executive Committee of the PAC, A. B. Ngcobo, was released from a Durban prison after serving a very short term for not carrying a pass. I thought this was a great opportunity to meet with him in Durban and inform him, as my leader, about the state of affairs in the organisation on the Witwatersrand and the money from Ghana that Ellen and Andrew had embezzled. Because the pass laws were back in force, I decided not to drive or take a train to Durban. I had no pass to start with, and Park Station always had quite a number of uniformed police and detectives milling around looking for suspicious black people to arrest for imagined, potential, or real transgressions. Instead, I flew from Jan Smuts Airport, as it was then called, down to Durban Airport on South African Airways. I was the only black person on that flight. One of the ways in which I disguised my activist persona was by being well groomed and smartly dressed. I looked like an educated and rather well-off young black man who was gainfully employed, and not like an Africanist or a troublemaker of any sort. In other words, my appearance and demeanour did not make white passengers and flight attendants feel uncomfortable, so long as I sat at a distance from them.

I arrived in Durban and quickly arranged to meet A. B., as he was commonly called, at the Durban Botanical Gardens round mid-morning. We met and I diligently went over my report to him. He did not say much except that he would try to come to Johannesburg at some later date. That afternoon I visited Emkhumbane (Cato Manor). When I got there, a branch meeting was being held primarily to hear from me the latest news about what was happening in and around Johannesburg and Sharpeville in particular. At this meeting, I told the chairperson about the money taken by Ellen and Andrew and how I had reported this to A. B., a member of the National Executive Committee. With a hint of cynicism, the branch chairperson predicted that A. B. was already on his way to Johannesburg and had left before the branch meeting had even started. And he was correct. Why the rush,

I wondered? I later found out that it was the money Ellen and Andrew were holding for the PAC. Edwin and I never heard a word about that money even from A. B. This was my first experience with the dishonest and scandalous conduct of some of the leaders of the PAC, especially those who were in exile, who pocketed large sums of money donated to help support the liberation struggle at home and abroad.

By the 8th of April, both the PAC and ANC were banned. On the 10th of April, the regime announced that blacks unable to produce passes on demand would be immediately arrested. The pass laws were back in full force. Before the first week of April up to the 8th of September 1960, I worked secretly and closely with several branches of the liberation movements of other countries that were located in Johannesburg. There was the Southern Rhodesia African National Congress (SRANC), which was also banned in 1960 but was replaced by the National Democratic Party (NDP) of Southern Rhodesia during the same year. Two other political parties that I worked very closely with were the Malawi Congress Party (MCP) of Nyasaland and the Basutoland Congress Party (BCP) of Lesotho. Africans from Southern Rhodesia who worked and lived on the Witwatersrand were also actively engaged in providing support for the SRANC. So were those from Nyasaland whose remittances to the national offices of the MCP were indispensable during the struggle for their country's independence.

My engagement with the MCP was deeper and more extensive than with the other organisations. I had helped motivate for the merger of its southern and northern Transvaal branches into a single branch. My relationship with the leadership of the MCP was extensive and very different from my relationship with the leadership of the BCP. With the latter, my working relationship was confined to its two senior leaders, Ntsu Mokhehle and Makalo Khaketla. They were close to Robert Sobukwe, and their party was an ideological ally of the PAC's. Both Ntsu and Khaketla were trusted couriers of the PAC who carried written and verbal messages from the remaining structures of the PAC to its emissaries abroad, Nana Mahomo in London and Peter Molotsi in Accra. Then there was Ashley Peter Mda, also in Lesotho.

He was immensely helpful to me during this difficult period in advising me on a number of strategic organisational issues. He had an intimate knowledge of the PAC and the tactical direction it had to take given its dire situation with most of its leaders being in prison. He had a wealth of experience and knowledge in resistance organisations. He provided invaluable advice on how we could regroup and rebuild the organisation in the face of heavy odds. The objective, now that the government had escalated its repression to the point where it was determined to kill those of us who were prepared to stand up against its oppressive rule, was to try to garner more support as we continued to wage the resistance struggle.

15

Hiding and Flight

After the tragedy of Sharpeville, I continued to do political work to help re-organise and align the different liberation organisations. Several attempts were made at forming a coalition between the PAC, the ANC, and the Unity Movement. All failed. It was difficult to work effectively because I was wanted by the secret police and, of course, no longer carried a pass. I was also not staying at home in George Goch anymore because I could easily be found there by the police. Instead of moving into a township, however, I decided to find a backroom in the city where the risk of being arrested was lower. Black people were not expected to live in the city unless they were domestic servants who lived on their employers' premises in the servants' quarters or in backrooms or hostels. I found and rented a back room in Doornfontein's poor white neighbourhood, very close to the station. This neighbourhood was similar to the poor white neighbourhood in George Goch. My landlord was a poor Afrikaner who was happy with the rent I paid him. He never asked me where I worked or what I did for a living.

This hide-out was a short distance from the Doornfontein railway station, to which I returned after attending meetings in different parts of the Witwatersrand. Whenever I returned from political meetings at night, often after the 23h00 curfew, I could sprint from the station to my back room. If, on the other hand, I returned to my room by car (getting a lift from a friend, for example), I insisted on being dropped off a little distance from where I lived because I did not want even my 'comrades' to know my address, in case they were followed or arrested and 'persuaded' to reveal where I could be found. There were, I knew, some informers amongst our 'comrades'. I also always chose to be dropped off on a one-way street and would walk or run in the opposite direction from the oncoming traffic. If one of the cars coming my way was a police car, it would have to turn around against traffic. These streets were narrow and making a U-turn would be difficult, which would buy me precious time to escape.

I chose two one-way streets in particular. These were streets lined with apartment buildings occupied by whites that had black security guards stationed at their main entrances. I cunningly cultivated friendly relations with these security guards and tried to find out whether they were politically conscious and might perhaps be supportive of my political activity. If they were, I would enlist their help, asking them if they would give me refuge in the buildings they were guarding should I ever come running from the police. I also asked whether, should the police came looking for me wanting to know if I had run into the building, they would be prepared to deny it. And indeed, on two occasions, after returning late at night from meetings I had in Alexandra, and being dropped at a spot I had chosen, the scenario I had contemplated and pre-empted played out. The security guards I had befriended protected me even as they endured verbal abuse from the police, who did not believe them. I remain grateful to these men for their solidarity in protecting me from being arrested.

On another occasion, I had just left a friend's place at the corner of Nugget and Banket Streets and was walking towards Wolmarans Street on my way to Park Station when I suddenly noticed a police truck – a 'khwelakhwela'. A tall policeman, dressed in civilian clothes, was locking up the khwelakhwela's canopy after having just thrown inside some black person he had arrested. As he was securing the padlock, I noticed he had a gun in a holster hanging around his waist but hidden by his jacket. When he finished with the lock, he turned and faced in the direction I was coming from, walking, it so happened, straight towards him. Using his forefinger, he indicated that I should come to him. I averted my eyes and kept walking as if heading towards him, but at the intersection of Banket and Bok I turned left, though without increasing my pace, as if I had not noticed his motioning to me.

I recall this man's heavy breathing as he caught up with me and pulled me back by my shoulders, lifted me off the ground, turned me around, and put me back down, now facing him. He was a huge man and his face was red with anger. He wanted to know why I had disobeyed his order to come to him. In the very good Afrikaans I had learned at Emmarentia Hoërskool, I said that I thought he was beckoning someone behind me. He blurted out that I was talking 'kak' (Afrikaans for 'shit'). Then came the dreaded question. 'Pas jong?' My pass. I did not have one. I lied again in good Afrikaans, saying that I had inadvertently left it in my friend's room in a building just up the street. He said this did not matter; I was under arrest. He unlocked the canopy and threw me into the khwelakhwela, which he again locked up.

In the canopy were five men sitting on crude, makeshift wooden benches. One of these was a clergyman dressed in a black suit and a stiff white collar. He could have been a NGK clergyman, like my father. I quickly asked if anyone had a box of matches. In my pocket was a letter I had received from A. P. Mda, the teacher and elder activist, who often wrote me long letters of advice on how to continue organising. These letters were of great help to me because he understood my predicament in trying to unite an organisation whose national and regional leadership had been decimated by the arrests. The advice he gave me and the solidarity he extended kept me energised. At the end of each letter he sent me, before he signed off, he would remind me to burn the letter as soon as I had read it. This time, I had not done so because I wanted to read some of it at a meeting of PAC members in Orlando, Soweto to which I was en route. But now I was under arrest. Fortunately, one of my fellow-prisoners had a box of matches, which he handed to me. I went to the corner of the canopy, took out the letter, and burned it. It burned very quickly because it was written on the very lightweight paper used for airmail letters.

Once the evidence was destroyed, I began proselytising to my fellow prisoners about the struggle against the pass laws. They were bewildered at what I had just done and, of course, by the political agitation I seemed to be involved in. I was still in the process of politicising these men when suddenly the canopy door opened and the big Afrikaner said that he wanted the young man he had just thrown in to come out. Everyone looked at me. I got out. He told me he was going to accompany me to my friend's place so I could show him my pass. He locked up the truck and we walked together to the building where my friend lived. To get to my friend's room, which was on the servants quarters' level – located on the roof of the building, as was typical in South Africa and still is – we had to enter through the basement and take the lift used by black people, goods, and garbage collectors. We walked into the basement and waited for the lift together with a few black people. When it did arrive, it emptied a full complement of domestic workers and a few black men carrying garbage drums. The smell that accompanied this cargo was repulsive, a mixture of rotting garbage, body odour, and the odour of the old lift itself. The policeman couldn't stomach it. He pulled me aside and told me never again to go around without my pass. The lift left us while he was admonishing me. So, I was saved by the presence of my people, the garbage, and the overwhelming smell. He walked off grumpily, and I waited until the lift returned with the usual load. I got in and went to the roof of the building, from where I watched the policeman walk back to his truck and drive away. Then I quickly went back down and resumed my journey to Park Station to catch the train to Soweto, looking out for any other policemen, whether in uniform or in civilian clothes but behaving like detectives.

~

Another close brush with arrest had to do with the death in prison of my colleague, George Siwisa, who was the president of the PAC's Witwatersrand Region when I served as his deputy. George was one of those arrested on Monday the 21st of March. Sometime during April, I received a message that his daughter wanted to see me urgently, so I went to see her. It turned out that she had been contacted by the police in Johannesburg and told to pick up her father's clothes at the Johannesburg Central Police Station (which was renamed John Vorster Square in 1968 until September 1997). It was on that visit that she was told that her father had died in prison. The cause of death was not given. When she asked where he was buried, the police said they had no idea. Because I had worked very closely with him, she not only implored me but instructed me to find his body. She wanted a proper funeral for him. This was a daunting and risky assignment. She was the only child of the Siwisas and was adamant about having an honourable funeral for her father, who was also our hero. This was understandable.

Hiding and Flight

With the help of my political network, I found out where he was buried. It was in an African township in the East Rand (I don't remember the name of the township). He was buried in a pauper's grave. Through other contacts I obtained an exhumation order from the Ministry of Health, and once I had this order, I asked an old elderly friend of the Siwisas, Mr J. Walaza, to accompany me so that he could help identify the corpse. At the entrance to this township, like that of the Eastern Native Township, was the white superintendent's house. We had to get his permission to open the grave. He was furious and hopping mad and wanted to know why we had come to his township to dig up a dead man. He was extremely agitated. Why couldn't we let him be, was his question. We politely explained that we had been tasked by the dead man's only child, who wanted to arrange a decent burial for her father, with exhuming the body. And, of course, we also had the exhumation order from the Minister of Health. He gave us the permission and told us to get our business done quickly before too many residents returned from work. It was late in the afternoon.

For some reason, the graveyard was located in the middle of the township and surrounded by a barbed-wire fence no more than a metre high. The residents' houses on all sides faced the graveyard. Walaza and I had asked a hearse to accompany us in case the dead man was our colleague. Naturally, when the residents saw the hearse and only two men in a separate car, this was a very unusual sight for what they thought was a burial. When we got to the grave site, the grave diggers were packing up their tools and leaving; their day was over. We asked them to help us dig, but they would have none of that, so Walaza and I dug out the coffin. It took some time. The driver of the hearse helped lift the coffin out and set it a little distance from the gaping hole. We had come with some basic tools including a screw driver and a hammer. The coffin was simple plain wood very crudely nailed at all corners. We opened it. The smell was putrid. Inside was the totally naked, decomposing body of a man. Tied to its big toe with a piece of thin wire was a small tab of paper with a number. This was the pauper's number.

Walaza and I had planned how to conduct the identification of the corpse. One of us would go and look and come back and then the other would do the same. After these two separate viewings, we would then compare our observations. Just as I was studying the corpse, reporters from *Drum Magazine* drove into the cemetery in a mad rush. David Sibeko jumped out of their car and was instantly looming over my shoulder, his camera clicking at high speed, and shooting at every corner of the coffin without looking because the stench was too much. Walaza took his turn and came back, and we then compared what each of us had seen. It was indeed the corpse of our friend. The reporters drove away quickly with a scoop for their publication before we could ask them to help load the coffin into the hearse or help fill the gaping grave with the sand we had dug out. With these jobs done, and before the residents of the township returned from work, Walaza and I left the scene and drove back to Johannesburg to tell Siwisa's daughter that we had found her father's body and that she should go to the funeral undertaker whose hearse had transported the body. That was as much as I could do for her and the late George himself. He was well when he was arrested. No explanation was given by the police as to how and why he died. George was given a respectable burial on the 3rd of July 1960. Again, it was too risky for me to attend.

The incident I'm about to recall was decisive. It began on the afternoon of Thursday the 8th of September and ended the next afternoon on Friday the 9th of September 1960 when I left the country. Because of the role I played in unifying the northern and southern branches of the MCP in the Transvaal, I was chosen to be one of the delegates of the South African branch of the MCP which had to attend the first annual congress of the party to be held around the 27th of September in Nkhotakota in Nyasaland. (This name means 'Corner Corner' in the Chichewa dialect.) This town was located in the Central Province of the country. Attending this conference offered me the opportunity of possibly meeting our two representatives abroad and briefing them about what had transpired since their departure, before the Sharpeville shootings. Only the secretary general of the newly constituted Transvaal MCP, Kondi Khulisewa, knew about this hidden part of the agenda for the trip. He had arranged a 'chitupa' for me. This was an identification paper used by mineworkers when travelling from home to the mines and back. I assumed the name of Johannes Ndoane, a mineworker who was returning home to Nyasaland.

In preparing for this journey, I had written reports on all the liberation organisations that I had been in contact with or working with in and around Johannesburg for the past six months. I went to the offices of a recently launched government-owned magazine called *Bantu* where I had a trusted secretary friend whom I asked to type my hand-written reports for me. I promised to pick these up at five o'clock in the afternoon when the offices closed for the day. I was three minutes late – she had left! I hardly knew where she lived. Khulisewa and I had planned on my catching the special third-class train the following day, which transported black mineworkers from Johannesburg to Southern Rhodesia and beyond. It was scheduled to depart from Park Station at three o'clock in the afternoon. I now faced a serious dilemma. Where and how did I find the young lady with my typed reports? Was her home in Alexandra or Orlando? If she lived in Alexandra, did I go looking for her at the Noord Street PUTCO bus terminal, or if she lived in Orlando, did I go looking at Park Station? I chose Park Station because I suspected she was from Orlando East or West. I dashed off to the Park Station's ticketing counters for blacks. I could not find her. Instead, I ran into my elder sister, Beauty, the first born in our family. She was very excited to see me because I had not been seen or heard from for months since Sharpeville.

Sis Beauty wanted to know where I had been hiding and what I was up to. I was very close to Sis Beauty. In our family, we all looked up to her because she was the firstborn – caring, smart, strong, attractive, and a leader. She had been one of the first few black women to work at what was called The Helping Hand Club for Native Girls in Johannesburg at an area called Fairview. This area had no restrictions on African residents who were being trained as domestic servants. These servants took courses in reading English, arithmetic, first aid, dress-making, laundry, home nursing, and cooking. Sis Beauty taught cooking and baking. This earned her the nickname 'Khekhe' meaning 'Cakes', given to her by my father, who enjoyed the cakes she often baked and brought home. I would sometimes accompany her to The Helping Hand Club. I remember one afternoon when we both boarded a train from George Goch to Jeppe, which was the next station on the Park Station line. We got into a very crowded third-class coach where there was just enough standing room close to the door as we entered. One burly but quiet African man was uncomfortably close to us. My sister and I began gossiping in English saying how uncouth some of our people were as we breathed on top of one another. Just as we were manoeuvring our way to the door getting ready to disembark, this burly, quiet man made a searing observation in Zulu directed at us when he said, 'Abanye abantu baya klitisiyiza,' which may be translated as, 'Some people are critical.' We were very embarrassed and could not get to the door fast enough.

The ticket office where I met Sis Beauty was teeming with people buying train tickets for the many destinations the trains headed to from Park Station. Under immense pressure and feeling quite anxious, I revealed to her that I was leaving for Nyasaland the next day for a MCP Congress but would return once it was over. She looked at me with great doubt in her eyes and told me she thought I would not return. She insisted that I go with her to her home in Umzimhlophe (White City), a part of Orlando West, for dinner. I told her that I really did not feel safe spending a night in the township because of the frequent police raids. She understood and reassured me that I would be allowed to leave shortly after dinner to return to my hideout in the city. So, we took the train to White City and had dinner at her house where we talked quite a bit about my political adventures. As I was about to leave, she suggested that I stop to see my brother whose house was a short walk from hers. I reluctantly agreed. By this time, it was early evening and getting dark.

When I got to Stanley and Ruby's house (Ruby was my sister-in-law), I found it packed with activists engaged in heated debates about the aftermath of the Sharpeville shootings. Many of them I did not know. I recognised only a few of them as PAC activists. For a short while, I sat and listened quietly and did not say a word. Most of the issues they were passionately discussing revealed that they were on the whole uninformed about the facts and realities that the banned political organisations were facing. I then entered the fray with the intention of clearing

Hiding and Flight

up some confusion. That was when they realised that I was the vice president of the PAC of the Witwatersrand Region. While establishing my *bona fides*, I lost track of the time and missed the last train going back to the city. I realised this when I heard the train slowly rolling past from the Phefeni station on its way to Umzimhlophe then to New Canada on its way to Park Station. I was very upset because I was now forced to sleep in an unsafe environment, the township. The meeting broke up and people went their different ways.

I asked Stanley and Ruby to please wake me up round five in the morning so that I could catch the first train leaving Phefeni for the city. Instead, we were woken up by a fierce banging on the front door. It was the police, and it was a few minutes after five. We had overslept! I quickly pulled open the curtains in the guest bedroom where I was sleeping only to see that the house was surrounded by Special Branch policemen dressed in civilian clothes. The thought of jumping out the window was out of the question because all the windows had fixed, close-set burglar bars. I was trapped. All I recall is saying a quick prayer because I was now definitely going to be arrested. Stanley walked to the door and opened it. Four of the policemen leapt into the house and went straight to his bedroom as if they knew where it was located. After they had entered the bedroom and allowed him to get dressed, I heard one of them say 'moenie jou horlsie vat nie want jy kom nie terrug nie' ('do not take your watch because you are not coming back'). I could hear this clearly from the room in which I was at that moment propped up against the head board of the bed, having resigned myself to finally being arrested. All White City houses had domed-shaped concrete roofs; most of them did not have ceilings. So, anyone talking in any room could be easily heard throughout the house.

In a few minutes (which felt like a lifetime), I saw Stanley and Ruby being herded into the bedroom where I was sitting up. Stanley and Ruby's eyes looked like they were going to pop out. They were very frightened. I myself was in a world of turmoil when one of the policemen asked who I was and why I was there. My response was that I was John Dube and had come from Springs in the East Rand to visit my friends, Stanley and Ruby. He did not ask for my pass, and in any case I did not have it. If I had had it and been willing to show it to him, it would have revealed my real name and where I lived. Fortunately, no one in this police contingent was familiar with the name John Dube, nor did anyone catch the significance of a name associated with the founding member of the ANC. They turned around with Stanley and Ruby in front of them and headed for the front door.

Just as they were about to open the door and step out, one of them noticed Stanley's long, beautiful radiogram. Out of curiosity and perhaps envy, he pulled open a drawer. During the years that my brother had been a radio broadcaster, he had accumulated a large collection of vinyl records, which filled the drawers of the radiogram and other boxes in the house. But in the drawer the security officer had opened, on top of the collection of records, was the latest issue of *Bantu* magazine. All I heard was a jubilant shrill from one of them saying, 'Dit is nou wat ons soek!' ('This is what we're looking for!'). For them, this was a significant discovery, and for me, it signalled the end of my road in my homeland.

I jumped out of bed to see what this find was all about. How I waded into and pushed through the four security agents and Stanley and Ruby to see what had been found I don't recall. But when I saw the cover of the magazine, I instantly realised what had happened. When paging through the magazine, they had discovered the reports I had missed collecting the previous day at five in the afternoon. Apparently, when I did not show up at exactly five to pick up the typed version of these reports, my friend had somehow found my brother and entrusted both the typed and handwritten versions to him in the hope that he would pass these on to me. The night before when I showed up unexpectedly and found him engaged in heated debates with other political activists, he forgot to tell me that he had my incriminating reports in the house. Had he told me, I would not have spent the night in the township. Now my valuable work was in the hands of the secret police.

With a certain cautious brazenness, I asked to see what they had found. A little taken aback by my intrusiveness, they allowed me to see what they had discovered. They showed me the

Hiding and Flight

two types of reports. In a split second I noticed my handwritten reports alongside the typed ones. I interjected what I thought was an important observation: I told the security officers that the handwriting on the reports was definitely not that of my friend, Stanley; I knew his handwriting. What they were looking at was the handwriting of Stanley's younger brother, Morley. I was trying to save my brother from serving a long prison sentence because of me. I went on to say that even if my friend had tried to write like his brother, he could not. This conversation was conducted in fluent Afrikaans, as always under such circumstances. My unsolicited intervention was followed by a quick and angry response by one of the officers, 'Waar is die bliksem?' ('Where is the scoundrel'?). Very reassuringly, I replied that the scoundrel was at his home in George Goch. They said that they had been there several times but could not find him. I urged them to go there because it was still very early in the morning, round 6 a.m. With an air of confidence like someone very familiar with Morley's movements, I said they would find him there. They were excited and felt reassured as they left in a hurry with my brother and my incriminating reports. I knew that I had just sealed my fate. It was time to leave the township and the country.

My first problem was what to do with my sister-in-law, who was sobbing, and her little daughter, Dudu, who was turning one in four days' time. I tried to explain to Ruby what I intended to do, but she could not hear or understand a thing. Her immediate concern was what she was going to do now that her husband had been arrested and was not coming back. I realised that every minute was now precious because the police would definitely not find me in George Goch, and that a larger search would be started that day, now that they were in possession of my reports which mentioned my departure plans that afternoon and several names of political activists I had worked with since Sharpeville. So, I securely locked both mother and daughter in their house and ran back to Sis Beauty's house to tell her what had happened. Fortunately, she was home, and I quickly told her what had happened since I had left her house the previous night to visit my brother and his family. I handed her the keys to the house and asked her to please go and see what she could do. I left in a real hurry.

My first stop was the Lever Brothers' depot in Auckland Park where a close friend worked as a sales representative. This was David Kau, who was much older than me; he and his wife, Irene, were like a brother and a sister to me. David had a car which he usually parked at the depot during the day when he was out selling company products using a company vehicle. I got to Lever Brothers quite early, before he had hit the road, and explained what had happened that morning. I asked to borrow his car in order to alert the individuals whose names were in the confiscated reports that the police would be looking for them, explain what had actually happened, and warn them that these officers would be very angry because I had sent them to George Goch on a wild goose chase. He understood my predicament and gave me the keys to his car. We also arranged where to drop off the car and its keys once my mission was accomplished. I managed to alert all the individuals that I had unintentionally compromised. To this day, I still wish my brother had remembered that he had my documents in the house when I stopped in to visit. I have convinced myself that had he told me that they were there, I would not have slept in the township that night, and that if this mishap had not occurred, both our lives could have taken different turns. Whether for better or worse I don't know, but what is very clear is that the meeting held the previous night was host to an informer who tipped off the security agents. Was it sheer coincidence that the security agents showed up when I was there? It simply isn't plausible.

~

After returning David's car and leaving it in the Lever Brothers' car park and the keys in his office, I rushed to meet Kondi Khulisewa in Jeppestown where he worked and told him what had happened the previous day and night. Two travel documents had been prepared two days before. One identified me as Johannes Ndaone who came from the village of Mwambula in the Blantyre district, the Chief of which was Somba. This travel document was issued by the Nyasaland Government Representative's Office in Jeppestown on the 7th of September 1960. It also said that Joannes

Hiding and Flight

was returning home at his own expense by train to Blantyre station in Nyasaland. The other was a Permit No. 227/60, also for Joannes Ndaone, who was allowed to travel through the Province of Mozambique on his way to Nyasaland. It read, 'He will cross the Mozambique border at Manica and Mutarara.' It too was issued on the 7th of September 1960 by the Curator of the Portuguese Natives. This document was a backup in case my routing changed for some reason. Kondi and I quickly retrieved the two documents and hurriedly left his workplace and headed for Park Station.

It was round two o'clock in the afternoon on the 9th of September when we neared the station. We were very cautious in approaching the ticketing office for blacks because we suspected that the Security Police would be on the look-out for me. They had found out from my reports that I intended to catch the train carrying miners, which was scheduled to depart at three o'clock in the afternoon. We were amazed at the number of Special Branch officers and policemen who had surrounded the station entrances on both sides and were milling around the ticketing offices looking for someone they did not know, except for the four officers who had seen me at my brother's house earlier in the morning. It was evident that they were determined to prevent me from catching the train. The clock was ticking as Kondi and I tried to figure out what to do. I was desperate, and Kondi was extremely anxious. Both of us were scared.

I suddenly remembered that this train's first stop was the Mayfair Station where it picked up more mineworkers who often came from the mines around Langlaagte and from Crown Mines and were returning home beyond the borders of South Africa. I looked Kondi in the eye and sternly told him that we had to run and catch this train in Mayfair. He was astonished at my suggestion. He said it was impossible to run to the Mayfair train station in time to catch the train. Mayfair was quite a distance from Park Station. I insisted that we try because that was the only chance we had, and like the trooper he always was, he agreed. We set off running immediately until we got onto the Main Road which ran parallel to, but above, the rail line to Mayfair. After a short distance, I spotted uncle Dan Twala driving his two-door Volkswagen Beetle, going in the same direction. I hailed him and

The Way Home

asked him to give us a ride to the Mayfair station, which was on his way. He did. He wanted to know why we were running to the station. I told him we were seeing off a friend who was catching a train bound for Bechuanaland (at that time a British Protectorate).

We got to the station, got out of the car, thanked him, and asked him to convey my greetings and best wishes to the Twala family, my in-laws through Stanley's marriage to Ruby Twala. I totally forgot to tell him that I had left Ruby, his niece, and her baby locked up in their home earlier in the morning, let alone why. Left on the pavement, just before a short flight of stairs to the ticketing office of the station, we decided that Kondi should go into the station first to check if there were any policemen around the ticketing office. There was not one. We then descended the stairs with some confidence and walked up to the ticketing office where I bought a one-way ticket to Bulawayo in Southern Rhodesia. Again, before walking down a longer flight of stairs to the platform where the train would stop, Kondi went down first to scout for cops. Again, there were none. What struck both of us was that we were the only two individuals on the whole platform. In fact, there was nobody on the opposite platform for trains going to Park Station either. We had a few minutes to celebrate having outwitted the police and the security apparatus. We stood there facing each other, wordless, perhaps trying to figure out what was going to happen. When would we next see each other? So much hung in the air between us.

Just then, the coal-fired locomotive appeared from around the bend, slowly belching out black smoke and white puffs of steam and pulling a number of third-class passenger coaches carrying only mineworkers to their homes in British Protectorates. Kondi and I shook hands and bid each other farewell. I had no luggage; all I had was what I was wearing, the chitupa, and some money. The train stopped, and a white train conductor alighted from the caboose to see who was getting onto the train. Only one person got in – me. He blew his whistle, and the train pulled out of the station. I leaned out of the window and waved goodbye to Kondi. He stood there alone waving back, getting smaller and smaller as the train gathered steam and left the station. I remember this parting with a heavy heart. It turned out to be the last time that I saw him. He was clever, energetic, incisive, and a passionate Africanist. I did not realise that I would never see him again. My journey into exile had begun.

Part Two

Stateless

1

Across the African Continent

Bechuanaland Protectorate

The train didn't stop until it reached Mafikeng early the next morning. A Saturday morning, the 10th of September 1960. Eager to know what was in the news at home, I bought a newspaper from a man about my age walking up and down the platform selling newspapers and snacks. I was about to open and read the newspaper on a bench when I realised that it might seem unusual for a black mineworker to be reading a newspaper, so I quickly folded it and sat on it. Looking around, I noticed there were a few men, black and white men, dressed in civilian clothes but behaving like detectives, walking on the platform alongside the coaches, eyeing the passengers, and this scared me. Mafikeng was the extraterritorial headquarters of the British protectorate of Bechuanaland (now Botswana). It served as the capital of the protectorate from 1894 until 1965 when Gaborone was made the capital of what became Botswana. The South African and British security services collaborated very closely. Perhaps my luck was that in the eyes of white detectives, I looked no different from the black man sitting next to me. The train soon left again, bound for Francistown, where it arrived the following day, Sunday the 11th of September. From there it proceeded to Plumtree, where I was asked to show my chitupa to be allowed to enter Southern Rhodesia. I went through without a hitch. I did not read the newspaper I bought in Mafeking until the train reached Bulawayo later in the afternoon, round 3 p.m. There was nothing of interest to me in that newspaper.

Southern Rhodesia

Once in Bulawayo, I asked someone in the street – an African person; I would not have asked a white Rhodesian – for the offices of the National Democratic Party (NDP), and there I managed to locate a couple of officials of that party. The NDP was the precursor to the Zimbabwe African People's Union (ZAPU). Inside the offices, I introduced myself to two officials and declared my political affiliation and position in the PAC. They were both clearly affected by my arrival. The news of the Sharpeville massacre was still reverberating throughout the region. The two officials were Wirayi Dzawanda 'Willie' Musarurwa, a respected journalist, and Enos Nkala, later a founder of ZAPU. They proposed that I immediately proceed to Salisbury, because they felt that Bulawayo was unsafe, and Salisbury, which was further away from South Africa, would be safer. They gave me two names of NDP colleagues in Salisbury who, they said, would look after me. The hospitality they extended to me was a sign of the general solidarity that existed among African nationalist movements of the period. Before I left them, Musarurwa and Nkala gave me a last piece of advice: they advised me that should anyone ask where I had come from, I should say I was from Gwanda. I later learned that Gwanda is situated in the south-western district of Southern Rhodesia, near the border with South Africa. It is the capital of the province of Matabeleland South. Many black people who live there speak Ndebele, which is very close to isiZulu.

I arrived in Salisbury on the morning of Monday the 12th of September. It was a public holiday called Occupation Day. The white settlers were celebrating decades of having occupied the land they had forcibly taken from the indigenous African people. I met the colleagues that Musarurwa and Nkala had told me about, and they gave me a place to stay. That night, in a strange bed, I thought anxiously of home. What would they be thinking? The only thing that put my mind somewhat at ease was that I had told Beauty about the MCP Congress in Nyasaland. She would tell the rest of the family. I trusted that, in time, they would understand that I had left for my own safety and theirs. I did not know when I would be able to communicate with them. But now it was time for me to look ahead – and to survive.

On Tuesday, the next day, Musarurwa and Nkala arranged for me to meet Herbert Wiltshire Pfumaindini Chitepo at the University of Nyasaland and Rhodesia (now the University of

Zimbabwe). Chitepo was the first black barrister in Rhodesia. He had qualified as a barrister-at-law and was called to the Bar at Grey's Inn in London, whose alumni included Winston Churchill. Chitepo was also a research assistant at the School of Oriental and African Studies in the University of London. When I met him, he was secretly advising the NDP.

In addition to sheltering me, Musarurwa and Nkala were concerned about my safety in Salisbury. Political activities were heating up in Salisbury, and they suggested that I proceed to Nyasaland as soon as possible. I would be safer there than in Southern Rhodesia. Southern Rhodesia borders South Africa, and their respective security agents and police forces had close ties.

On the 14th of September 1960, out of curiosity, I went to the African township of Highfield to hear what Sir Edgar Whitehead, the then Governor of Southern Rhodesia, had to say to its residents. However, although Sir Edgar had been invited to speak at the meeting, he was not given the chance. If the militant NDP could have gotten their hands on him, he would have been a goner. He was rescued by escaping through a window close to where he was standing and waiting to speak. He managed to get into his car and quickly drive off as a hail of stones was thrown at his car. It was under such conditions that the NDP leadership persuaded me to leave Salisbury quickly.

Musarurwa and Nkala bought me a one-way air ticket from Salisbury to Chileka Airport in Blantyre, Nyasaland. I boarded a DC-3 plane which had one white pilot and carried a few passengers and an interesting variety of cargo, which included a live goat and some chickens in a cage. I had never seen anything as strange as this. I could have been travelling in an old Leyland bus bound for a distant rural village in the reserves somewhere. But I was a passenger flying in a small plane from Salisbury to Blantyre, the commercial capital of Nyasaland.

Nyasaland

We landed at Chileka Airport in Blantyre on Monday the 19th of September 1960. Stepping onto the tarmac, I felt a mixture of emotions. I was certainly relieved to have made it here, out of

Southern Rhodesia and another step away from South Africa. At the same time, I felt a sort of vertigo at getting further away from home. Once in the town itself, I went looking for the hotel where I was to stay with two other members of the MCP delegation from the Transvaal. Kondi had given me the address of the place, and I easily found the hotel. It was a small hotel run by an enterprising member of the MCP. Its clients were Africans. When I got there, the two other delegates from the Transvaal MCP had already arrived. The three of us had been chosen and mandated to attend the annual national conference of the party in Nkhotakota, which was scheduled to take place towards the end of September 1960. Nkhotakota is in the country's central province. To familiarise myself with my temporary surroundings, I took a walk around the neighbourhood. Not far from the hotel, I found a prison in which some of the leaders of the MCP were detained. I was excited at the prospect of visiting and seeing them in person. One of them was Orton Chirwa. So, without informing anyone at the hotel, I walked to the prison.

At the prison gate, I was refused permission to enter. Rather disappointed, I walked back to the hotel and told the hotel owner what had happened. He looked infuriated. He was astonished at my stupidity in announcing my presence to the British Police of Nyasaland. He reminded me that the little chitupa I was carrying would not stop them from arresting me and deporting me to South Africa. How could I hope to convince them that I was a Nyasa when I could hardly string together a single sentence in Nyanja? My enthusiastic curiosity had gotten me into serious danger. This was aggravated by an argument I'd had earlier with the leader of our delegation over being a member of the delegation when I was not a Nyasa. This was regardless of the fact that I was nominated at a MCP branch meeting at home where he was present. The hotel owner told me to get ready to leave very early the next morning before the police came looking for me. My travel arrangements were made for me that very night as I sat and listened quietly. I was very afraid.

I was woken up very early the next morning while it was still dark and taken to the Blantyre railway station, where a one-way ticket to Chipoka was bought for me. Chipoka is at the southernmost tip of Lake Nyasa (now Lake Malawi). The hotel owner gave me some pocket money, and I got into the train with a little pack of food that I had bought to eat on the way. I had no luggage and was still wearing the same clothes I'd had on since I left home, almost two weeks before. I usually washed some of these clothes, especially my underwear, in the evening and had them dry and ready to wear the next morning. Ironing anything was out of the question. I got into a train that was pulled by what I thought was one of the oldest steam engines I had ever seen. It was owned by the Nyasaland Railway Company. I had seen many steam engines in South Africa but not one as ancient as this. It really belonged in a railway museum. The passenger coaches were the usual third-class 'reserved' for natives.

This train pulled out of the Blantyre station before sunrise. It dragged along very slowly and deliberately. We had not been travelling for more than an hour before it was shunted to a small siding. By now it was getting light outside. The train I was on made way for a smart and polished diesel engine that was pulling two neatly painted green coaches which had Her Majesty's insignia on their sides. One was a sleeping coach; the other was a dining car, and in this dining car sat a white man. He was alone and dressed in an impressive white tunic like a high-ranking soldier. On this long table, but at a distance from where he sat probably waiting for breakfast to be served, was a white pith helmet sporting a long, swan-feather plume. His tunic, helmet, feather, dining tablecloth, and plates were all white. He looked very important. I later found out that this was Proconsul Glyn Smallwood Jones who was acting governor of Nyasaland while the actual governor, Sir Robert Perceval Armitage, was on leave for three months. The Proconsul was also heading to Chipoka to catch the same boat I was going to board. But his train had to get there before ours. He was the last colonial governor of the Protectorate of Nyasaland before it achieved independence and became the Republic of Malawi.

A few minutes later, our slow and lumbering museum piece carrying Her Majesty's protected subjects pulled out of the shunting line. Haltingly, it puffed its way until at some point going uphill became difficult. It would try going up but would suddenly slow down and roll backwards faster than it could go forward. The engine driver instructed the train conductor to tell Her Majesty's subjects to get off and walk up the hill so that the train could make it up. We all got off and walked alongside the train until it was over the incline. Some of the passengers trotted alongside the train close to where they had left their luggage. I did not because I had no luggage. Once over the hill, the train stopped to allow us back into the coaches. This experience confirmed my initial observations about this steam engine being a relic of the past. The train could not leave immediately because a few passengers had run off into the nearby village to buy provisions, so we waited until all the passengers had been accounted for before resuming our journey. All I could hope for was that we would get to Chipoka on time before the boat departed. Fortunately, we did.

I bought a third-class, one-way ticket to Nkhotakota. When I got to the mooring and saw the little ship called 'Ilala', a sense of adventure welled up in me. Here was a quaint little white ship that I was to board to Nkhotakota, somewhere up north in the central province. It had three classes of accommodation: first, second, and third. Third class was at sea level where there was a notice posted on the wall as you embarked – you couldn't miss it. It said that this class was for 'Natives and Cattle'. Above this class was the second class for whites only. The topmost level was the first class for very important and wealthy white people. The Proconsul Glynn Jones was, of course, in the best of the first-class berths. My third-class sleeping space was very close to the steam engine and the coal room. I don't know how I managed to sleep amid the sound of the droning engines, which ran day and night except when the ship had stopped at a port to discharge or take on passengers and cargo.

Not much of any food was available for so-called 'natives' on the ship. Everyone carried his or her own small provisions. I had very little. For supper I was invited by the black crew to share its rough porridge and some gravy-like stew consisting of some kind of worms, like mopane worms but smaller. What was scary was that these worms floated on top of the thick brown sauce and wriggled as if they were still alive. Next to this dark mixture, which was cooked in one black tripod pot, was another pot containing the rough porridge that went with the wormy stew. I was afraid of the worms but not the porridge. What if I got sick on the Ilala in the middle of Lake Nyasa? Perhaps I could survive if I ate the porridge and gravy but without the worms. This was very faulty logic dictated by my hunger; hunger is not very discerning. The gravy was in fact a residue derived from the worms. I dug into the porridge and dipped it into the mix so as to avoid the worms that floated on top of the thick brown sauce. We all dug into the porridge pot with our bare hands and my colleagues took mouthfuls of the worms and gravy without blinking. They were familiar with what they were eating, unlike me.

The Ilala finally arrived in Nkhotakota, and many people got off. Some of them were going to the MCP annual conference; others had come home. I was met by my host, a local African policeman whose house I was to hide in for some time until the conference I had planned to attend was over. My host's house was on the west side of the lake; the conference was being held on the east side. However, I was barred by the hotel owner in Blantyre from going to this national MCP conference because of my visit to the prison in Blantyre. His instructions were to lie low and out of sight until the conference was over and all the delegates, including the two who were part of the delegation I had come with, had departed. This was for my safety. The plan to meet my senior PAC officials at the conference was unfortunately scuttled. For a few days, I would wake up as if I were going to work with my warden. He would head for the port, and I would head for the hill from where I watched the marquees across the lake and the movements of the delegates attending the conference. This conference was the 1960 MCP's Annual Conference and began on the 27th of September. Most importantly, it was at this conference that Hastings Kamuzu Banda was elected as president of the MCP.

I was not alone on this hill from where I observed the conference. There were several goats that grazed there every day. Initially, they did not take kindly to me; they just stood there and stared at the newcomer. But as the days passed, they got used to seeing me hanging around. Perhaps they were a little puzzled that I was not grazing too. For me, the pity was that I had a lot that I wanted to talk about. I knew they could hear, but whether they could understand what I had to say, I doubted. If only we could communicate, I thought, I would tell them about my tribulations and anxieties, and they could fill me in on life in the Central Province's town of Nkhotakota. Perhaps we would also engage in some interesting political discussion regarding their situation and mine. Once the conference was over, and the marquees had been dismantled, I knew that it would be safe for me to resume my journey. When I was reassured that the British Nyasaland Police had left, my host and I walked back to the harbour where he saw me off on the Ilala going further north. I disembarked at its last stop, in Mbeya, the border town between Nyasaland and Tanganyika.

Tanganyika

I exited the port without a passport or valid travel document. All I had with me was my chitupa which was valid for travel only up to Malawi and not beyond. I was now getting into Tanganyika, another country. I mustered all the courage I had and told my sad story to the immigration officials on the Tanganyika side of the border, asking them to please let me into their country. My story was convincing, and my plea was accepted. I was free at last from the tentacles of both the British police and the South African security agents. It was late in the afternoon when I left the harbour at Mbeya and walked towards what looked like the town. I planned on asking someone where the main Mbeya railway station was located because I wanted to catch a train to Dar es Salaam. I had to carefully select whom I would ask.

On my way to the station, I saw an Arab man wearing a turban, floral shirt, and a wrap-around from his waist down to his ankles. He wore beautifully crafted sandals. What was frightening for me was the long and curved dagger which was in a sheath affixed to a leather belt which hung from his waist. This was the first time that I had set my eyes on an Arab, not one in the American movies which I often watched in Johannesburg's bioscopes for blacks (Rio, Good Hope, Odeon, and Lyric). In these movies the Arabs were portrayed with drawn daggers like the one I had just seen but were menacing and ready to decapitate their adversaries. Recalling these chilling, racist clips from American movies heightened my anxiety and fear. It was much later that I found out that the dagger was called a *janbiya*, a dagger with an ornate hilt or handle that is worn on a belt tied round the waist. I was relieved when this was explained to me later. However, I did approach someone who was *not* carrying a *janbiya* to ask for directions to the train station. When I arrived at the station, it was almost dark. I sat on a bench waiting for the train to Dar es Salaam and wondered how I would get there with no money.

A smartly dressed man who looked like he was some kind of professional had noticed me. He came over and asked where I was going and where I had come from. It seemed that my general appearance told him I was a stranger, uncertain of his destination. I told him how I had gotten off the Ilala at the port and intended on reaching the Tanganyika African National Union (TANU) offices in Dar es Salaam. After hearing my reasons for going to Dar and listening to the story of my evasive journey from South Africa, he invited me to his home in Dodoma. The train to Dar stopped at Dodoma on its way. I accepted the invitation from this total stranger, and he paid my fare and took me to his home. My generous host was Mr S. J. Mwenda, a clerk at the East African Railways and Harbours offices in Dodoma. How I wish I had kept in touch with this Good Samaritan! At his house, I had a bath, was dressed in clean pyjamas, had a lovely dinner, slept in a nice, comfortable bed, and literally passed out for the night. I woke up the next morning very refreshed. I washed and was given clean clothes to wear. My old shoes were still fine. I had breakfast with this man and his wife and was given money and taken to the Dodoma train station where they bade me farewell. This whole experience is unforgettable! This was my first taste of Tanzanian hospitality and solidarity.

TANU's solidarity with refugees from South Africa and the hospitality that it extended to us were overwhelming. Its president, Julius Nyerere, vice president, Rashidi Kawawa, secretary-general, Oscar Kambona, and the party as a whole were totally committed to Pan-African solidarity and unreservedly and generously supported African liberation movements. Oscar Kambona commanded great respect and exerted great influence on the liberation movements that had representatives and bases in Tanganyika. Political exiles who sought refuge in Tanganyika were then his responsibility. He later became the first Minister of International Affairs of an independent Tanzania. Three other Tanzanians who were very helpful to me as well as other South African refugees were Ally Sykes and his two younger brothers. They were all senior members of TANU. When I arrived in Dar, I very quickly met a few South African refugees who were comfortably lodged in the International Hotel. They were being treated to free room and board, which included breakfasts, lunches, and dinners in what was the best hotel in town! What a life for a refugee! We were idle and almost on holiday, except that each day brought anxieties because we did not know what the following day would bring. Everyone lived with a hope of leaving Dar for some unknown destination depending on what his organisation's representative could organise and arrange. It did not take TANU officials long to notice that putting us up in a hotel without any definite plans was expensive. We were moved and accommodated in a house in Buguruni, a rural township approximately seven kilometres from downtown Dar.

The house in Buguruni was a fair size and had been converted into a dormitory with very basic facilities. We all missed the hotel but understood why we had to move out. Even at home in South Africa we did not live such a luxurious life. In Buguruni, we had a cook who prepared breakfast, lunch, and dinner. These meals were quite ordinary in the sense that they were the types of food people in the neighbourhood ate. Meal times were rigid and had to be adhered to. If you were late for dinner, you slept on an empty stomach. This resulted in a few break-ins into the pantry where food was usually locked up. Breaking into the pantry incensed the cook to the point of condemning all of us as thieves. We had to censure those responsible for the break-ins because we did not want the cook and the other helpers to think that all South Africans were crooks. Besides, we were political refugees who should be grateful to the Tanganyikans for providing us with a sanctuary and for feeding us too. We let our colleagues know that honest, respectful, and good behaviour were important in consolidating our relationships with TANU, with the community in which we were housed, and with our cook, of course!

I met one Geoffrey Mokoka in Buguruni. He came from Sophiatown and was a member of the PAC. He had left South Africa before I did. He told me that he left home out of sheer frustration with apartheid and was very curious about what it was like to live in Ghana, an African country that had achieved independence from Britain. He was fascinated by Ghana and the prospects of other African countries also achieving independence. Geoff was also basically a restless soul but an optimistic Pan-Africanist. The distance from Buguruni to Dar did not stop him or limit his daily wanderings. For lack of anything to do every day, city-types like Geoff and I spent hours walking on the beaches of Dar. This helped us retain some sanity and hope. During one of these visits to the city, we met and befriended a Tanganyikan who worked for one of the Scandinavian Embassies. This friend often invited us to the Ambassador's residence when His Excellency was out of town. He could see that we were destitute and often hungry and felt sorry for us. It was at this residence that we enjoyed great sandwiches and cold Carlsberg beers. It was also during one of these visits that we hatched a plan to leave Tanganyika and head north to Kenya and, perhaps later, Egypt.

The idea to go north was planted in our minds by the visit of a PAC representative, Peter Molotsi, who was based in Accra, Ghana. Peter was very patronising towards Geoff and me. He was impressed by how clean and neat we looked, despite not having any other clothes to change into, and showered us with praise for how disciplined we were. It made us angry, but we did not show it. The fact that we usually washed the only clothes we had and hung them to dry overnight, then woke up to iron them, did not strike him as inconvenient enough to offer to buy us even two sets of underwear. He left Dar without saying anything about how his office or that of his London counterpart, Nana Mahomo, would help us. We realised that we were on our own and shouldn't expect anything. That was when we began figuring out how to get out of Tanganyika and head north to Kenya.

For some reason, we had to be vaccinated against smallpox. I was issued an International Certificate of Vaccination or Revaccination Against Smallpox No. 20995 at the Vaccination Centre of the Municipal Council of Dar es Salaam, Tanganyika on the 27th of October 1960. Our friend at the Ambassador's residence helped us with bus fares, some pocket money, and a packet of provisions to eat on the road. One morning Geoff and I got up as usual and had our regular skimpy porridge with milk for breakfast and left as if we were going to loiter in the city, wander about on the beach, and return before dinner. Fortunately, we had no luggage. No goodbyes were said to the fellow South African refugees we lived with. We headed straight to the main bus terminal in the city and boarded a long-distance bus to Nairobi in Kenya. Waiting for that bus to leave, I felt my heart painfully divided. The further north I travelled, the more my relief grew. But I was also moving deeper and deeper into the unknown, which brought with it a foreboding anxiety of its own. Where was I going to end up? Would I ever see my family again? To quieten these impossible thoughts, I would focus on the here and now: the next town, the next meal, the next place to sleep.

Kenya

We had no idea of the distance between Dar es Salaam and Nairobi, which turned out to be slightly more than 900 kilometres. The trip took many hours and had only a few stops. The frightening parts were, first, the road, which was narrow and rough; second, the bus, which was old and rickety; and third, the fact that for the entire trip we had just one driver. There was no second driver to relieve him. It is astounding that this journey did not have any accidents. The bus was packed with passengers carrying all sizes of luggage, with some of the big pieces strapped on top of the bus's luggage rack. It was a long, scenic, interesting, and adventurous journey for the two of us who came from urban environments. One of the most unforgettable stops was at a small town called Moshi, located almost mid-way between Dar and Nairobi. This little town is covered with green trees nestled at the base of Mount Kilimanjaro. The air was fresh from the mist and the dense, green trees. It was one of the prettiest places that we stopped at on our way to Nairobi. We stopped there for a few minutes only, but looking up from where we had stopped to the top of the snow-capped mountain was breath-taking. What I saw of Moshi is still etched in my mind.

Across the African Continent

From Moshi the bus continued its long journey to Nairobi. Another different but also memorable experience was driving through another national park. This was the first time that I had seen so many different kinds of animals roaming free over a vast and open plain. Neither Geoff nor I had ever seen anything like that before. The rest of the journey up to Nairobi was not as spectacular as the wild natural reserves we had seen after we left Dar. We arrived in Nairobi in the early evening after travelling almost all day. We were exhausted and anxious about where we were going to sleep that night. The bus terminal where our journey ended was teeming with people and buses and quite chaotic. Buses parked wherever they could stop and disgorged their passengers and heaps of luggage. In the same vicinity, we located a house which looked like a huge dormitory with many beds lined up in rows one next to the other. It was more than just a bunk house. It was also used as a big brothel frequented by transient passengers. We were tired and slept in our clothes and with our shoes on. We were among the first to leave the place in the morning.

The search for the offices of the Kenya African National Union (KANU) Solidarity House was the first order of business. We both had learned a little Swahili during our short stay in Dar es Salaam. We had heard about KANU and its leaders like Jomo Kenyatta and Tom Mboya when we were in South Africa, and we were certain that when we found one of them, we would be welcome. After asking a few people to direct us, we found the KANU offices, and when we arrived, we were indeed well received by three senior leaders of KANU. They were James Gichuru, Thomas (Tom) Mboya, and Pio Gama Pinto. Gichuru was the chairman, Tom the secretary-general, and Pio was a leading member of the National Executive Committee and the only East African Goan in the leadership of the organisation.

On this first day of our visit to the KANU offices, Pio introduced us to Oginga Odinga, the vice chairman of KANU who, we were told, had just returned from the Soviet Union on a KANU mission. Where he was seated appeared a little out of place and distant from where we were meeting with his three colleagues. He appeared a little isolated from his colleagues. He graciously welcomed Geoff and me and gave us each a metal badge which had KANU colours and a face that resembled the face of Jomo Kenyatta but on closer inspection looked more like Joseph Stalin. He had many of these badges made in the Soviet Union. We later found out that there were different ideological leanings within the leadership of the organisation. Oginga was definitely to the left; his colleagues were not.

The organisation was busy preparing for the upcoming KANU elections and imminent release of Jomo Kenyatta from prison. Pio, who turned out to be a brilliant strategist and organiser, quickly took charge of Geoff and me and arranged that we be accommodated in the servants' quarters of his brother's house. His younger brother, Rosario, lived in one of the middle-class suburbs of Nairobi. At his home, Geoff and I were out of sight of the Kenyan police who were still under British control. If they had found us, we would have been returned to South Africa. Pio then drafted us to work in Rosario's printing shop in the city where we found ourselves busy making plastic badges with a distinct image of Jomo Kenyatta imprinted on a KANU flag as a background. These badges were much lighter than the metal ones Odinga had brought with him from the Soviet Union. They were also easier to pin and display on the lapel of jackets or women's collars. More strikingly, there was no mistaking Kenyatta's face. Sheltering us at the back of Rosario's home and having us work in his shop meant that we did not have time to be loitering on the streets of Nairobi like we did in Dar. And of course, Nairobi was far from any beach and from Mombasa, which faces the Indian Ocean.

Rosario's servants' quarters were comfortable but small. Apart from sharing a single bed, Rosario had organised that we have a shortwave radio. We religiously listened to the BBC's overseas service. This service was targeted mainly at English speakers in some of the outposts of what was once the British Empire and later became the Commonwealth. Listeners in Kenya received the broadcasts via a relay station located in Cyprus, a member of the Commonwealth. This relay service was opened on the 1st of May 1957. Regardless of the selective news it beamed, Geoff and I felt a little connected to the outside world as seen and reported by the BBC in the evenings. We knew what time the news was broadcast and would wait in great anticipation, hoping that we could get a snippet or two about South Africa. There was nothing. We often washed and hung our only clothes to dry overnight as we listened to these broadcasts while waiting for our dinner, which was delivered after Rosario's family had had theirs. Sometimes it seemed that we were being served leftovers, which were not appealing. But it was food, at least. The uncomfortable experience of sleeping on empty stomachs forced us to eat what was shared by generous and sympathetic people who provided us with a roof over our heads. Some mornings we would ask for an iron to press our shirts and pants before being driven by Rosario to work in his shop. He also drove us back to our hideout after work.

In between working during the day and hiding at night, I would often be driven by both Tom and Pio to meet some Indian businessmen, some of them aspiring politicians jockeying for positions in KANU, which was destined to form the government of an independent Kenya. These visits took place during the night and mostly on weekends. Their purpose was to ask for financial assistance for me and Geoff so that we could leave Kenya and go to Egypt. It was during these visits, when I would recount my experiences both at home and on my journey into exile, that I felt what it was like to be a beggar. It was painful to observe how comfortable individuals could listen and follow your sad story with what appeared to be sympathetic attention yet at the end of your outpouring tell you how sorry they are but they cannot help.

Geoff and I had heard that Gamal Abdel Nasser's United Arab Republic (UAR), the sovereign union between Egypt and Syria, was a safe and welcoming haven for refugees like us. Nasser was also a Pan-Africanist, and during his tenure Cairo had become the epicentre of African liberation movements. His government had provided these movements with offices in Zamalek, an upmarket neighbourhood of Cairo. One morning Pio came to his brother's house to fetch me because there was someone I had to meet and tell my story to. I was driven in a Volkswagen Beetle to the Stanley Hotel in the city. This hotel was the fanciest in town. I had to crouch in the back seat of the car and be covered with something like a tarpaulin so as not to be seen. When we got to the hotel, I was told to get out and walk confidently into the restaurant and head straight to the last booth where I would find a 'Negro' male waiting for me. I followed the instructions.

I found the man who was waiting for me. He was light-skinned and of average build and height but did not look well. This was Frank 'Curly' Montero. He was a Kennedy emissary sent to organise and arrange air lifts for Kenyan students destined to further their education in the United States. After a short introduction and rendition of my sad story, he simply said he understood my situation and felt very sorry for me. All Geoff and I were asking for was money to buy two one-way, economy-class plane tickets to Cairo. I left this brief encounter thinking 'there we go again – begging with no result!' And nothing came of it. I was picked up by Pio and whisked back to work. Geoff as usual was waiting with anxious anticipation to hear the outcome of my meeting. My face said it all. He was not surprised.

A couple of days later, both Tom and Pio arranged for us to meet them surreptitiously. We were informed that we were to visit the Indian High Commission in Nairobi where we would be issued travel documents allowing us to leave Kenya and enter the UAR. The air tickets were ready for us to travel as soon as we had collected the travel documents from the Indian High Commission. We were told in the clearest of terms that we were to surrender these travel documents to the Indian Embassy in Cairo the day following our arrival. How could we not do so after our brothers in the struggle had shown us such Pan-African solidarity? We thanked both for their help and went to collect the travel documents and the plane tickets. We also had to obtain yellow fever vaccination certificates before leaving the country. My Revaccination Against Yellow Fever certificate was No. 90304, issued by the Colony and Protectorate of Kenya on the 27th of January 1961. Tom and Pinto again reminded Geoff and I for the last time to return the travel documents to the Indian Embassy in Cairo the day after our arrival. These documents were like *laissez-passers*. We left Nairobi unceremoniously on an afternoon flight bound for Cairo.

Across the African Continent

United Arab Republic

The United Arab Republic (UAR) was a short-lived political union between Egypt and Syria that lasted from 1958 until 1961 when Syria seceded, though Egypt continued to be officially known as the UAR until 1971. Around the same period, Kwame Nkrumah in Ghana also motivated for the formation of the Ghana-Guinea-Mali union in 1958. This union brought together into a loose regional organisation two former colonies, one British, the others French. This was the first union on the African continent. Nkrumah and Nasser were Pan-Africanists who shared a similar ideology, vision, ideas, and practised solidarity with the liberation movements that were waging struggles against colonial rule and apartheid with the goal of achieving freedom and independence.

When Geoff and I landed in Cairo in the evening, we hailed a taxi and asked to be driven to a cheap hotel where we could spend one night only because we had very little money. It was not difficult to tell that we were broke. We had no luggage and were not dressed for the weather, which was very cold. All we carried was a brown envelope containing the two travel documents, our yellow fever vaccination certificates, and the remaining stubs of our two air tickets. The taxi driver drove us to a cheap hotel where we shared one room for one Egyptian pound for the night. The man at the reception desk asked where we had come from and whether we had any luggage; we told him we had come from Nairobi and did not have any luggage. We had to use our Indian High Commission documents to check in. We were asked to pay for the night in case, I think, we disappeared during the night. We did look like a doubtful pair. So, I paid the pound, and we were left with one pound between the two of us!

We got the room and were about to sleep because it was late when, suddenly, I had a severe allergic attack. My whole body broke out in hives that itched like fire. I was in bad shape. Poor Geoff stood there flabbergasted. I honestly thought I was going to die. I got up, dressed quickly, and walked downstairs. Just as I was about to go through the revolving door at the main entrance of the hotel and walk out to find the nearest hospital, the receptionist caught sight of me and stopped me. He wanted to know where I thought I was going so late at night. I told him that I was sick and was going to look for a hospital nearby. He advised me not to go out and wanted to know whether I had one pound. I said I did. He said he would call a doctor to see me and that I should go back to my room. I heeded his advice.

Back in the room Geoff was still pacing up and down, not speaking, confused and worried. He was dumbfounded, and I was frightened and itching fiercely from the swollen hives. It was not long before the doctor arrived. I was lying in bed when Geoff let him in. I recall seeing a short rotund man of average height wearing a black suit, a white shirt, a dark tie, and a black barret. He looked like a European. He came in and greeted both of us, put his case on the side of my bed, pulled out his stethoscope, and started examining me. In a few minutes, he diagnosed me as having developed an allergic reaction to something I had eaten. He reassured us that I would be well in no time and shouldn't worry. He opened his medical kit, took out a syringe, extracted some liquid from a small vial, cleaned the spot, and injected the medicine. As he was putting away his medical instruments, he asked where we had come from. We told him we had just arrived from Nairobi in Kenya but were originally from Johannesburg in South Africa. He knew something about both countries because he had trained to be a medical doctor in England. We paid him the pound, and he gave us his business card and told me to visit his rooms the next day so that he could be sure I had recovered. By the time Geoff saw him off at the door, I was sitting up and almost fully recovered. Whatever he had injected me with worked like magic. I will never forget my first night in Cairo. This doctor was Ahmed Galal Hilmy. His consulting rooms were in the old section of Cairo, and he lived at 75 Oraba Street in Heliopolis.

The Indian Embassy's travel documents were returned the next morning. We later visited Dr Ahmed Hilmy at his consulting rooms – I had fully recovered. After this visit, we went looking for the offices of what we were told was the African Association building at No. 5, Ahmet Hishmat Street on the island of Zamalek. We did not have any money to buy food, let alone catch a bus to a place we hardly knew, so we walked and stopped to ask for directions. The language barrier was a handicap, but we finally got to Zamalek. It turned out to be an upmarket area on an island in the middle of the Nile River but connected to the inner city by bridges. It was an integral part of the city of Cairo. We located the African Association offices; they were not difficult to find because it was generally known that the address we were looking for was a busy hive of young African men from different countries.

When I saw the African Association building, it represented for me the embodiment of Pan-Africanism and the solidarity that went with it. President Gamal Nasser had given Dr Foud Galal, a senior member of his government, the responsibility of overseeing all the operations of this centre. Dr Galal was also an advisor on African Affairs to Dr Monique Leslie Akasi who in 1959 had written that 'Egypt was an African and Arab State.' This was evident from the various liberation organisations housed in the centre. When one examined the political and ideological orientation of these organisation, it was evident that they shared a common cause and objectives and had very similar experiences and problems in the struggles they were waging in their respective countries. What the white South African government was doing to black people in South Africa was not very different from what it was doing to black people in what was then called South West Africa (now Namibia). What the white governments of Southern and Northern Rhodesia and the Portuguese government were doing to black people in Angola and Mozambique also had many similarities. The need for solidarity did not escape the African nationalists. It was there, in Zamalek, that I met Sam Nujoma and Emil Appolus.[8] Virtually all the refugees whose organisations were hosted in the African Association building were waiting to be deployed by their leaders or representatives. Some wanted to further their education while others chose to go for military training. Very few had their own plans unrelated to the liberation struggles in the countries they had come from, though they were not ostracised for not being involved in the struggle.

---

8 Nujoma and Appolus were both founding members of the South West African liberation movement, SWAPO (South West African People's Organisation). Nujoma was SWAPO's first president and Namibia's first democratically elected president.

The African Association had offices for different liberation movements in various countries. There were representatives' offices for South Africans, South West Africans, Southern and Northern Rhodesians, Ugandans, and others. Geoff and I inquired about the representatives of liberation movements from South Africa. We were told that there were two representatives from the African National Congress (ANC). It was quite early in the morning and they had not yet arrived, so we waited outside their office. The PAC did not have an office and had no representatives either. We did not wait long before the two ANC representatives arrived. We did not know them, nor did they know us, but because we were South African refugees, they took us into their care. We gave them a full account of who we were and how we had arrived in Cairo. They confirmed that there was no PAC representative at that time but that they would take us in nonetheless. The two ANC representatives were Mzwai Piliso and Ambrose Makiwane.

We lived in their house until we found a small room on top of a high-rise apartment building near the African Association offices which we rented. The ANC office helped us get financial stipends which we used to pay our rent and buy some basic items. Our room was on the roof of this building, which housed the domestic maids working in it. We shared a single bed. Apart from it, other treasured belongings were a primus stove, a couple of pots, a pan, two metal dishes, two old military cups, and some spoons. We also had some linen for our bed, a couple of face cloths, and two towels. What was really awful about this room was sharing a small bed and preparing scanty, basic meals using a primus stove. To sleep two of us on a single bed we had to sleep head to toe, each looking at and smelling the other's feet. Geoff was a restless sleeper; sometimes I would be woken up by a kick in the face. But it was better than sleeping on the bare concrete floor. We simply had to put up with each other.

Geoff and I spent some evenings watching various sporting activities played by young Egyptians on the Zamalek sports field, which was well lit and which we could see from the top of the building where our little room was located. Those of us who sometimes had a little more money would venture into the night clubs to watch belly dancers. Movies were a no-go because our

Arabic was almost non-existent. In the evenings, the boats that carried passengers, tourists, and cargo during the day were moored along the banks of the Nile. Some of these, which moored under the bridge connecting the island of Zamalek to the city centre, were very busy at night. They served liquor and were frequented by prostitutes. I met a few important African liberation leaders on some of these boats. We had all gone there for drinks.

Pan-African solidarity promoted and practised by leaders such as Kwame Nkrumah, Gamal Nasser, Julius Nyerere, and other leaders contributed to the strengthening of the Pan Africanist fulcrum built over decades by black intellectuals in the diaspora and the continent. These leaders took a personal interest in keeping track of, and offering advice and guidance to, liberation organisations. Their influence on, and commitment to, the liberation and independence of the entire continent did not go unnoticed by the big powers, East and West, who were determined to exert their own influence on these movements. Consequently, there was no liberation movement that was not being courted by these powers. There were many ways in which they did this, but the most effective was by providing financial assistance in one form or another. In most cases, this took the form of scholarships in their countries.

Most of us were aware that we were pawns in the Cold War contest and were therefore quite vulnerable. We had to be careful about taking sides in the contest between East and West. Those of us who did take sides usually ended up facing disastrous consequences which, in turn, hurt the organisations we belonged to. Embassies from both the East and the West were aggressive in recruiting political refugees from the African Association. It was in this atmosphere that we came to know, and become friends with, Sally Burgess, an official in the Consul Section of the American Embassy in Cairo. Sally was a small woman, engaging, even gregarious. It was Sally who introduced me to lavish evening parties in the desert around the Great Pyramids of Giza with the Great Sphinx gazing majestically over us. I learned to ride a camel at one of these parties. But I also had a feeling of disquiet. Being a pawn in the heady international political and ideological contest staged in the Cairo of the early sixties could easily have developed into an adventure with unpredictable consequences. Walking around Cairo, waiting for some help from the PAC while attending embassy parties where there was free food and lots of drinks, made me feel uneasy, adrift.

We all had a lot of time on our hands waiting to go somewhere. Some of us would visit interesting sites like the museums and parts of the old section of the city during the day. I even visited the Port of Alexandria and its fantastic museums. But Geoff and I became increasingly restless. We sent word to the PAC representative based in London, Nana Mahomo, asking to leave Egypt, and he finally came to Cairo. We gave him an extensive briefing, which covered the period from the Sharpeville shootings up to our present situation, including our respective journeys, our meeting with Peter Molotsi in Dar es Salaam, and how we got to Cairo from Nairobi. He appreciated our long oral report. He then asked what it was we wanted to do and where? Geoff wanted to go to Ghana as soon as possible, whereas I wanted to train as a fighter pilot in the Egyptian air force. Geoff's wish was accepted. Nana was startled by my request. He rejected it firmly and instead proposed that I enrol at the local and prestigious Al-Azhar University. I was stunned. What went through my mind was having to learn to read, write, and speak Arabic. Al-Azhar was at that time a renowned centre of Islamic and Arab learning in the world, and I was neither an Islamist nor an Arab, so I rejected this offer. We had to find a compromise. And the compromise was that I would go to London where we would decide on what I could do and where. It was agreed that Geoff and I would go to London by ship, which we would board at Port Said. We were excited by the prospect of London, a place we still thought, somewhat naively, was the centre of the world.

I still feel occasional anger at Nana's refusal to arrange that I be trained as a fighter pilot. I also wonder what would have become of me had I enrolled at Al-Azhar. I found out much later that in the same year that I was in Cairo, 1961, the Al-Azhar University was taken over by the government of President Gamal Nasser. A wide range of secular faculties were added for the first time: business, economics, science, pharmacy, medicine, engineering, and agriculture. Before 1961, Al-Azhar was a religious university and centre of higher learning.

When it was confirmed that I was going to leave for London, Dr Hilmy and his family arranged a farewell lunch for me. It was touching. I was leaving an environment that I had begun to like and find quite familiar. I had formed friendships that I truly treasured, and by this time, I could speak passable Arabic. But now I had to go. Geoff and I were contacted by a travel agent of the Peninsular & Oriental Steam Navigation Company (P & O) and told that our tickets to travel from Port Said to Southampton by ship were ready. This port was east of Port Alexandria. I had hoped that we would depart from Alexandria, the largest port in Egypt and the second biggest city in the country. I had visited Alexandria earlier with an Egyptian whom I had befriended in Cairo and whose home was in Alexandria. He had shown me some memorable places in parts of the al Montaza district, which is the major centre of the city. Some of the museums that I visited, like the Alexandria National Museum, were wonderful. I was hoping to return and explore other historic sites that I had been told about. Unfortunately, this was not going to happen: it was now time to leave the continent.

2

Another Continent

Crossing the Mediterranean Sea

After collecting our tickets for the steam ship, we went to the Cairo Ramses Railway Station, where we bought two one-way train tickets to Port Said. Later that afternoon, we boarded the P & O liner bound for Southampton in England but scheduled to stop briefly at the Port of Marseilles in the south of France. For me and Geoff, this was our first time on a ship. We were curious rather than excited about this experience. Even though we were booked in the lowest class of cabins, we were allowed to walk around and survey the facilities on the ship. These were mind-boggling. What was most impressive was the large dining-hall, which was lavishly decked out. And the food! The menu was impressive. The variety, number of courses, size of servings, and drinks were unbelievable for two poor refugees. We sat at a long table with white people who did not seem to be bothered that there were two blacks sitting with them and being served like them. Perhaps it was because Geoff was lighter skinned and could have been an Egyptian and I was a little darker skinned and could have been a Nubian.

The evening before docking in Marseilles, we were all having a good time, enjoying the food and wine, and totally oblivious of the fact that we were on a ship sailing across a sea. The dining hall was packed. We had been served drinks, starters, and the main course and were waiting for desserts, coffee, and tea when suddenly the ship began to heave up on its bow and down on its stern. Before we could figure out what was happening, it began to list to one side and then the other. I will never forget seeing so many plates, glasses, cups and saucers, forks, knives, and salt and pepper shakers all sliding down to the ends of the tables when the ship first heaved up. What followed was an incredible sight of table cloths sliding in whatever direction the ship was listing. The diners too! The din of breaking plates and glasses and sliding chairs was accompanied by the scramble of frightened diners who had instantly gotten up and headed for the doors leading out of the dining hall. Those who got out fast enough, wobbled to the nearest handrail on the side of the ship and leaned over to vomit. It was a sight to behold. The ship moved like a big whale up and down and sideways. I was fine and rather amused at all the people who could not hold their food and drinks. Geoff left quickly for our bunk; he was not feeling well either. I walked around exploring parts of the ship that I was allowed access to. I was curious and wanted to see how rough the sea could get. Somehow, in the course of my wanderings, I found myself at the bar.

Behind the counter, the bartender was waiting on a customer who seemed to be quite relaxed as he sipped his drink. This calm and unfazed customer happened to be an Egyptian, and I joined him. Fortunately, he and the bartender spoke English. We talked about the rough sea and other things as we enjoyed our free drinks. As we got tipsy and merry, I gathered that the Egyptian was returning to London where he was responsible for looking after the Egyptian Embassy, which had been closed due to the diplomatic fracas between Egypt and Britain that began in July 1956 when Egypt nationalised the Suez Canal Company. The bar tender was very generous in refilling our glasses and keeping us happy while we kept him company. We almost forgot about the rough sea and the unstable ship. I hardly remember when I went back to my cabin to sleep. But I recall the following morning vividly.

The storm was over and the sea was calm and quiet. Most of the passengers looked worn out and haggard. Many stood quietly holding on to the rails of the ship and looking at the Port of Marseilles as it approached. No one had gone for breakfast after the previous night's mass regurgitation. Almost everyone wanted to get off the ship and walk on land. Disembarking at the port was a solemn and very orderly process, and setting foot on land was very healing for most of us. Walking around the Port of Marseilles was a great relief for everyone including the crew, who had had a lot of cleaning up to do. We all strolled around the port's shops window-shopping, and some passengers treated themselves to French snacks and food. When we boarded the ship for the last leg to Southampton, the mood among the passengers was a little livelier and relaxed. One could sense that we were all quietly hoping that we would not run into another storm. And luckily, we didn't.

United Kingdom

When the ship docked at the port of Southampton, Geoff and I were met by Jacob Maleka, a PAC cadre who was sent by Nana Mahomo, the PAC representative in the United Kingdom, to meet us and bring us to London. Jacob was cautious and eager to get us to our destination as soon as possible. It was a cold, damp day. All the locals were in dark coats with their collars turned up against the weather. There was little time to look around as Jacob hurried us along to a nearby train station.

Catching the above-ground train from Southampton was no big thing. Getting off a few stations down the line, and going underground to catch the Tube, was something else. It was novel and very exciting. What was fascinating to us, as on the ship, was feeling like seemingly ordinary passengers amongst a predominantly white crowd. For me and Geoff, the ride on the Tube took first prize. In the early evening of our first day in London, Jacob decided to introduce us to a London pub, which was on the same block as the Transport and General Workers' Union offices.

In the pub, Jacob bought us a pint of bitter beer each. We did not like the taste of it at all. Geoff and I must have stood out in the pub because a couple of patrons came over and asked where we had come from. We told them we had just come from Port Said in Egypt. The next question was where we were going to stay. Jacob, our guide, told them that we would be staying at the Harold Laski hostel, which was walking distance from the pub. We were thrilled. I had first heard this name mentioned in the Africanists' debates on socialism at the time that I was reading George Padmore's book in South Africa. I thought, 'Wow, what an appropriate place for us to be staying.' This hostel was named after a renowned British political theorist, economist, author, and former professor. Laski had been a professor at the London School of Economics and chairman of the British Labour Party for a short period. He was Britain's most influential spokesperson for socialism during the interwar years (1918–1939). Furthermore, he was a Marxist and believed in a planned economy based on the public ownership of the means of production. Laski had a major and lasting impact on socialism in India and other Asian and African countries. According to John Kenneth Galbraith, the eminent American economist, Laski was 'the centre of [Jawaharlal] Nehru's thinking'. Some of this historical background I unearthed later.

Before Geoff and I left the pub, the patrons who had asked us where we had come from alerted us to some incidents that had occurred at the hostel in the early hours of the morning. This hostel was frequented mostly by transients who were passing through London. We were advised to sleep with our clothes and shoes on because these transients were early risers, and when they got up to leave, they quietly picked up any movable items lying around! This came as a great shock to us. On our first night in London, a place we thought was the centre of the world and civilisation, we had to sleep with our only set of clothes and shoes on with laces tied tight. We had done this once before on our first night in Nairobi, but this was in a major city, and neither Geoff nor I had ever slept with our clothes and shoes on at home. We finished our dinner of steak and kidney pies and bitter beer – a far cry from the lavish dinner on the P & O liner from Port Said to Southampton. In the end, the night was uneventful, and we slept fairly well.

The next morning, we woke up feeling somewhat dishevelled, washed our faces, and went in search of the South Africa United Front (SAUF) offices. Jacob had told us how to get there, and we arrived early in the morning before the offices opened. The SAUF was formed in Addis Ababa, Ethiopia on the 19th of June 1960, just three months after the Sharpeville massacre. The public statement announcing SAUF's formation in London was made at a meeting on the 23rd of September 1960. This meeting was sponsored by the Anti-Apartheid Movement, Christian Action, the Committee on African Organisations, the Movement for Colonial Freedom, and the Africa Bureau. Oliver Tambo (ANC), Nana Mahomo (PAC), Fanuel Kozonguizi (SWANU), and Dr Yusuf Dadoo (SAIC) were present and represented their constituent organisations. The South West African Peoples' Organisation (SWAPO) was admitted later, in January 1961, but never really participated. It later withdrew before SAUF was formally dissolved in January 1962 in Dar es Salaam and in London in March of the same year. I was then in London, having arrived only a few months earlier from Cairo. The internal rivalry between the PAC and the ANC was the primary reason for the dissolution of the SAUF.

SAUF's offices were on John Adams Street, across the street from the Charing Cross railway station on the Strand. It was a typical wintery London morning – cloudy, damp, drizzling, and quite depressing. Geoff and I got there pretty early and waited under a shallow, narrow entrance to the office on the ground floor facing a restaurant across the street. A medium-sized Bedford truck stopped at the curb outside the restaurant. Its driver and helper, both short chubby white guys wearing blue overalls, got out of the truck, and started off-loading crates and bags of vegetables which they carried into the restaurant. As they were off-loading, a few vegetables fell and landed under the two back wheels of the truck. They were a cabbage, a couple of carrots, and a potato.

We had not had any breakfast, and the previous night's pies and bitters had not been a real meal. We were very hungry. Without saying anything to each other, our eyes fixed on these vegetables. Then, a few moments later, we both wondered aloud whether we should salvage them or not. I was against picking them up, but Geoff wanted to dash across the street and get them. My argument was that he might be suspected of stealing and taking food from the truck, and in any case, I said, you don't scavenge, especially in London. We speculated that the truck might reverse and squash what would have been a substitute for breakfast, and we were still arguing about whether or not to retrieve the vegetables when the two guys came out of the restaurant and jumped into their truck. The driver started the engine and backed up, reducing what would have been our breakfast into pulp. We were sore and sorry! Geoff was mad at me. We didn't talk to each other until the secretary working in the SAUF offices arrived and let us into the offices.

Nana Mahomo arrived soon after we had made ourselves comfortable in the offices. Wearing the dark sunglasses that were his trademark, he greeted us and asked about our journey and the previous night's experience. After a short chat, he gave us some money to have breakfast at a restaurant a few steps from the entrance on the ground floor. It was a treat. Then we returned to the office for further discussions. Geoff was determined to leave for Ghana as soon as possible, so the necessary arrangements were made. I now wanted to go to university, but Nana wanted me to go to Algeria and open a PAC office there. I refused, and my arguments were, first, that I was not sufficiently prepared to take on such responsibility; second, that I was not keen to learn a new language, French; and finally, that Nana himself, as I reminded him, had spent a couple of years at the University of Cape Town, which had helped prepare him for his work on behalf of the PAC. By this time, I realise, I was settling into exiled life. In London my existence had, for the first time since I escaped South Africa, begun to assume a quality of permanence. It was because of this that I could start thinking of studying and of building a life for myself. Thankfully, Nana conceded, and an appointment was made for me to visit Oxford University's Ruskin College, where a scholarship was available. This was a much better deal.

Geoff left a few days later for Accra in Ghana, where he was to be under the care of Peter Molotsi. Within a couple of days, I got into a train at the Charing Cross station bound for Oxford. The train ride was pleasant and the scenery beautiful. Oxford was attractive. My interview at Ruskin was short and went well. There was, however, one feature of the college's academic programme that made me uncomfortable: attending classes was not compulsory. All I had to do was register for the subjects I wanted to study, read the prescribed material, and write the set examinations for those subjects. This made me feel uneasy and a little scared. I imagined how political errands in the London office could very easily take precedence over my academic work. I suspected that the probability of failing and dropping out was high. Another PAC cadre took up the risky Oxford scholarship after I had left for the United States, and he did not graduate for these very reasons.

Privately, my hope was for a scholarship to study in the United States. The counsellor I had met in Cairo, Sally Burgess, had been in touch with me about a scholarship that was being organised by the Southern African Students Program (SASP) and administered by the African American Institute (AAI), a group established in 1953 to build and develop relationships between the US and African countries. The USSR had established the Patrice Lumumba Friendship University in 1961, offering scholarships to students from Third World countries. Some of the recipients were black South Africans who were fighting the apartheid regime. The SASP scholarship was a direct response to the Soviet scholarship, though I didn't yet understand this. All I knew was that I was interested in studying in the US, even more so after I understood the loose, rather *laissez-faire* way in which the Oxford scholarship was run. Sally understood this and was making some enquiries on my behalf.

~

From the time I left home in a hurry in September 1960 to February 1961, my pace of life as a refugee was quite slow and unpredictable. A faster pace started in London and was to accelerate until I left for the United States in mid-August 1962. The political errands and engagements were many and some were quite demanding, as both the ANC and PAC were busy mobilising the British politicians and public to support the anti-apartheid movement, which was at the forefront of campaigns designed to isolate South Africa from the international community. The British Labour Party, which was the governing party during this period (1961–1966), was more supportive of the movement. In fact, it was under the Labour Party's government that I was able to travel between the United States and Britain without a passport. All I had at this time was a British visa allowing me to enter Britain. I used the back of this paper to get other visas that permitted me to travel to a few countries in Africa and Europe. How I travelled in and out of the United States without a passport is another story.

SAUF leaders did not encourage refugees to be financially dependent on it for support of any kind. I therefore had to find a part-time job to pay for a place to stay and to buy some basic necessities. The first place I stayed at was the International Voluntary Services (IVS) hostel near the Camden subway station. IVS was a British branch of Service Civil International (SCI), which was a volunteer organisation dedicated to promoting a culture of peace by organising international voluntary projects for people of all ages and backgrounds. These volunteers were engaged on a short-, medium-, or long-term basis depending on the duration of the different projects in the different countries. The IVS's Secretary General during my residence there was Mr Frank Judd. Frank has since forged impressive public and professional careers over the years and is now Lord Judd of the Labour Party. He wrote that among the most exciting and enjoyable periods of his life was his tenure with the IVS. He said the following: 'What was special about IVS was its scope. Peace was seen as rooted in solidarity, mutual service, and a sense of community which knew no bounds.' His senior staff members were Roy and Judy Payne and others who were dedicated to their jobs and responsibilities, which included hosting several resident volunteers, young male and female adults who came from various parts of Europe, Asia, and Africa. My first encounter with Sri Lankans was at IVS. The secretary of the SAUF, Janet Goodricke, was also a boarder at IVS. This was very helpful because she helped me navigate my way through the London subway and bus systems.

The IVS hostel had several rooms which varied in size. There were single rooms mostly for women; men shared one large room with several beds in it. There was a common lounge and fully furnished kitchen with a big rectangular table and benches. Each lodger had to prepare his or her own food – breakfast, lunch, and dinner. Those who could not or were too lazy to cook relied on fast-food outlets and fish and chips. The tastiest and most enjoyable meals were prepared by our Indian or Ceylonese colleagues. For these meals, those interested usually contributed money for the ingredients of the meals. These communal dinners were very interesting because we got to hear who came from where, why he or she was passing through IVS, and what their final destination was. There were occasions when we delved into each other's personal experience, especially in cases where individuals came from countries experiencing conflicts of one kind or another, like South Africa and Ceylon (renamed Sri Lanka in 1972).

After dinner, whether communal or not, the male contingent went to bed with some trepidation. This was because of the prospect of interrupted sleep, particularly in the early hours of the morning. For the period that I lived at the IVS hostel, there were four or five of us in the one room that looked like a dormitory. I remember Paul, Upali, Frank, and, of course, myself. Paul W. H. Johnson was British and apprenticed in law at the London Inns of Court. Singaravelu Upali came from Ceylon and was a refugee like me. Frank, whose surname I don't remember, was British. He was a gruff, working-class Londoner who was employed delivering things in the city and its surrounds. Frank hated his job. He had to wake up earlier than all of us because he had to travel quite a distance to get to work. Before going to bed he would set his alarm clock for five or five-thirty in the morning. What drove us crazy was that he had one of those ancient alarm clocks with a ring that woke up almost everybody on the second floor of the building – except Frank! He would stretch out his hand and stop the ringing but then immediately fall back asleep. The rest of us could not. He had difficulty waking and dressing up to leave. And once up, he would start cursing out loud as he quickly splashed his face with water, wiped it, and left. We complained to management about Frank, his alarm clock, the noise he made when he got up, and his cursing.

But before this complaint could be dealt with, Frank went and bought a medium-sized bathtub made of corrugated iron. He put his alarm clock inside the tub, then on top of the tub he strung a tightly knit mesh made from ordinary string. This device was meant to prevent him from reaching the alarm clock bell and turning it off when it rang. However, Frank was unaware that this contraption would in fact amplify the noise and that the mesh would prolong the damned ring. We realised that Frank was daft. So, before he could operate his new contraption, we decided to demonstrate the effect of his design. Voila, we were correct. He was forced to abandon his plan and return the bath tub to the shop the next day. He then decided to tie the alarm clock to the headboard of his bed so that it hung just above his pillow; this way he could reach it quickly when it went off. How we wished he could just leave the hostel. As it turned out, I left before he did.

When I left IVS, I had been putting in some time at the SAUF offices and had started working for Richard Houser. Houser was married to Hephzibah, sister of the celebrated violinist and conductor, Yehudi Menuhin. Yehudi is considered one of the greatest musical geniuses of the past century, and it is said that when Albert Einstein heard him play, he remarked, 'Now I know there is a God in heaven.' While in London, I was privileged to attend several of his concerts. Hephzibah had a younger sister named Yalta, who was also an acclaimed pianist, painter, and poet. She was married to Joel Ryce. Both Yalta and Joel were professional concert performers, so between Yehudi, Yalta, and Joel, I was invited to many concerts and soirées where I was treated to beautiful music. Menuhin visited South Africa later in 1956 and was shocked that he was billed to play to white audiences only. He insisted on playing to a black audience as well, and did so in Soweto and Alexandra. He later returned to South Africa to celebrate Nelson Mandela's release from prison.

Richard Houser was an Austrian Quaker, sociologist, social commentator, planner, permanent lecturer at Nottingham University, and an advisor to a variety of institutions in Europe and the United States. Jacqueline Kent, an award-winning biographer, wrote in her book, *An Exacting Heart*, that Hephzibah and Richard 'usually had at least twenty projects running at once, including counselling marginalised ethnic minorities, prison inmates and victims of domestic violence; undertaking social surveys for the British Home Office; working with the peace movement in India; and trying to establish human rights centres to mediate between paramilitary groups in Northern Ireland.' I can attest to the accuracy of this observation. Later I learned that another assignment Richard had was to de-Nazify Mussolini's army in Italy after the Second World War.

I was unaware of the many projects they were involved in when I visited the Houser's beautiful home, located not far from the Baker Street Tube station. My first assignment was to join a very small team of coffee tasters. There were three or four of us, Richard included. Our job was to taste coffees made from a variety of ground coffee beans using different kinds of sugar, granulated and refined. This was a Cadbury project. The working environment and conditions were fantastic. We were working in a lovely, beautiful, furnished home with a soothing ambience and drinking rich, exotic coffees. I almost forgot I was a refugee. The team members methodically sipped individual coffees made from different beans, added certain sugars and milk, and then recorded the tasting results in a methodical way. The system we were using was well thought out. The first tasting was in the morning as soon as we got to work round 8 a.m. The second took place two hours later round 10 a.m. Lunch time was the third, followed by four o'clock teatime, which, for those of us who did not live in the house, was the last. For a couple of weeks, this job was great fun. I had never in my short life enjoyed drinking such fancy coffees. But it did not take long before I began to get the jitters! I had no idea what was happening to me. I mentioned this to Richard, and he immediately took me off the coffee tasting project. Apparently, I had begun reacting to too much caffeine and sugar, so I was then assigned to another project in Notting Hill.

My job in Notting Hill was to conduct research into the living conditions of poor people who lived in properties owned and operated by Peter Rachman. Richard Houser had been contracted by the London City Council to undertake this job. Nana had also introduced me to Martin Ennals, who was a friend of his and a human rights activist. Martin worked for Amnesty International in London, another organisation that supported the liberation movements in Southern Africa. I consulted Martin about Notting Hill and Peter Rachman's role in that neighbourhood, and Martin was very helpful in briefing me.

Peter Rachman had built a property empire in West London consisting of over one hundred blocks of mansions and several night clubs. Over time, he proceeded to subdivide these large houses into flats and rooms for renting and prostitution. To maximise his rental income from his Notting Hill properties, he drove out most white tenants and replaced them with newly arrived Caribbean immigrants. The white tenants who lived in his properties were driven out because they had statutory protection against high rent increases. Recently arrived black immigrants from the Caribbean, on the other hand, did not have that kind of protection, and there were many of them who were desperate to have a place to stay, whatever the cost. Notting Hill thus earned itself the title of 'Rachman's West Indian ghetto'.

Peter Rachman went on to become a slum landlord who was portrayed, in the popular media, as the evil head of an empire based on vice, violence, and extortion, the festering heartland of which was Notting Hill. This was long before the famous and wealthy made it their home. A woman who lived in one of his rented properties is reported as having said that: 'There are landlords who mend their broken windows with cardboard instead of glass and don't care that the water is passing through a light in your child's bedroom. They are happy to protect the rent while their tenants live in danger and squalor.' A description of where I lived confirms what this lady said. The types of people I got to know, and in some cases befriended and hung out with, also reveal the change that occurred when Notting Hill degenerated into a slum in the late 1950s and early 1960s, by which time Rachman had largely moved out of slumlording.

The history of Notting Hill before Rachman moved on is very interesting and vividly illustrated by the murder of Kelso Cochrane. Cochrane, a thirty-two-year-old Antiguan immigrant, was murdered in Notting Hill on the 17th of May 1959 shortly after midnight while walking home. The Notting Hill of that period was dominated by Oswald Mosley's Union Movement and Colin Jordan's White Defence League. These organisations were racist and had a history of promoting racial riots in the area (the most devastating of which had taken place in 1958). Following Kelso's murder, the British government commissioned an investigation into race relations in Britain. The chairperson of this inquiry was Amy Ashwood Garvey, the first wife of the Jamaican political activist, Marcus Garvey. Amy had founded the United Negro Improvement Association with her husband in 1914. Commenting on the inquiry, Father Trevor Huddleston, the anti-apartheid Anglican bishop, said, 'If it should lead, as it still may, to a radical searching of the conscience on the part of ordinary citizens, then much good will have come out of evil.' After the murder, and its fallout, Jamaicans, Trinidadians, Barbadians, small islanders, and Africans were united in their determination to stay in Notting Hill and establish a new Black Afro-Caribbean identity. These immigrants had tended to gravitate to this area for the previous two generations.

The building I moved into and lived in was owned, I was told, by a West Indian. It is more than likely that he bought it from Rachman. Its Victorian façade looked drab, worn, and dirty; its colour was a dull grey. A few steps from the sidewalk and up the stairs led to the entrance of the building, which was a big wooden door. Inside it was dreadful. The building was imploding. The room that I was being offered to rent was on the fourth floor, the top most floor of the building, and getting to that floor was a dangerous climb. The staircase was old, falling apart, and wobbled as it tilted away from the wall on your left towards the banister on the right, most of which was missing. The tilting and missing sections of the banisters started on the ground floor and ended on the fourth floor. It was safest to keep to the wall as you walked up what remained of the stairs. On the third-floor landing, I discovered a bathroom with an old and dirty-looking toilet with half of what was once a white bath tub. The other half of the bath tub was missing. When I reached the fourth floor, I walked into a very sparsely furnished single room that had a single bed with a horrible-looking mattress and pillows which I could not use. My first reaction was the fear of bed bugs!

I immediately noticed that I had to find some basic items like a mattress, sheets, pillows, blankets, a primus stove, a paraffin can, a kettle to boil water, a couple of pots for cooking, a tin washing basin, soap, towel, face cloth, and other things including something to kill any and all bugs. I had done this before in Cairo. Water was available only on the third-floor landing from the broken bathtub. I don't recall how many tenants lived in this dreadful building, but all of us got our water from the faucets in the bathtub on the third floor. Taking a bath was out of the question, of course, because half the bathtub was missing. Where to shower or bathe, then? I had my full baths on certain days during the week in the public baths in the city that looked clean enough. Some of the folks who sat next to me while we waited our turns had some ripe odours. We all needed to bathe.

On the fourth floor where I had a room, I had an interesting and strange neighbour across the hallway. I don't know whether he was from the West Indies or West Africa. We never exchanged a word, even when we accidentally bumped into each other in the hallway. He was short, dark, stocky, and had strong African features. I do not know what he did for a living, nor did he know what I did for a living. What was absolutely astounding to me was what I saw through the open door when I passed his room. His room was full of all sorts of odd and old things, trinkets, and gadgets which he seemed to have collected. He usually sat in the middle of this vast, mixed collection with his back to the door while watching his black-and-white television, listening to his radio, and playing his old gramophone – often all at the same time. And all three were turned up quite loud. How he followed or appreciated any of them amidst that cacophony still puzzles me. I often think he was off his rocker but can't be sure because we never talked to each other. The noise from his room was not too loud once both our doors were shut.

I got to know the neighbourhood quite well as I visited some local pubs where I quickly made acquaintances with white people my age. Coming from South Africa, I aroused the curiosity of many people and invariably faced questions about why I had come to London and why I had chosen to live in the slum of Notting Hill. I did not know who I could trust, so to questions like these I gave dodgy but plausible explanations. These encounters in the pubs, and subsequent visits to the living quarters of some of my acquaintances, I often found depressing. Among these acquaintances was a pleasant and sociable young white couple who had a child that was several months old. They were destitute and consumed more drugs and alcohol than food. They lived in a hovel compared to my single room. Their place tended to be a meeting place for other drug-addict friends they associated with. They all got together to smoke pot or inject each other with drugs with the same needles they had themselves just used. The practice was usual and casual as was the smoking of marijuana. Meals were often fast foods that they bought or that some of their friends brought with them in the evenings. This couple and most of their friends lived on the margins; economically and socially, they were London's poor but not yet homeless. Peter Rachman collected rent from such people and others. He achieved notoriety after a couple of revelations surfaced in London high society following his death in November 1962 at the age of 43. A member of parliament, Ben Parkin, in the course of the debates dealing with housing in the city of London, coined the word 'Rachmanism'. This word entered the *Oxford English Dictionary* and means 'the exploitation and intimidation of tenants'. The *Rent Act* of 1965 was introduced to give tenants security, but this also had the unfortunate consequence of reducing the stock of private, rented housing.

While working in Notting Hill, Richard would also drag me round to places like the Bethnal Green Asylum, a mental institution. This was Richard's way of showing me the different projects he was involved in. Visiting this facility was unnerving, and on one visit to Bethnal Green, Richard led me to a room where some inmates were having a meeting. Richard had organised this group of mental patients into a collective so that they could deal with some of the problems that they faced and that needed to be addressed by the prison authorities. Watching how they had a chairman, an agenda, minutes of the previous meetings, matters arising, and then items on the agenda all seemed very normal and was very surprising to me.

At another meeting I attended with Richard there were moments when the discussions got quite heated and frightening. At some point during the proceedings, the chairman responded to one of his colleagues, saying 'he's mad!' This was followed by roaring laughter during which some said, 'But aren't we all mad?' The chairman distanced himself by saying he was not as crazy as most of them, and although there was some truth to his observation, that retort very nearly broke up the meeting. But it finally ended well, and the next meeting was scheduled. When we left the room, Richard and I shared our observations of the meeting. He made some professional remarks about the mental conditions of the inmates, which revealed that he had been working with this group for some time. My only remark was that I feared the prospect of the meeting degenerating into a brawl and objects being thrown around. Richard pointed out that there were two security personnel stationed just outside the meeting room in case things fell apart.

Another incident that remains etched in my memory was Lord Bertrand Russell's ninetieth birthday celebration at a concert held in London on the afternoon of 19 May 1962 at the Royal Festival Hall.[9] Nana had been invited to the event and was on the programme. He had been tasked with presenting Lord Russell with a gift from the African community of London and had asked me to be there as well. I was comfortably ensconced in my seat next to some people I knew when, a few minutes before the event started, Janet Goodricke, the secretary of the SAUF office, hurriedly approached and whispered to me, saying Nana could not be found anywhere and that I had to stand in for him. I foolishly allowed myself to be persuaded, and Janet took me to the back of the stage of the hall. Peeping between the stage curtains, I got a glimpse of Lord Russell sitting comfortably at one end of the stage and looking not very excited about the goings on around him. In fact, at times he seemed to be nodding off. I found myself standing behind Vanessa Redgrave who was standing behind the Duke of Bedford (Bertrand's cousin, Ian Bedford). The two were also going to go on stage to wish him a happy birthday and present him with some gifts. Others who were on the programme were Victor Purcell, Mrs Sonning of Denmark, and Ernest Willis, the Swiss sculptor.

The Duke was calm and relaxed. Vanessa, on the other hand, was fidgeting nervously as we waited to go on stage. This unsettled and surprised me. The previous night I had gone to the Aldwych theatre on the Strand to watch a play, *As You Like It*, in which she had the leading role. She was magnificent as usual. To see her now so nervous, standing right in front of me, sent tremors through

---

9 Philosopher, logician, mathematician, historian, social critic, and political activist, Russel was also a leader of the Nuclear Disarmament Movement, a leading anti-war activist, and an anti-imperialist who derided US involvement in the Vietnam War. In September 1961, at the age of 89, he was arrested for breaching the peace by taking part in an anti-nuclear demonstration in London. When he appeared in court, the presiding magistrate offered to exempt him from jail if he pledged to 'good behaviour'. Russell's reply was 'No, I won't.'

my own nervous system. I could not understand why she had stage fright on this occasion, when the previous night she had been in total command. When I asked her about it, she said she always got jitters before she got on stage. That only made things worse, and by the time it was my turn I had lost it completely. When I got past the curtain and looked out at the audience, I was mortified. I did not know that the hall was so big and could accommodate so many people! What struck me most were what seemed like the millions of eyes and white faces staring at me. I had never seen so many of them under one roof in my short life. Not in South Africa, certainly. I lost what nerves were left from stage fright. I do not remember what I said as I handed the beautifully carved African head to Lord Russell. The head was a piece of art but weighed a ton. I never forgave Nana for leaving me in the lurch.

It was during that summer, the English summer of 1962, that I received a letter from an office in the US Department of State to say I had been granted a scholarship to study in Pennsylvania, and that the documents would soon arrive. In due course they did, and I began the process of bidding farewell to those with whom I had stayed over the past year. Of these, I was most sad to leave Martin Ennals, who had become a close friend.

The last outing I remember happened in early July 1962, when my former roommate at IVS, Paul Johnson, invited me to visit his home somewhere outside London. I don't recall the name of the place, except that his home was next to Henry Moore's, the English sculptor. We went next door to see some of Moore's work in his garden. Paul had rented a little Lambretta scooter, and we rode all over the place, stopping frequently at local pubs to eat and taste some of the excellent local brews. On the same tour, we visited Stonehenge and later Oxford University, where we went punting. Paul knew how to punt; I was just a passenger enjoying the scenery on both sides of the stream. It was summer and the grounds, riverbanks, and stream looked their best. Many people were out picnicking and enjoying the balmy weather. I can still recall the scene vividly, one of the last images I have of England from my time there as a stateless person and a refugee. It must have been about a month after that, in the second week of August 1962, that Martin Ennals, wearing his usual tweed jacket and grey pants, accompanied me to Charing Cross station early one morning and saw me onto a train bound for Southampton. A ship bound for New York would be departing from Southampton port, and I had a place upon it.

Part Three

America

1

Arrival In New York

The great ship docked with a low, terrific noise, and after ten days on the water all the passengers prepared to disembark. What I remember most clearly from my arrival in New York was the sense of relief I felt when I was processed, moments after stepping onto dry land, without any questions. I had been travelling with strange documents for over two years and naturally felt concerned that I would be refused entry and told to return to where I had come from. But the port official simply took my document – titled 'Special African Program No. P. I. 3016, Naturalisation Service No. 11/22/55, File No. 314.6.300 ED' – looked at it, and said, 'All right, welcome to America.' I felt a swirling mix of emotions, intensified by the time spent on the water. Besides relief, I felt excitement and nervousness at finally arriving in the United States, a place I had known, though only in imagination, for most of my life. I was further from home than ever before, but I was also, at last, in a place where I intended to stay, at least for a while.

Saying goodbye to the four friends I had made on the journey – George, Hank, Norman, and Giuliano – was bittersweet. Over the days of our voyage, we had formed a certain bond. It may be of some interest to the reader to know who these four men were. George Houser was a Methodist minister who became a leading civil rights activist and was a veteran supporter of African liberation movements. He was also a co-founder of the Congress of Racial Equality (CORE), which was formed in 1942 in Chicago, and of the American Committee on Africa (ACOA), which was formed in 1953. I would see him again before long. Norman Fruchter would become a well-known novelist, filmmaker, and academic; among other things, he worked as assistant editor of the *New Left Review* and editor of *Studies on the Left*. Hank Heifetz was a graduate of Harvard University and the University of California, Berkeley, who became a poet, novelist, documentarian, critic, and noted translator of Spanish, Sanskrit, and Tamil. Finally, the Italian, Giuliano: Giuliano Amato had joined the Italian Socialist Party in 1958. When I met him on the ship, he was headed to Columbia University Law School in New York City. There he earned a Master's degree in Comparative Law and went on to become a professor and member of the Italian Parliament for eighteen years. He was subsequently a member of the Democratic Party in Italy and was Prime Minister of Italy twice, from 1992 to 1993 and then from 2000 to 2001. Before we parted ways, they gave me some of their contact details, and I told them the name of the student program I was a part of, and we promised to be in touch.

Navigating through the throngs of people at the port, I made my way with some of the other African students to the meeting point we had been told about. As we walked, the towering buildings, the honking of horns, and the hurried pace of those around me compelled me. I was stunned by the massive size of the buildings in that area. London has buildings, but they are dispersed and not nearly as tall as these were. And the pace in London was not as fast as the pace I walked into in New York. It is an energy I still sometimes feel in New York to this day. Everything seemed larger than life, a stark reminder of the decision I had made to leave my home. As we stood at the meeting point, scanning the crowd for the person who would guide us to our next destination, I felt a sense of wonder at the journey that lay behind me and the one that lay ahead.

A small group of staff members from the United States Mission to the United Nations met our group of African students and took us in private cars to a hotel where we were to spend the night before heading to our different destinations the following day. Once we got to the modest hotel, we were taken to our rooms and told that in a couple of hours we would be picked up and driven to the United States Mission, where a welcome dinner had been arranged for us. We were also diplomatically asked to 'freshen up' and dress nicely for the occasion. We tried, but I think we still looked like what we were: refugees who had just landed.

Arrival In New York

The United States Mission to the United Nations is located on First Avenue, just across from the United Nations Headquarters. For some of my fellow Africans, I recall, getting into the elevator of this gigantic building was a frightening experience. This was the first time that they had walked out of an elevator high up in a building only to see floor-to-ceiling glass walls girded by steel and aluminium frames. Outside was New York City at night, and seeing the bright city lights, the cars down below, the enormous buildings, including the United Nations Headquarters opposite, was breath-taking. The floor had a soft, thick-pile carpet. When you stepped on it, your shoe sunk a little causing you to almost lose your balance if you weren't careful. Two African students who were wearing new shoes that they had bought in France before boarding the ship were still breaking them in when they had to make their way across this cushy carpet. As I recall, they did not have an easy time of it.

We were ushered into a large ornate room, lavishly decked out under sparkling chandeliers, an elaborate arrangement of tables covered with embroidered white tablecloths, chairs, shining silverware, and glittering wine and water glasses, beautiful fresh-cut flowers – the works. By the time we were all seated at our assigned tables, you could tell from our facial expressions that we were all mesmerised by the scintillating room, the well-dressed hosts, and the fine food. None of us was used to such opulence.

At each table was seated a couple of white Americans, a woman and a man. I was escorted to my table, introduced to my hosts, and seated. Jean and Bob Bach, a well-dressed couple in their fifties, graciously welcomed me, and we soon entered into conversation, the same conversation that was going on, in different versions, all over the room: Where had we come from? How had our travels been? Where were we going to study in the United States? While we chatted we were treated to starters, drinks of one kind or another depending on one's preference, the main dish, desserts, and tea or coffee. It seemed that the idea behind this dinner was to introduce us to American hospitality and affluence – the beginning of our socialisation process. The food was delicious and much more enjoyable than what we had

had on the ship. The portions were inordinately large, surpassing what I had grown accustomed to in England.

Jean Bach had blonde hair and a strong voice. She was a radio and film producer, and one got the sense that she was sophisticated in some way, but you didn't know how exactly. Bob, her husband, who worked in television, was down-to-earth and more soft-spoken than his wife. It was Jean who asked the questions; she was inquisitive. Our conversation started with my experience on the ship, and I had a lot to tell them about that. It then switched to where exactly I came from and why I had left home. I told them that I was politically active in the movement that resulted in the Sharpeville shootings of protestors. They knew about the Sharpeville massacre; they were well-informed. Their curiosity reminded me of my encounter with George and the others on the ship, and I began to feel uncomfortable. *Who could I trust?* I told them a truncated version of my story and deliberately left out my adventures as a refugee. I remember they made the observation, which was accurate, I think, that I seemed a little more relaxed than the other African students. I acknowledged that by saying I grew up in the city of Johannesburg, had lived in Cairo for a short period, and had just arrived from London where I had lived for over a year. I knew a little about big cities, I said. My demeanour was polite and subdued. Being very reticent and a little secretive, I did not talk too much, nor did I ask too many questions either. I remember them as being an impressive couple, friendly and courteous, and I was pleased, sometime later, to become reacquainted with them.

The evening did not end particularly late, but I remember feeling very tired in the car that took us back to the hotel. It had been an overwhelming beginning. The next morning, immediately after breakfast, we were informed about our individual departure plans. Lincoln University, where I was headed, was located near the town of Oxford, in the state of Pennsylvania. What Pennsylvania would look like, I realised, I had no idea.

2

Lincoln University

Lincoln University was the first institution outside of Africa founded to provide a higher education in the arts and sciences to young people of African descent. It was also the first degree-granting, historically black university in the United States and was founded by a Presbyterian minister, John Miller Dickey, together with his wife, Sarah Emlen Cressen, in 1854. They gave it the name Ashmun Institute, naming it after Jehudi Ashmun, a religious thinker and social reformer. This name changed to Lincoln University in 1866, in honour of the assassinated President Abraham Lincoln. Of its other distinguishing features, two stand out. One is that it is located just north of the Mason-Dixon Line, and was therefore often referred to as the symbolic boundary between slavery and freedom in antebellum America. The other is that its founders were committed, as they wrote in their founding documents, to the 'elevation of an intellectual elite, divinely ordained, through whom would be exercised on the lower classes among their fellows, the saving grace of God's plan for redemption.' And this intellectual elite did play a crucial role in the struggles for freedom from slavery.

The college attracted highly talented black students from numerous states in the country, especially during the long decades of legal segregation in the southern states. Many of these students went on to achieve great things in academia, public service, the arts, and many other fields of endeavour. Some of its leading alumni included Thurgood Marshall, who served at the US Supreme Court of Justice; Dr Horace Mann Bond, the first African-American president of the university; Langston Hughes, the Harlem Renaissance poet; Dr Nnamdi Azikiwe, the first President of Nigeria; and Dr Kwame Nkrumah, the first President of Ghana. These and other outstanding graduates of this university made it very attractive, effective, and suitable for educating prospective African-American and African political leaders. This is why the programme believed Lincoln University was an appropriate institution to host students like me.

~

To get there from New York I had to catch a Greyhound Bus at the Port Authority Bus Terminal in Midtown. Port Authority took up two whole city blocks, and was a formidable proposition for me, since I was so new to the city. I had never seen such an enormous bus station: hundreds and hundreds of buses going to all sorts of different places, near and far. I remember I went to the ticket counter and told them I was going to Lincoln University. They charged me for the ticket and told me what platform to go to and the number of the bus to catch. (At the hotel that morning, the people who were helping us had given us money to get to our different destinations.) I was the only person going to Pennsylvania.

I boarded the bus. There were a number of people in the bus already, most of whom were black people – I had no clue why. The bus was very comfortable, and it drove down and out and, because you move slowly in New York, I got another look at the city before we hit the highway. I remember craning my neck to try to see the tops of the buildings. Then we joined the highway and picked up speed.

Driving down to Lincoln via Philadelphia, I recall stopping at a gas station, as they called it, where we could get stretch our legs and get a little something to eat. I remember seeing families of Amish people with their horses and realising I had really left New York behind. A short while later, I began to see signs indicating that we were approaching the university.

~

What immediately caught my attention, on entering Lincoln's main gate, were the beautiful red brick buildings of different sizes, neatly laid out among the spacious lawns with their lush green trees. To the right, as you went deeper into the campus grounds, were the classrooms, library, dining hall, dormitories, chapel, recreation hall, and a couple of regular houses. A few of the African students were accommodated in one of these two-storey regular houses.

When I arrived at the university, late in August 1962, I found maybe a dozen other African students already there. These students came from several African countries such as South Africa, Angola, Mozambique, Uganda, Kenya, Nigeria, and what were then still called South West Africa and Southern Rhodesia (later Namibia and Zimbabwe). Most of these students were members of nationalist organisations in the countries they came from.[10] Most Kenyan students had arrived earlier under the East African Airlifts Programme, which was funded by the Kennedy Foundation. The students at Lincoln University who came from Southern Africa were, as I was, in the Southern African Students Program (SASP), established and funded by the American government and administered by the African American Institute (AAI). The period beginning in the early 1960s witnessed the acceleration of decolonisation on the African continent. Emerging African states were being courted by both the East, especially the USSR, and the West, the USA in particular. The Cold War fuelled this competition for the hearts and minds of newly independent nations. Educating and socialising prospective African leaders – demonstrating how American democracy and its institutions functioned on the one hand, and how Socialist societies worked on the other – became a strategic foreign policy investment and tool for both the East and the West.

On campus, the programme was directed by Professor John Marcum. Like the president of the university, Dr Marvin Wachman, Marcum was interested in and informed about African liberation politics and movements. Marcum had been an advisor to John F. Kennedy during his presidential campaign of 1960. At Kennedy's request, Marcum and Averell Harriman had even travelled to the African continent on a fact-finding mission.

~

---

10 The major organisations represented were South Africa's ANC and PAC; Mozambique's FRELIMO; Angola's MPLA and FLNA; South West Africa's SWAPO and SWANU; Zimbabwe's ZAPU and ZANU; and the Union of the Peoples of Cameroon (UPC).

I shared the ground floor of a dormitory house with Jacob Kuhangua who came from South West Africa. He was also a political refugee. He was a member of the South West African National Union (SWANU), which had also been banned in 1960 when the PAC and ANC were banned by the South African government. Jacob was a very thin person and short like I was. He was very bitter about being away from home, so his attitude was difficult to bear. He was a good person to talk to, even if he was sometimes grouchy.

I had one room to myself, and Jacob occupied the other. We shared the bathroom. This kind of accommodation was a far cry from places I had lived in during the previous two years, travelling as a political refugee. Sharing a space with someone I could relate to was a great help, and we could also tolerate what little idiosyncrasies the other had, unlike Frank's alarm clock in London, for instance. But sharing had its downside, and that was how often we found ourselves looking back and reminiscing about home. We had nowhere else to go on the weekends, so we would sit in our room and talk about where we had come from. We both missed home, despite the oppression we had been subjected to there.

~

The scholarship programme provided refugees like me and Jacob with a monthly stipend with which we could buy some necessities like toothpaste, toothbrushes, soap, other toiletries, underwear, shirts, socks, shoes, and some clothes in the next small town of Oxford. Most of the items I bought I did not have during my long journey into exile. I could even save some of the money because there were no distractions in the neighbourhood like theatres or cinemas or stadiums at which to watch football or baseball. For these types of activities, you had to travel to Philadelphia. There was no regular daily bus system that could take you there and back. And no refugee had a car, motorcycle, or bicycle. You were at Lincoln to study and contribute to the liberation struggle. In a way, you could not forget why you were there, and some of the names of the halls like Nkrumah Hall also reminded you of your obligation. The history of the university itself, in which I soon became well versed, gave you a sense of purpose and mission.

The daily routine from Monday to Friday was getting up, fixing my bed, quickly entering the bathroom to use the toilet, brush my teeth, occasionally shave, jump into the shower, and get out to give Jacob, who would normally be patiently waiting, his turn. We usually left our rooms together to go to the dining hall for breakfast, after which we attended classes. It took me some time to grasp and understand the pronunciation and spelling of American English. Lunches and dinners were enjoyable, and the variety of menus and big portions that were served I had never seen or experienced. I learned to love hamburgers and french fries. I often remembered the days when I went without a meal in Nyasaland. The contrast was stark.

We spent evenings studying and doing work we were expected to present in class the next day, talking about where we had come from and often trying to make friends with the African American brothers. Those who were keen to get to know us called us 'homeboys'. For some reason, we from Africa did not reciprocate accordingly; I think the historical meaning of this expression escaped us. There was ample time to reflect on and figure out why and how I had chosen to come to the United States and Lincoln University in particular. Invariably, I would look back and trace where I had come from and why I had landed up in the United States. This was emotionally draining and reminded me of how disconnected I was from home. I longed to know what was happening back home, and to tell my family where I was, but I knew that sending a letter would compromise both them and myself.

The first letter I received from home came from Nobuntu Msila, the PAC courier who informed me that the police were still looking for me. I have no recollection of how she got the address for me at Lincoln University, but she knew I had reached the US from London. The letter essentially said that she had heard that I was in the US and that she hoped I was doing fine. I remember distinctly that it was an aerogramme – a short-form letter that travelled by air. I think she found out where I was through

PAC networks. I wanted to write back to her but felt I might put her in danger by replying, so I didn't. I generally did not get any letters at all. Maybe there were one or two other letters after that, but I knew I could not write back. It would be too risky or might implicate the person receiving the letter.

~

The primary objective of the programme at Lincoln University was to expose African students to the political and economic systems and social norms of the United States. The thinking was that the African students were potential leaders of independent African countries and would adopt governance structures, institutions, and development policies that accorded with those of the United States. The US was cultivating African friends and allies. This was confirmed when, as early as in the fall semester of 1962, a number of us were taken on a bus trip to visit the Department of State in Washington, DC, where we were introduced to the former Governor of Michigan, G. Mennen 'Soapy' Williams, who was then Assistant Secretary of State for African Affairs in the John F. Kennedy administration. Soapy Williams's address to us showed how determined the United States was to build relationships with emerging and independent African states. We had a spirited exchange with him about our different political concerns regarding the United States's influence and interests in our countries. The high point of this debate was between him and Edson Zvobgo, a refugee from Southern Rhodesia (as it was then called) about the support the Rhodesian and South African governments were receiving from the US government. At the close of this visit, Secretary Williams predicted that Edson would become a politician.[11]

This visit to Washington, DC, I recall, occurred round the same period, when on the 1st of October 1962 Federal Marshalls

---

[11] The prediction, in fact, came true. Edson was a founding member of Zimbabwe's ruling party, the ZANU-PF, and its spokesperson at the Lancaster House talks in 1979, which paved the way for Zimbabwe's independence in 1980. Between 1980 and 2000, Edson was Minister of Local Government and Housing, Parliamentary and Constitutional Affairs, and Mines and Minister without Portfolio in the governments of Robert Mugabe. He was demoted to the latter position because he often stood up to Mugabe.

had to escort James H. Meredith to class at the University of Mississippi, where he was to be the first black undergraduate student to be enrolled. By forcing Meredith's enrolment, President John F. Kennedy sent a message that Washington was determined to enforce federal law if intransigent states stood in the way. It is chronicled that his position drove the Democrats in the Deep South to the Republican Party. The Meredith incident was when the penny really dropped for me. (And not just for me: I remember discussing this with some of the other newly arrived African students, and we all had the same realisation.) Segregation was alive and well in the United States, just as it was in the countries we came from. We were just beginning to be aware of the similarities but were not yet familiar with the history and depth of white supremacy and segregation, and the resistance to both, in the United States.

During a short period of two semesters at Lincoln University, I found myself travelling to colleges and universities in Pennsylvania such as Swarthmore, Cheyne State College, and the University of Pennsylvania on speaking engagements about South Africa. I also often travelled to New York City for meetings and visits to the United Nations (UN) and got to know the Port Authority bus station quite well. At the UN, I met with African ambassadors to the UN who supported the liberation movements in Southern Africa. They were interested in getting first-hand briefings and information about conditions in South Africa in order to inform the concerns they raised in the UN forums. It was at one of these briefing sessions that I remember meeting Eduardo Mondlane, the founder of Frelimo, the Mozambican liberation movement. He was then teaching at Syracuse University. Another person I got to know and interact closely with was Enuga Sreenivasulu Reddy, who was the driving force behind the Special Committee Against Apartheid at the UN. In fact, it was Reddy who often organised these briefings. I travelled to New York so often during that period that I started to think that my political activities in helping to mobilise against the apartheid regime might be better served if I went to school and lived in New York City.

~

Then, one day early in the autumn of 1962, John Marcum sought me out on campus to let me know I was being invited to attend what was called The American Negro Leadership Conference on Africa (ANLCA). The meeting was to be held over three days, November 23, 24, and 25, at the Arden House Campus of Columbia University just outside Harriman, New York.[12] My invitation had come directly from Theodore E. Brown, who was the director of this programme.

The invitation had some instructive information on it, which I pored over excitedly. It would bring together leaders of America's top 100 Negro organisations for the purpose of analysing 'The Role of the American Negro Community in US Policy in Africa'. The work of the conference would be informed by nine background papers prepared by eminent scholars and authorities on Southern Africa. Sponsors included the Congress of Racial Equality, National Association for the Advancement of Colored People, National Urban League, Negro American Labor Council, Student Nonviolent Co-ordinating Committee, and other organisations. Among the call committee were James Farmer, executive director of the Congress of Racial Equality (CORE), Martin Luther King Jr, and some other familiar names. One of these was Tom Mboya. He and Pio Pinto, the leaders of KANU, had introduced me to an African American man in Nairobi at the Stanley Hotel in January 1961. The other was George Houser, my old shipmate. And finally, there was John Marcum himself, who drove me down from Lincoln University with him.

In the days before the conference, I had read the 'Preamble to its Resolution', which helped me understand a bit more about the conference's rationale. 'The American Negro community in the United States,' this preamble stated, 'has a special responsibility

---

[12] I later found out about the origins of the ANLCA, its founders, and what their objectives were. It was formed in 1961 when several major organisations, such as the National Association for the Advancement of Colored People, the Congress of Racial Equality, the American Society for African Culture, and the National Urban League came together. They were subsequently joined by many other groups. Together, they represented several different constituencies of African Americans who were concerned about US policy towards Africa and wanted to influence it for the betterment of African countries.

to urge a dynamic African policy upon our government. Although we have a serious civil rights problem which exhausts much of our energy, we cannot separate this struggle at home from that abroad. If the United States cannot take vigorous action to help win freedom in Africa, we cannot expect to maintain the trust and friendship of newly independent and soon-to-be independent peoples of Africa and Asia.' This conference went on record in launching a more aggressive determination on the part of African Americans to make their influence felt on the policies pursued by the US government in critical areas of the African continent.[13]

The morning the conference was due to start there was a slight delay because the main speaker had not yet arrived, and I remember standing around outside the hall trying not to look like a bewildered spectator. During this wait, I overheard some interesting observations. One of the delegates remarked on the irony of the fact that that it was the first time that most (if not all) the leading black organisations had gathered under one roof, but that they had come together to discuss conditions affecting Africans in sub-Saharan Africa and not their own conditions in the United States. And here they were being asked by the US organs of state, and prominent white politicians, to contribute to the formulation of US policy in Southern Africa. Put like that, it puzzled me too. It was evident from this that the US Department of State had motivated the holding of this conference.

When the keynote speaker did arrive, a throng of individuals surrounded him, making it impossible for me to see him, and almost carried him on stage. We all took our seats and settled down. The programme director introduced the speaker, who began with an apology for being a little late. I could not concentrate on

---

13 Carl P. Watts, in his doctoral thesis titled *The Rhodesian Crisis in British and International Politics, 1964–1965*, says that, in the announcement for its first ANLCA conference, the organisation explicitly linked the domestic civil rights campaigns with African issues. A part of this announcement reads as follows: 'We believe the 19 million American Negro citizens must assume a greater responsibility for the formation of United States policy in sub-Sahara Africa. Negroes are of necessity deeply concerned with developments in Africa because of the moral issues involved and because the struggle here at home to achieve in our lifetime equality without respect to race or color is made easier to the extent that equality and freedom are achieved everywhere.'

what he was saying because he looked somewhat familiar. I was struggling to place him until he mentioned something about Kenya and the African students' airlift he had organised with the help of the Kennedy family foundation. That was when it dawned on me: this was the man I had met at the Stanley Hotel in Nairobi in January 1961. This was Frank 'Curly' Montero. Frank's presentation was crucial because he had been on a fact-finding mission when I met him and was now reporting back on that mission's findings. His report was essential in providing the very latest information for the planned discussions and workshops.

The next three days were a whirlwind and an intellectual wonder, which I still remember. I was inspired and impressed by the level of discussion and the commitment to the continent I had only recently left. Looking back from more than 60 years in the future, I still feel fortunate to have been invited to this historic conference. It had an important and lasting impact on me in that it revealed how much support our struggles in Southern Africa had had in the United States, especially among African-Americans and the organisations they represented. And this is also where I reconnected with Frank Montero, who would become an important figure in my life in exile.

One of the first resolutions dealt with the need for 'across-the-board' educational assistance to the people in those areas in Africa which were of concern to the conference. These areas were South Africa, South-West Africa (now Namibia), Angola, Mozambique, Congo (the current Democratic Republic of the Congo), the Central African Federation (Northern and Southern Rhodesia), and Kenya. Two other supporting resolutions addressing the educational needs of the countries just named urged American Negro participation in the United States Programmes in Africa and gave instructions to the convenors of the conference to seek a meeting with the President of the United States on Human Rights Day, December 10, 1962, to present the findings of this conference. They did indeed meet President Kennedy and presented the findings of the conference. A change in attitude and direction emerged, in that the US took a sterner line towards the oppressive minority regimes of Southern Rhodesia and South Africa. The successful outcomes of this conference were indicative of how well organised and prepared it had been.

Attending this gathering less than three months after my arrival in the US was a fortunate coincidence and an induction into the struggle of African Americans against white supremacy. It helped dispel many of my romantic perceptions about the US, which I had nurtured in my earlier days in George Goch when I avidly followed what I read in magazines put out by the US Information Agency library in Johannesburg. This bracing introduction to the realities of black life in the US reminded me of what was taking place at home. The similarities were frightening, especially in the mid-western and southern states. And this was the country I had chosen to further my education in when several other refugees like me chose to go East, to the Soviet Union, the German Democratic Republic, and other socialist countries. I rationalised my choice by saying that it was not a bad idea to gain the experience of living in 'the belly of the beast', though I obviously did not know the nature of this beast. I started on a steep learning curve, which continues to this day. But so does my appreciation and understanding of the solidarity of black people in the diaspora along with other progressive groups who supported black issues of freedom, equality, anti-racism, and civil and human rights everywhere.

~

A month later, I spent my first Christmas holidays in New York City with Stephen Pearson and Sally Burgess, whom I had befriended in Cairo. Sally worked in the US Embassy's Consulate office and had called to invite me to spend a few days with them during the holidays and to inform me that she and her partner Steve were engaged and planned to get married on Saturday the 29th of December.

Of the two, Sally was the more outgoing. Steve was on the quiet side, and also very understanding of what Sally would prefer to be done. Steve was a little chubby, short, and a nice guy to be around. While in New York on that Christmas break, I also visited compatriots who lived in Manhattan, including Hugh Masekela and Jonas Gwangawa. Then I topped it off with Sally and Steve's wedding. That day was cold – it had snowed the night before – but this did not bother me. I had already been initiated by London's cold, damp, foggy weather. The wedding celebration was held at New York City's Harvard Club – Steve was a Harvard graduate. I was very impressed with the club, its décor, the lavish lunch that was served, and the dancing which followed. For a while, I totally forgot that I was a refugee.

Steve and Sally were eager to have me move to New York City. They lived on the Upper East Side of Manhattan, and among a number of interesting places they introduced me to that December were the Metropolitan Museum of Modern Art and the Presbyterian Church on Madison Avenue, where they worshipped. On one occasion, they invited me to a morning service where Viktor Frankl, the author of *Man's Search for Meaning* and founder of logotherapy, was speaking. Frankl was an Austrian neurologist, psychiatrist, and survivor of several Nazi concentration camps. I had read his book and had been moved by his experiences in the camps and his ability to write about them. He was a tall man, thin, even gaunt, with white hair and striking features. After his talk, I went up to him, introduced myself, and we had a chat about his book, particularly the part in which he dealt with the meaning of loss – loss of dreams, possessions, family, livelihood, and homeland. This was all of deep personal relevance to me. Frankl knew something about South Africa, and I got the sense that he knew something about being subjected to the kind of oppression that some of us had endured. He was very encouraging about the struggle; he felt we should go on. I could not help but be in awe of this man. I admired his fortitude and his determination to survive. Somehow, it looked as if there was some hope for people like me.

The only time I felt in danger when visiting with Sally and Steve was when they took me with them to ski in upstate New York. It was very cold, and I had to wear thermal underwear, thick socks, snow boots, well-insulated gloves, a woollen scarf, hat, and other protective gear. When we got to the slopes, they rented the skis for me and organised lessons from the resident instructor, for which they paid. In one of the lessons, I nearly hit a tree skiing downhill. That incident intimidated and discouraged me from taking additional lessons; and that is how my interest in learning to ski ended.

Apart from those days with Sally and Steve, I had lots of free time on campus. Most of the American students had gone home for the long Christmas holidays, but all of the refugees from Africa had stayed on campus. Some of us were lucky enough to be invited to Christmas lunch or dinner with generous and hospitable families who felt sorry for us because we were far from our homes, families, and loved ones. That part of the holiday was very sad, because it reminded me of home. I began to reflect on where I had come from and how I had got to where I was and started to ask myself where I was going. With the free time I had, I travelled back and forth in time and space.

3

Columbia University

During those first winter semester holidays at Lincoln University, I had ample time to reflect on the journey that had brought me to the United States. Looking back and reminiscing about my past was sometimes painful and depressing. I had to find a way to bury the past in my subconscious so that I could embark on a new journey with my studies and the life ahead of me. Still, when called upon to speak about my country, the hurt would invariably surface. I had no choice but to be engaged in the struggle against the forces that had made me a refugee and an exile. I decided to leave Lincoln University at the end of the spring semester and go to New York City and hopefully get into Columbia University.[14]

I had talked to John Marcum, the director of the SAPS programme about my intention of moving to New York City, given the frequency of my visits there for one meeting or another on issues related to South Africa. He understood my situation and facilitated my application and transfer to Columbia University. Of the goodbyes that I made, I particularly remember going to bid John Marcum and the president Marvin Wachman farewell and to thank them.

~

When I arrived in New York City, I moved into the Beaux Arts Hotel at 310 East 44th Street between 1st and 2nd Avenues. This was about half a block away from the United Nations headquarters

---

14 Before leaving the subject of Lincoln University, there is one final memory I would like to record. In the Lincoln sports gym, there are a few pictures of black American football players hung on the walls. I was surprised to see that two or three of these big men, clad in full football gear with shoulder pads and helmets, were black South Africans from the then province of Natal. The dates on these pictures were from the turn of the nineteenth century, that is, in the late 1890s. These pictures registered in my mind, but I did not ask who these individuals were or how and why they had come to Lincoln University.

and two streets south of the offices of the African American Institute (AAI). The AAI was the administrator of the scholarships that the US government had granted African students who had been recruited to study in the United States. The apartment in the Beaux Arts belonged to Mr Irving Brown who was away in Europe for most of the time. He had suggested to Nana that I stay there, for free.

I later found out that Irving was the AFL-CIO (the American Federation of Labor and Congress of Industrial Organizations) representative in Europe. His primary role in the AFL-CIO was to organise against the Confederation du Travail, which was a very powerful trade union federation affiliated with the communist party in France. This project was partly funded by the CIA. Initially, I was a little uneasy about living comfortably downtown in a fancy hotel with guests who were mostly diplomats from various countries and who had been deployed to the United Nations, while I was a student on a scholarship studying at an Ivy League institution in New York City. From time to time Irving's son, Bobby, would also stay there with me. He was also a student at NYU and had a penchant for French literature and poetry. And he was quite good at both. He idolised certain French poets and writers, recited some of their works, and emulated them to the point of assuming their deportment, expressions, and postures.

~

As soon as I had settled in at the Beaux Arts, I went to visit some of my South African compatriots whom I knew had arrived earlier in the United States and had decided to live and work in New York City. The ones I met first were Hugh Masekela, Jonas Gwangwa, Willie (Keorapetsi) Kgositsile, Miriam Makeba, Dollar Brand (Abdullah Ibrahim), Caiphus Semenya, Letta Mbulu, Spencer Tlholoe, and Bethuel Setai. Bethuel and I were both students at Columbia University.

In the city, Hugh and Jonas's apartment at 310 West 87th Street uptown was the most popular place to see our homeboys, have a good time, talk about home, share our experiences in this new environment, and commiserate about our condition as exiles. The other place where we tended to gather was Miriam

Makeba's apartment in the city, also uptown. Miriam had arrived late in 1959 and was already performing and earning a living, unlike most of us who were still studying. Visiting both places was very therapeutic and comforting. Miriam often invited us to her rehearsals for her performances at Lincoln Centre, Carnegie Hall, or other prestigious venues. When she was not busy, she would invite some of us for lunch and great food, which reminded us of home. It was in this atmosphere of longing for home and wondering if and when we would return that Miriam and Hugh decided to get married in 1964. They then moved to a suburb in New Jersey, and the frequency of these get-togethers declined.

At the university, we met Herbert Vilakazi who had come from Connecticut where his anthropologist father, Absolom Vilakazi, was teaching African Studies. Herbert was tall and thin, dressed always in a shirt and tie, and very deliberate in his manner of speech. Whether he spoke in English or Zulu he always had the same deliberate manner. You could tell he came from an educated family. Another exile who stood out, in the sense that he was not intimately connected to the ones mentioned earlier, was Sikhulu Shange.

Sikhulu Shange was a businessman, entrepreneur, social justice activist, and an ardent promoter of black music. He operated out of Harlem on 125th Street opposite the famous Apollo Theatre. Shange and the refugees mentioned earlier were the members of the first community of exiles during the sixties who lived in and around New York City. This group consisted of people who were mostly musicians, performers, artists, and university students; one was a poet. They were exiles like me. We were busy and focused on our different fields of work but also very active in the anti-apartheid struggle. Home and the developments there were always on our minds. I was also kept informed to some extent by buying the weekly international issue of *The Star*, which was available in a small shop that sold various foreign newspapers on the south side of 42nd Street around the corner of Sixth Avenue.

I must return to why I said Sikhulu Shange stood out. Most of us lived and worked in Midtown and went to institutions in the same area. Shange, however, lived and worked uptown in Harlem.

He was tall, well-built, and a strong-looking man with the demeanour of a Zulu warrior. He sold music records and all sorts of electronic gadgets related to music. His shop was called The Record Shack. He consistently wore a variety of African colourful shirts, dashikis, and other robes made out of African prints. It is said that he embodied the 1960s style and Harlem pride. When he was not attending to his customers or rearranging his stock, he would be sitting on a stool at the entrance to his shop with a big stick called a knobkerrie. At one end of it was a round knob. This feature made it an awesome weapon which deterred anyone from trying to steal anything from the shop. Of course, there was always some interesting music playing in the background. He was said to be a fixture in the heart of Harlem.

There was an unforgettable incident involving Shange that occurred at the wedding of two other refugees. The wedding celebration was to take place further uptown in the Bronx. I had been tasked with the job of slaughtering a goat for the occasion, a procedure I had mastered early in my teens under the mentorship of my father, though what I had been asked to do was illegal in the state of New York. While my accomplices and I were cleaning up the evidence, we saw Shange walking in wearing a cap, carrying a big brown disposable bag and a stick, but also wearing a raincoat, which was surprising in the summer heat of July! We asked why he was wearing this even before we greeted him. It turned out that he had left his Harlem residence dressed in the traditional Zulu attire still worn in the rural parts of KwaZulu-Natal. For Harlemites, this was the Shange they knew and found very interesting. He walked to the subway station where he bought the tokens to board the subway going to the Bronx. The train arrived, but when he entered the coach, he frightened the passengers and they started screaming as they bolted out. The coach was empty, Shange told us, and he sat there alone. But the train would not leave the station. It did not take long before the police arrived. They wanted to know where he was going and why he was not dressed properly. He explained in some detail why he was dressed as he was and where he was going, but they told him that he had to get out and go and put on some 'regular' clothes so that the train could proceed. They also wanted to know what he was carrying in the brown bag. It was his trench coat and long pants, among other things. The police were relieved and then asked him to put on the raincoat and long pants, so he did, and the train continued on its journey with a few passengers in the coach where the Shange drama had played out. We all cracked up as Shange told this story. For the occasion, he changed back into his traditional Zulu dress and saved the 'regular' clothes for the subway ride back to Harlem.

~

Towards the end of 1963, I left the Beaux Arts hotel and rented an apartment on West End Avenue called the Lincoln Towers. Because the rent was high, I shared this apartment with three other PAC members, Bam Siboto, Peter Davidson, and Nga Machema. We were all refugees going to school. Peter and Bam were full-time students at Manhattan College, a private Catholic liberal arts college in the Bronx. Across the hallway on our floor lived Arthur Forrest and his wife, Rita. Both were very friendly. Arthur was a producer of *The Dick Cavett Show*, among others. Arthur became a confidant of Peter's to the point that, when I would admonish Peter for hanging out with friends who smoked pot, Arthur would tell me that I wasn't Peter's dad. Peter's habits led to him returning home to Swaziland before completing his bachelor's degree. I had no idea that he had gone back home until one Sunday morning when I received a call from him. He said he was at JFK International Airport. He was asking for a place to stay as he was resuming the scholarship he had abandoned. That was when we learned that he had gone home only to be told to go back to finish his studies. I was able to come to his rescue.

Another more dangerous adventure Peter nearly undertook at Nana Mahomo's urging was going to Angola to help Roberto Holden's National Liberation Front of Angola (FLNA), which had been fighting for independence from Portugal since 1962. FLNA received support from the United States National Security Council, which was reacting to the Movement for the Liberation of Angola (MPLA), a left-wing, social democratic organisation led by Agostino Neto, who was supported by European and Soviet communist parties (see *The Angolan Revolution* by John Marcum). Nana had called us – Peter, Bam, Nga, and me – for a meeting to deploy us. He suggested that perhaps we should consider going to assist in the Angolan revolution by joining the FLNA. I was not going anywhere, I told him immediately. Bam said he wanted to help his countrymen in the Transkei by joining the Matanzima Administration, which had accepted the idea of independent Bantustan states. When Nga said he was willing to go to Angola and join forces with the FLNA, Peter said he was too. I there and then told him he was not going anywhere. Decades later, over a sumptuous lunch at his home, in the presence of his entire family, he told all of us how my advice had saved his life. What can I say? I had first met him in London, then got him a scholarship in New York, and then he had wanted to disappear in Angola. I was not going to let that happen.

The group of refugees or exiles that had arrived in the United States and lived around New York City were very conscious of their individual and collective security. One incident that illustrates this occurred one day at Hugh and Jonas's apartment. Another refugee and I were in New York City and decided to drop in and visit Jonas, who was home. We had bought some lunch and beers around the corner of Broadway Avenue and 87th Street and were seated on the floor enjoying our meal when the doorbell rang. Jonas answered it to let someone in. When this person walked in wearing a uniform that resembled a policeman's, we quickly scrambled trying to hide the beers. Jonas burst out laughing reminding us that we were in the United States and not in South Africa. His friend had just come from a Reserved Officer Training Corps programme at some college. He was rather surprised at what we were trying to do. We, of course, were really and truly embarrassed.

~

When I started at Columbia University, the head of the Department of Political Science, Professor Laing Gray Cowan, a prominent Africanist scholar, persuaded me to major in political science. He and his department were keen to have me, and offered to allow me to take three courses of independent study. This meant I did not have to attend classes to receive credits; all I had to do was write a series of papers on different aspects of my political experiences leading up to Sharpeville and on my travels after escaping into exile. I accepted this offer and enrolled in other courses such as Rhetoric, Ancient History of Egypt, Government, Music Appreciation, and Journalism. The latter I could take only during the summer term. During the regular semester, journalism courses were offered to graduate students only. The thought of studying journalism excited me, and I soon learned, first-hand, how it could be a vehicle through which one could document, and participate in, the struggle for justice and civil rights that was happening across the country.

On Thursday the 16th of July 1964, a white policeman, Lieutenant Thomas Gilligan, shot and killed James Powell, a 15-year-old African-American boy in front of his friends and about a dozen other witnesses in Harlem. James Powell was a ninth-grader who lived in the Bronx. He was in Harlem attending summer school at the Robert F. Wagner Junior High School on East 76th Street. This incident instantly drew onto the streets about 300 students from a nearby school, who had been told of the shooting by their principal. What followed set off six consecutive nights of angry protests that affected neighbourhoods in Harlem and Bedford-Stuyvesant in Brooklyn. About 4 000 New Yorkers participated in these protests, which led to attacks on the New York City Police Department.

When these protests erupted, I had just enrolled in the journalism course offered to undergraduates during the summer. The journalism teacher, who knew about my recent history, assigned me to cover the story as it unfolded. That I was the only black student in the class probably also played in a role in his choice. I was cautiously excited; this was going to be my first visit to Harlem – that is how new I was to the city. My assignment was to find out what was happening – not only why the boy had been shot, but what kind of social, economic, and political circumstances might have fuelled the violence. Our class met once a week on Saturdays. This assignment was given to me on Saturday the 18th of July, two days after James Powell was killed. I visited Harlem on Monday the 20th of July.

Harlem is walking distance from Columbia University. I was a little afraid and unsure of myself as I entered the neighbourhood.

The police presence in the streets was strong, and the grievance and anger was still simmering everywhere. The Congress of Racial Equality (CORE) had pickets held by blacks, whites, and Hispanics throughout the neighbourhood. People were chanting and demanding an end to police brutality. The Civilian Review Board had called for discipline in the police force. The month of July can be very hot and humid in New York City. Its tarred streets and tall concrete buildings seem to capture the heat. But Harlem somehow seemed worse affected. The heat was enveloping.

I had not been in Harlem for long when I caught sight of a black woman who was leaning out of a large first-floor window watching everything on the street below. There were several children sitting or playing on the fire escape leading up to the window. I walked closer, greeted her, explained that I was a journalism student, and asked if I might ask her one or two questions. She instantly noticed that I had a foreign accent and asked where I had come from. I told her. To her South Africa was Africa, and vice versa, but my being black and from Africa was enough for her to invite me into her living space on the margins of a wealthy city like New York. While the children regarded me with curiosity, the woman said I should come inside and leaned out further to point out the entrance to the building. The elevator had long stopped working. Walking up the ill-lit stairwell to the first floor, I noticed the extent of the neglect and deterioration of the building; it reminded me of the Notting Hill slum in London. Her door was wide open. She ushered me into her kitchen area, where she sat me down to ask what exactly I wanted. The kitchen was tiny. Next to an old gas stove were no more than three pots and pans. All were washed, empty, and hung upside down on a rack to dry. I told her where I was studying and what assignment I had been given. She nodded. She knew all about the shooting of the boy. She had heard about it and read all about it in the newspapers. We then talked about the living conditions in and around Harlem where black folks and Latinos lived. She walked me to the window and pointed out her two sons, both in their early teens, who were playing in the street. Their father, she said, had long since absconded. She had no job but had to raise these two kids, feed and clothe them as well as herself, and pay the rent. And all this from a monthly welfare cheque. Her refrigerator, I noticed, was almost empty but for milk, soft drinks, and a few wilted-looking vegetables. Furniture? A single bed for her and a couple of old thin mattresses with skimpy blankets on the floor for her boys. I could not imagine how this family coped with the North American winters. From what she told me and from what I saw and surmised, I felt sick to my stomach. I thanked her for her time and hospitality, then left to call my friend Susan Fitts, a young American woman who worked as a guide at the United Nations. I had to talk to someone who could console me.

I went looking for a public telephone and finally found one on a street corner. As I stepped into the booth and dialled Susan's number, I found I was in tears. Over the course of one morning, all the naïve expectations I had developed in South Africa about what the United States would be like had been totally shattered. Susan tried to comfort me, but it still hurt. I felt confused, lost. I got onto a bus that was going down 5th Avenue in the direction of where I lived. On the way downtown, the passengers getting into and out of the bus, and the buildings I saw from my seat at the window, told me the same story. When I got onto the bus in Harlem, virtually all the passengers were black and appeared to be working class. The buildings along the avenue looked old, drab, and in need of repairs. Somewhere around 110th Street, though, the black passengers began to dwindle and were increasingly replaced by white passengers, who appeared more affluent, many of them dressed like professionals of one kind or another. The buildings also started to look more modern, sprightly, and better maintained. By the time the bus arrived at the corner of 5th Avenue and 42nd Street, where I got off, there were very few black passengers left, and none of them were poor.

Feeling depressed, I began writing my investigative report slowly and carefully, trying not to let my emotions run away with me. What I had experienced in Harlem and observed on the bus was beginning to sink in. This was more like home than anyone had ever told me. I submitted my report the following Saturday, which would have been the 25th of July 1964. My paper was well-received, more out of curiosity than estimation of its quality, I suspect. The professor and the white students were no doubt fascinated to hear how a black student from South Africa viewed Harlem and what he thought of the protests. By the time the unrest ended, one person had died and 465 people had been arrested. Property damage was estimated to be between one to two million dollars.

Late in September of the same year, Lieutenant Gilligan, who had shot James Powell, was cleared of any wrongdoing by a grand jury and all charges were dropped. He maintained Powell had lunged at him with a knife. But the knife was never found.

~

Despite the trauma I experienced in covering the Harlem riots, I enjoyed the journalism course offered that summer. When the spring semester started, however, and I took some political science subjects, I began to feel uncomfortable. I could not see how graduating with a bachelor's degree in political science would keep me alive in the United States. But I could visualise myself as a journalist; and besides, I was doing well in my writing and rhetoric courses. When I asked whether I could switch to the School of Journalism, I was told that admission to the School required a bachelor's degree. I felt trapped. I was older than most, if not all, the white students in my classes. More importantly, I was on a scholarship which would end once I completed my first degree. What was I going to do with a bachelor's degree in political science in the US? I began to consider moving to another university downtown, namely New York University. It had a School of Commerce where I could enrol in an undergraduate programme and earn a bachelor's degree in economics. That type of degree could help get me a job, I thought.

But I was feeling pressure to stay at Columbia. John Marcum at Lincoln University, George Houser at the American Committee on Africa (ACOA), Professor Cowan in Columbia's Political Science department, and a few supporters of both the PAC and the ANC at the United Nations, particularly those who led the Special Committee Against Apartheid, emphasised the importance for me of obtaining a degree in political science, especially from Columbia. It was thus a confusing time for me. What was becoming clear, though, was the growing relevance, in American academic circles, of the struggle back home. Three publications put out during this period are indicative of how important the fight against apartheid had become in the UN and New York City. The first is *Racism in South Africa – A Call for International Action* (1965). This was an address by H. E. M. Achkar Marof, who was the Permanent Representative of Guinea to the UN and Chairman of the United Nations Special Committee on the Policies of Apartheid of the Government of South Africa. Earlier on in 1963, Ambassador Achkar Marof was elected Chairman of the Fourth Committee of the General Assembly, which dealt with problems of colonialism. The second and third publications from the ACOA were 'The South African Crisis and US Policy', and 'Partners in Apartheid – US Policy on South Africa'. Beyond the question of finding a job in the US, I also began to wonder how I could best serve this struggle: by studying politics or economics? It was a question to which I would soon find an answer.

4

Summer Visits to London

As I was navigating my way through this period, I was also preoccupied with African liberation politics and engaged with its supporters in the United States. During the summers of 1963, 1964, and 1965, I spent what money I had saved from my monthly stipend to go to London to work in the PAC office there, helping its representative, Nana Mahomo, and also reporting to him about the political activities I was engaged in in the United States. Being a refugee and a stateless person, I did not have a passport. I had persuaded the British Consul General in New York City to issue me with a visa for Britain. This visa was a large piece of paper that was blank on the back, but it served its purpose.

Nana was tall, somewhat lanky, and walked with a limp. He also had some sort of eye problem, so he always wore dark glasses. This suited him because he was a secretive person. He wore a warm three-quarter coat and put cognac in his coffee, which helped him keep warm, he said. His small office, which served as the PAC headquarters, was in the corner of a building facing Trafalgar Square. My responsibilities in the office included filing, occasional typing, fielding calls when Nana was out of the office, and helping to organise and schedule meetings.

Those summers in London were also a time of broadening horizons. In the summer of 1963, I had the privilege of meeting and talking to the late Cyril Lionel Robert (C. L. R.) James, an Afro-Trinidadian historian, journalist, socialist, and one of the leading theorists on Pan-Africanism. He was a friend of another eminent Trinidadian, George Padmore, who was also a journalist, author, and leading Pan-Africanist. Both Padmore and James were intellectuals, friends, ardent advocates, and organisers in the various diasporic activities in support of the African liberation movements and the struggle against colonialism. James had, among other publications, written the monumental study of the Haitian revolution titled *The Black Jacobins: Toussaint L'Overture* and the San Domingo Revolution. Padmore had authored *Pan-Africanism or Communism?* in which he attempted to counter Cold War suspicions that African independence movements were inspired by Communism. Padmore's book was read avidly by Africanists during my days as an African nationalist. Meeting C. L. R. James was incredibly inspiring. He gave me a copy of his latest book at that time, *Beyond a Boundary*, which he autographed and dated June 27, 1963.

During the 1964 visit, Nana gave me a rather unusual assignment. He wanted me to go to the Port of Southampton to inspect an ocean-going yacht that was for sale. Nana intended to buy it for the PAC. A white man, a friend of his, had to accompany me because he knew where the boat was moored. My task was to examine the boat, particularly its engines, since I had some experience with diesel engines from working at the Perkins Peterborough branch in George Goch. The ones on this yacht, large Cummins engines manufactured in the United States, were not dissimilar to the bigger types of Perkins engines with which I had some familiarity. The idea was to buy this boat for the purpose of shipping arms from somewhere in North Africa to a destination on the western part of the Cape coast, where the members of the PAC armed wing would collect them.

My report on the engines was positive, even though privately I was not convinced about the yacht sailing from somewhere in North Africa with a consignment of arms and ammunition to South Africa without being detected, intercepted, seized, or hijacked. Thinking back, I don't know if Nana ever bought the yacht. I do know that it never arrived in South Africa.

My visit in the summer of 1965 began with some drama, which played out at the Heathrow International Airport in London. I had flown from JFK International Airport, and when I got to the immigration counter, the officer looked at my document and refused me entry. I explained that I was a refugee from South Africa and was now studying in the United States and was coming to London for a visit during my summer semester break. The only identification documents I had were a British visa that was issued in New York and a United States Immigration Parole document that allowed me back into the United States. I did not have a passport because I was classified as stateless. The immigration officer waved at two policemen to come and take me to see the Chief Immigration Officer, and these men escorted me to the Chief's office.

Once in front of the Chief Immigration Officer's desk, I explained my situation exactly as I had done to the officer who had refused me entry. He listened patiently but with the face of a stern bureaucrat. When I finished my story, he motioned to the two cops who had been standing outside his office, with the door wide open, to come and take me back passed the immigration kiosk and put me on the next plane to JFK International Airport. I walked out of the Chief's office and sat down, and when the two cops tried to lift me, I lay down to make it more difficult for them to carry me. This tactic I had learned in the demonstrations that I attended and sometimes took part in both in London and New York. Some of these demonstrations were against the war in Vietnam, some for nuclear disarmament and other causes. The two policemen got agitated and angry. They picked me up like a heavy sack of soil and carried me, one holding my hands and the other my feet, passed the immigration counter to dump me on the next plane to New York. We were about halfway to the immigration kiosk when, very unexpectedly, the Chief Immigration Office jumped to his door, repeatedly yelling 'put him down and bring him back here!'

We were stunned, and the people who were witnessing this drama looked bemused. I was dropped like a bundle of dirty clothes but got up and walked almost triumphantly flanked by the same two cops back to the office where I was manhandled a few minutes earlier. Once in the Chief's office, he dismissed the policemen and politely invited me to sit down. Neither the policemen nor I understood what was happening. Apparently, the colleague who had come to pick me up at the airport found out that I was being deported back to New York and called the PAC office in London and told whoever was there what was going to happen. Nana Mahomo then called a Lord somebody who was a leading figure in the Labour Party and asked him to intercede. He did so by calling the Chief Immigration Officer and asking him to detain me overnight at the airport where I would be picked up by a car the next morning and driven to the US Embassy so that my parole status could be validated. This way I would be allowed to re-enter the United States and be allowed to stay in the UK for the summer.

After the Chief told me that I was being held at the airport overnight, I asked for my luggage. I was told that it was already on its way to New York on the plane I was to be put on. I was promised that it would be tracked and returned the next day. I was also assured that I would be provided with all the basic toiletries needed for the night and following morning. I was then driven to another part of the airport that had rooms for detainees. When I got there, I found a clean room with a bed and clean linen and the promised toiletries, plus a security guard who was to mind me overnight. I was served dinner, which came with a bottle of Beaujolais red wine sent by Nana. I invited my guard to share the wine with me. He was delighted and could not believe the generosity of his ward. The next morning when I had to leave, I could tell from his facial expression that he was a little sad and also struck with awe when a chauffeured Bentley sedan arrived to pick me up. Its driver stopped the car, came to open its back door for me, then shut it, got behind the steering wheel, started the car, and drove off with me in the backseat. For a moment, I recalled my days in Johannesburg as a chauffeur. How the tables had turned for a refugee.

The 1965 summer visit to the PAC office had a different agenda. I had planned on spending some time in the PAC office then meeting Sally and Steve Pearson in Paris. They were on a 'world tour' during which they had visited South Africa and met some members of my family. They were then heading for France. It was not difficult for me to enter Britain without a passport: I had done this before using their entry visa form. And, of course, the Labour Party was in power. But entering France without a French visa was not going to be easy. I again applied for a visa to enter Britain and it was granted. This visa was again on a large piece of paper with a blank back. So, when I got to London, I went to the French Consulate where I narrated my sad story of being a refugee and stateless person who wanted to go to France and join friends of mine who had news of my family in South Africa. They felt sorry for me and give me a visa. But where to put it? I then proposed that they stamp it on the back of the British visa. It was done. This was my travel document.

During the same summer in London, I met Patrick Duncan, the son of a former Governor General of South Africa, who had been a member of the Liberal Party in Cape Town and later joined the PAC in 1963. He was in the city on personal business, which included speaking engagements on South Africa. One of these was at the Royal Commonwealth Club. He had not informed Nana about these speaking engagements. It turned out he was also carrying a letter from Potlako Leballo, who was based in Tanzania and was then the leader of the PAC. The contents of this letter actually suspended Nana and effectively replaced him with Patrick Duncan. Nana did not tell me about this letter and its contents. I found this out only later on from Peter Davidson, who was then assisting Nana in the office. It seemed Patrick and Nana didn't get along at all.

As events unfolded, it was clear that the three of us each had separate plans. My plan was to meet Sally and Steve in Paris. Nana was doing his own thing (secretly, as usual) and so was Patrick. One day Nana came to the office carrying a brownish portmanteau and asked that I accompany him to a bank located on the Strand around Aldwych Circle. He handed the suitcase to me to carry. When we got to the bank and went to the deposit counter, he took the suitcase from me and put it on the counter. I was shocked when he opened it. It was packed with new and neatly wrapped notes of British pounds, French francs, and US dollars. He did not count the money because he had already done so at home. He then filled in the deposit slip and invited me to the counter where the tellers were serving customers. I refused. I simply could not get over what I was witnessing. I had never seen so much money except in a bank and not even in the teller's drawer. I knew that the few PAC representatives who were based in African countries were constantly asking for money from him but did not get it. Yet here he was banking piles of it in his own name in London. I could not help recalling how in April 1960, less than a month after the Sharpeville massacre, two PAC members had pocketed a large sum of money that Ghana had donated and shared it with a member of the organisation's National Executive.

5

New York University

When I returned to the United States from London at the end of the summer of 1965, I broke the news that I had decided to move to NYU. I knew I would one day return, if not to South Africa, then certainly to the African continent, and the best way I could imagine contributing there was as a development economist. The decision, in the end, had been a simple one. Some of my friends and supporters were angry and quite disappointed with me. How could I leave a prestigious Ivy League university like Columbia University and move down, as they saw it, to NYU? It didn't make sense! NYU? I repeated my reasons but was still met with dismay. I was truly on my own but nonetheless determined.

Just before moving to NYU, I received an invitation from a students' movement at the University of Michigan (UM), which was advocating for disinvesting in and divesting from South Africa. I inquired as to who else had been invited to speak on these issues. I was informed that because of the of the topics' importance, they had also invited a couple of white South Africans who supported the apartheid government. The intention was to get perspectives from both sides, those for and against apartheid. The former would be represented by a university professor and student leader from the University of Stellenbosch in Cape Town. I accepted the invitation. Many student groups, faculty members, and university administrations across America were wrestling with the dilemma of whether to invest in South Africa because of its apartheid policies. American companies were being solicited and pressured to stop investing in companies that traded and had operations in South Africa. The University of Michigan was renowned for its history of student activism. The riveting lecture that Dr Martin Luther King Jr gave in the Hill Auditorium on the 5th of November 1962 is historic. It was also the venue chosen by President John F. Kennedy to announce the launch of the Peace Corps Volunteers and where President Lyndon B. Johnson later first outlined his Great Society Program. It was against this backdrop that I accepted the invitation to go to Ann Arbor in Michigan.

On the morning of the event, just as the audience were taking their seats, I had to go to the men's restroom. At the urinal stalls was a young white man, a little younger than me. I don't know who told him that I was from South Africa, but in faltering English, he told me that he was uncomfortable with the task he had been assigned because he was to address the audience in English. I was a bit puzzled. Why did he take this assignment when he did not have the language skills to communicate with his hosts? To travel all this way from Cape Town to Ann Arbor and start your first morning there looking for an interpreter in the men's restroom? And to ask for help from a black South African 'nog al'! Unbelievable!

He was hoping that someone would interpret for him when it came time for him to speak. I did not offer to help. He was a student leader of an Afrikaner student organisation at his university and had come all the way to UM as its representative. In the morning's programme, he was scheduled to speak immediately after the professor who was accompanying him. I had found out a little earlier that there was one Dirk from the South African consulate in New York City among those attending. My suggestion to this nervous young man was that he ask his fellow Afrikaner, Dirk, to interpret. We both left the restroom.

When the young Stellenbosch leader's turn came for him to speak, he went to the podium and asked for an interpreter, saying that his English was not good. I proposed that his companion, the professor from the same university who had just spoken in English, help him. His companion refused. The audience was mesmerised at what was happening. I then followed up by asking Dirk from the South African Consulate in New York to help his fellow Afrikaner. He too declined. At this point, I was frustrated and angry. The audience was nonplussed. So, I offered to interpret myself. The rabid ultra-right student leader spoke the language he knew best and told it like it was. There was a need for the Afrikaners to triumph over what the British had done to them and also address The Black Danger (Die Swart Gevaar). This was the broad tapestry he wove and used to explain and justify the evolution of apartheid.

His Afrikaans was good; it was that of the elite class. And this man was well-chosen to deliver the gospel according to the apartheid regime. Fortunately, I had been taught Afrikaans by members of the same elite at the Emmarentia Hoërskool, had been taught English by Englishmen at Kilnerton High School, and had worked in the city of Johannesburg where both languages were used. As hurtful as was most of what this young man had to say, I made sure that my interpretation was precise. This turned out to be an excellent opportunity to show the audience the capabilities of black people despite their oppression.

In his determination to deliver the exact message he had been entrusted with, he explained the government's apartheid policies and how these had evolved during a period of conflict between the Afrikaners and the British and the fight of both against the Africans, resulting in bloody wars. He also emphasized how the Afrikaners were vindicated when they won the 1948 elections in which they defeated the ruling United Party, which was seen as the party of English-speaking people. The Afrikaners were now in a strong position to deal with the Africans whom they viewed as 'Die Swart Gevaar'. When it was my turn to speak, which was immediately after his vitriolic presentation, I set aside my prepared speech and homed in on just about every point the student leader had made. My repartee, which was totally unexpected, was based on refuting virtually all the incorrect and contrived points he had made. My focused rebuttal of his presentation was very helpful in informing the audience about the two opposing views they wanted to hear, as the university wrestled with the issues of disinvestment and divestment. My job was done. The irony of this incident did not escape the audience, which could not believe the drama that had played out in front of them. Later that evening, Dirk from the South African Consulate in New York City invited me for a drink. I refused. He responded by saying that he wasn't going to poison me, and I then told myself that for him to even mention the thought, I was better off keeping far away from him. Which I did.

The Way Home

~

When I moved to NYU, I decided to live closer to its School of Commerce,[15] which was located on the south-eastern end of Washington Square. I found a small but adequate apartment in a building near Tompkins Square Park. My apartment was on the second floor and looked out onto the park. It was essentially a large, one-room apartment that contained a sleeping area, a dining table and chairs, a small lounge space and a kitchen, and a bathroom neatly tucked away on the side. This was sufficient for a student. I had a few comfortable pieces of furniture, a couple of nice paintings, and a beautiful used Persian rug that was in good condition. I liked my new 'home'. There was, however, one snag. The apartment directly above me was occupied by a draughtsman who continually moved his wooden work table and easel back and forth over the bare wooden floor every evening and night. I had to wait for this irritating noise to stop in order to sleep. I complained about this to the caretaker of the building who told me that this tenant preferred not to have his apartment carpeted because it would hinder the moving of his easel and work table. I reluctantly accepted this explanation but asked that the tenant be mindful of how the noise affected me at night.

Before this matter could be resolved, I was introduced to Reverend Davis Given, who served at the Trinity Church at the intersection of Wall Street and Broadway in the financial district of lower Manhattan. This was an historic parish of the Episcopal Diocese of New York. He lived in an attractive duplex in a brownstone building at 76 Washington Place, which is half a block from the west side of Washington Square. The person who introduced me to Davis was a colleague of his, Harry Keaton, who was also an Episcopalian and a chaplain of the NYU Washington campus. Davis was looking for a reliable and trustworthy tenant who could live on the attic floor of his duplex. He was often away for weeks and months every year, either in the Navajo reservations

---

15 The NYU School of Commerce, Accounts, and Finance was established in 1900 to provide professional training for students pursuing careers in business. The school was and is still located on the University's Washington Square campus. It has grown, flourished, and changed for the better over the years. It is now called the NYU Stern School of Business, and has been immeasurably transformed.

in the northeast and southwest of the United States or in Bayreuth in Germany for its annual musical festival. When he was away, his apartment was vacant.

So, Davis arranged to visit me at my 10th Street apartment one Saturday morning when I was not attending classes. He evidently wanted to check out my living quarters and me. After this short visit, he invited me to have lunch at a nearby Hungarian restaurant around the corner on 9th Street. Over lunch, he explained his needs and asked me to visit and see where he lived. I had passed the test. I accepted his proposal with some scepticism because I was just beginning to settle into my new 'home'. But on seeing his place, I was very impressed. It was a duplex and had an attic on the third level that had two small rooms with bathroom facilities. I would sleep in one room, and the other would later be occupied by another student, Jesus Gerardo Gomez, from Mexico. On entering the house, everyone had to take off his or her shoes and put on a pair of slippers that he had supplied. The entire place was decked out in beautiful Navajo rugs with a variety of beautiful earthy colours, designs, patterns, and an ebony grand piano. His place was lavishly furnished and showed that he came from a very wealthy family. The latter was confirmed when one evening he invited me to dine with his mother, who lived alone on Park Avenue in the Seventies where she occupied the entire floor of a large building.

~

It took several minutes' walk across Washington Square Park to go from Davis's place to the School of Commerce. This area was called the Village, and it was a neighbourhood or community with shops for just about anything one needed. The social events that took place in the Square were also very exciting to me. The Village itself was alive with all sorts of activities, such as jazz concerts and demonstrations for one cause or another. It also had cinemas, theatres, public spaces for basketball, and a public swimming pool. Shops for all sorts of goodies were everywhere. From the Village one could go anywhere in Manhattan by public transport at just about any time of the day or night. Davis was an avid concert-goer and always had seasonal tickets for musical performances and operas staged at the Lincoln Centre in particular. When he was away, I inherited some of these tickets and had a treat of classical music, which deepened the exposure I had developed at Columbia University where I had taken a course in Music Appreciation. I went to some outstanding operas like Puccini's *La bohème*, Rossini's *The Barber of Seville*, and others by Verdi, Wagner, Vivaldi, and Copland. In addition to this exposure, I collected quite a few records of classical music.

The School of Commerce had very few black students. As far as African students went, there were only two of us: Demba Traore, who came from Guinea in West Africa, and me. Demba and I became friends, studying and hanging out together. Most of our white classmates were members of fraternities, but we did not join any because of the latent racial prejudices of most of the members, plus the fact that we did not have the time and money required to take off on short holidays or long weekends to go skiing. Besides, we did not know how to ski. Most of these students belonged to combines of one kind or another, whereby they helped each other by recycling written assignments due on Mondays. They had accumulated files of old papers with good grades submitted by its members, which were then used for any new assignment required by a professor in one or another course like economics, marketing, and statistics. These students were very entrepreneurial! Demba and I were not and were therefore on our own in many ways.

Luckily, there were other fortuitous events that cheered both of us up quite a bit. The most enjoyable and memorable were when African dancers from Guinea stopped to perform in New York City on their tour through the United States. Their energising, magnificent, and creative dance performances thrilled me and Demba and the other New Yorkers. The vibrant African music, colourful costumes, and impressive choreography were all stunning and made us Africans and African-Americans very proud. It was like saying, 'Look at what Africa can produce.'

Demba and I also attended concerts featuring Miriam Makeba, Harry Belafonte, Hugh Masekela, Abdulla Ibrahim (then called Dollar Brand), Max Roach, and other popular black artists. Miriam and Hugh were special to me because they were South

New York University

Africans whom I also hung out with. Others that I spent time with were Keorapetsi Kgositsile, Teddy Kgame, Jonas Gwangwa, and several other black South Africans who would pass through New York City. Sometimes Miriam would invite a few of us to watch her rehearse her repertoire of South African music for an upcoming concert, which included a gumboot dance. She continued to invite us for meals at her apartment, where we discussed our condition as exiles. These shared feelings and discussions kept us together and helped us to endure our exile with the hope of returning home sometime in the future.

In addition to my musical and other social forays, I was a regular visitor at a place in the Village called the Washington Mews where I had friends like Jean and Bob Bach whom I had met on my first evening in the United States. Jean was a prominent American jazz aficionado and radio producer who went on to become a producer of documentary films. Her husband, Bob, was a television executive and production co-ordinator. Of Jean, it is said that 'she was a fixture in the New York jazz world with an encyclopaedic knowledge of music, virtually unmatched connections and a reputation for giving great parties in Greenwich Village.' She and her husband introduced me to some very interesting friends of theirs. One of them was Arlene Francis, who was a regular panellist on a show called *What's My Line?* produced by Bob. This was one of the popular, leading CBS game shows at the time. She was also a leading radio presenter. Arlene invited me onto one of her radio chat shows to talk about South Africa and apartheid. This was the first time I had been on radio in the United States. I was a little nervous initially but relaxed as the conversation developed. This was also my first exposure to that cohort of the city's population that did not sleep at night. I was aware of some people who worked at night in the financial and legal firms on Wall Street but did not realise that some television staff worked at night also. Another indicator of the existence of night people was a large restaurant called Horn & Hardart at the corner of 3rd Avenue and 42nd Street which was open 24 hours a day, every day. This restaurant was noted for operating the first food automat in New York City and Philadelphia.

After meeting and getting to know Arlene, I was introduced to Bennet Cerf, the co-founder and chairman of Random House, a leading publishing firm in the United States. We often visited Bennet's home, which was upstate in Mt. Kisco, New York. Another friend of Jean's was Gloria Vanderbilt and her family, whom we would visit occasionally in her New York City home. For lively jazz and entertainment, Jean and Bob would invite me for cocktails at the Café Carlyle, and we would listen to Robert Waltrip Short, commonly known as Bobby Short, play the piano. The Café Carlyle was in the Carlyle Hotel on the Upper East Side at the corner of Madison Avenue and 76th Street. Bobby Short was an African-American cabaret singer and pianist best known for his interpretations of songs by popular composers of the first half of the 20th century. The café was a popular hangout for celebrities and famous people such as Gloria Vanderbilt and John F. Kennedy. However, despite frequenting such places and hanging out with celebrities, I did not lose my bearings as a political refugee and student or forget the reason that I was in the United States.

~

One of NYU's premises was Washington Mews, which has an interesting history going back to the 18th century. During that century it was developed into a two-storey building with stables. In 1881, the New York Department of Public Works ordered the construction of Washington Mews's first gates at each end in order to separate the Mews from the public streets. This area is bordered by 5th Avenue and University Place. Later, round 1950, New York University leased a good part of this property and converted the buildings along the Mews into offices and faculty housing. This is where I met Conor Cruise O'Brien and Stephen Spender, who were also living in the Mews opposite but adjacent to where Jean and Bob Bach lived. I often visited Conor Cruise and Stephen but not as regularly as I did Jean and Bob.

Conor Cruise O'Brien was the first Albert Schweitzer Professor of an interdisciplinary programme at NYU. This programme covered comparative literature and the history of ideas, and its scholarship and teaching emphasised the relevance of the humanities to present-day concerns and the nature and quality of interracial awareness. Conor Cruise was an Irish intellectual with a long career as a journalist, politician, literary critic, and public servant. He was formerly the UN representative in Katanga (a province in the DRC) and had served as Vice Chancellor of the University of Ghana. Visiting him was exciting, and this is where I also met Stephen Spender. Stephen Spender was an English poet, novelist, and essayist whose work emphasised issues that arose from the class struggle, such as social justice and the lot of the poor. An example of the latter is his concern for children from the slums, who he said should also have the opportunity of being educated and being part of the wider and better world.

Whenever I visited Conor Cruise and Stephen, we would have long conversations and share interesting bits of information and insights about African politics and the role of the British government in its dealings with South Africa and Southern Rhodesia. Both Conor and Stephen were supportive of the liberation movements in these two countries. It was on the armed struggle waged by the liberation movements that our views diverged. The downside of these discourses was that we drank a lot of beer, and I always had a hangover the next day. Luckily, these enjoyable but taxing meetings happened on weekends only.

Morley at Lincoln University. Photo taken as part of Southern African Students Program, 1962/63.

Snapshot of Morley in the USA during early 1960's.

Morley, second from left, with interns from the Louis Berger Inc program he directed. 1968.

Reverend David Nkosi and his second wife, MaDlamini, taken by Joanna Karvonides at the Institute for Race Relations, Johannesburg, August, 1970.

Morley and Joanna visiting with Ann and Frank Montero to discuss marriage plans. 1970.

Wedding photo, Joanna and Morley in traditional attires, 24 October 1970 at Montero home in Riverdale, New York City.

Paul Mokgoba leading his dance troupe at Joanna and Morley's wedding, 1970.

Morley in cap and gown after doctoral graduation from the New School for Social Research, 1984.

Family photo at United Nations International School where Thenjiwe attended primary school in New York City, 1986.

Stanley Nkosi's first visit and meeting with Morley since 1960. Mandla at the table with Stanley and Morley. Taken at Nkosi home in Hoboken, New Jersey in 1986.

Stanley's second visit to Morley and family, accompanied by his wife Ruby. Photo taken atop World Trade Center in New York City, 1987.

6

A Meeting and a Departure

The students at NYU's School of Commerce were there because they wanted to get into family businesses or join corporates. Their motivations were straightforward, clear, and quite practical. My former classmates at Columbia University tended to be more intellectually inclined. I quickly settled down at the School of Commerce and majored in economics. I also became relatively acculturated to the hustle and bustle of budding entrepreneurs. The economics and marketing courses were taught by passionate, flamboyant, and engaging professors. The Columbia University courses on Music Appreciation, Rhetoric, Ancient Egyptian Civilisation, Philosophy, and other social science subjects, taught by dispassionate and deliberate intellectuals, were a thing of the past. I now had to learn about the world of commerce, of which I had no experience. I immersed myself in my studies, especially after the AAI confirmed that there would be no scholarship available for me to go to graduate school. Demba Traore and I, the only two African students, both majored in economics because we intended to practise as development economists. We were committed to contributing to the development of our continent.

Many politically conscious students in American colleges and universities were both studying full-time and engaged in organisations, on and off campus, supporting progressive movements fighting for social and economic justice as well as a more peaceful world. Among these organisations were the South African Association of Students Abroad (SAASA), largely based in the northeast US, the Organisation of African Students at New York University, the Congress of Racial Equality (CORE), and Students for a Democratic Society (SDS). It was during this period, characterised by a vibrant political environment, that I met Joanna Electra Karvonides, the daughter of Pontic Greek refugees in the US, a bright student and an activist with progressive ideas.

I first saw Joanna through a glass wall of the cafeteria at the Loeb Students' Centre. The centre had places for students to study, hold meetings, and generally hang out. She was talking to a West Indian student called Elton, whom I knew, and once she had gone, I approached Elton and asked him who this beautiful white girl was.

A few days later I was in the cafeteria again (we called it the Commons) having a meal with Jerry Bornstein, a Jewish activist on campus and chairperson of the Committee to End the War in Vietnam, when Joanna walked by. She stopped to ask Jerry about an upcoming demonstration, and Jerry introduced us before she went on her way.

The next day, back in the Commons, I had bought my meal and sat down to eat in a cubicle, when I saw Joanna looking round for a place to sit and eat. I greeted her, and invited her to sit with me. We chatted for a long time. It was easy to tell we had similar ideological leanings. I remember that at one point Elton and some of his West Indian friends, who usually sat over near the window, came past and spoke to us. I thought Elton looked slightly surprised to see the two of us together. Little did Joanna and I realise that we had embarked on a long journey together. This was in the spring of 1966.

For our first date that weekend, I asked Joanna to accompany me to a party that a fraternity was having, to which I'd been invited. They were looking for new members. Being part of a fraternity was not something I was particularly interested in, but I was curious all the same. Joanna and I had this in common: she had no desire to be part of any sorority. We went to the party, where we were surrounded by mostly commerce students. It became clear from the atmosphere and the conversations that it really was not our scene, so we didn't stay long. Instead, we went to dinner at a neighborhood restaurant and afterwards walked around Greenwich Village, talking for hours.

It was evident, very quickly, that we shared similar views on the current social, economic, and political issues then prominent, and our early courtship was a very active time for both of us politically. We attended marches and meetings concerned with issues of civil rights and segregation, particularly in the southern states of the US, the war in Vietnam, apartheid in South Africa, Southern Rhodesia's Unilateral Declaration of Independence, the Anti-Dictatorship Movement against the Junta in Greece, and other struggles which progressive students were waging on campuses. We avoided engaging in civil rights demonstrations beyond the north-eastern parts of the US, particularly in the southern states. Petty discrimination in New York City we could manage and survive but not in the South.

Joanna was a history student at the Washington Square college and lived in a dormitory for women called Rubin Hall on Fifth Avenue, a few blocks away from the college. We started spending practically all our free time together. Most evenings, we prepared our meals together in the small kitchen of my duplex at Washington Place. These meals usually consisted of salads, rice, and meat or chicken stew with hot spices and jalapeño chili peppers, which Gerardo cherished, Joanna liked, and I withstood. Sometimes we went and bought sandwiches in the neighbourhood on 8th Street or ate at Tad's Steakhouse where a steak, baked potato, and salad cost only $2 (although the quality was a little dicey). Lunches we often ate at Chock Full of Nuts, a coffee and sandwich bar across the street from the university. Apart from preparing and sharing meals, we also went to the local art cinemas, theatres, jazz venues like the Village Vanguard, university functions, and the Carmine Street public swimming pool, which was clean and which we monopolised because we went during the day when most residents were at work.

Joanna wanted me to come to Maine to meet her family. She was at home during the summer of 1966 and told her mother and father that there was a person, perhaps she said her 'boyfriend', that she would like to invite for the long weekend over the 4th of July holiday. Of course, her mother immediately wanted to know who this person was and, specifically, whether he was Greek. Joanna told her, no, he's not Greek; he's from South Africa. As Joanna remembers it, her mother went completely ballistic. Not only was this person not Greek, he was black and African. Her mother could not comprehend this news. Joanna was deeply angry and upset at her response. She had been staying at her parents' home but had to move out. She took her things and stayed with her sister, Mary, for the rest of her time in Maine.

~

Studying in New York in the 1960s was a thrilling and unforgettable experience. While NYU was the centre of our lives as students, it was located in Greenwich Village. The Village was an area celebrated for its beautiful brownstone and brick houses and campus buildings. The larger area was home to wealthy families, professionals, artists, musicians, and students like us enrolled at NYU. This community shared a border with Soho (South of Houston Street), which was a neighbourhood that was home to many galleries and artists working and living in lofts. Walking distance from Soho and next to Chinatown was Little Italy, which was renowned for its Italian cuisine. Chinatown attracted many Chinese people from the neighbourhood and beyond because of its authentic dishes which were modestly priced and which even poor students like me could afford. Not far from these neighbourhoods were Jewish delicatessens and restaurants like Russ & Daughters, Katz's Deli, and Ratner's Deli on 2nd Avenue, a restaurant that served only kosher dairy (milchik) produce. The fish sold by Russ & Daughters and the meat at Katz's delicatessen complemented the kosher fair at Ratner's. All these neighbourhoods were within walking distance of each other and made up the ethnically diverse and cosmopolitan character of downtown New York City in which the Village was situated. Looking back, I realise it was while I was at NYU that I really became a New Yorker.

It was also during that heady time that I attended my last meeting as a member of the PAC, where I was billed as president of SAASA. This meeting, which took place in Washington, DC, was sponsored by the Consultative Council of South Africa (CCSA), whose offices were on East 43rd Street just across from the UN Headquarters. CCSA was formed around 1964 by church groups led by the Methodist Church. It served as a clearing house for information and action proposals for some thirty affiliated organisations engaged to varying extents in supporting liberation and independence movements in Africa.

The Washington, DC meeting was called a seminar on American Involvement in Apartheid, and the question asked was, 'What Can Be Done?' The programme ran from the 19th to the 21st of March 1966, the latter date being exactly six years since the Sharpeville massacre. The programme was designed to be used as a basis for planning future action. It aimed to assess the extent to which American capital and trade propped up the apartheid economy and to determine which types of capital and trade would be most vulnerable to pressure from concerned American organisations. The recommendations of this seminar were to be brought to the attention of the US government through targeted meetings with influential people in both the legislative and executive branches.

I opened the programme, speaking on the topic 'What is South Africa's Apartheid?', and tried to give a comprehensive account in order to set the scene as best as I could for what lay ahead of us. I was followed by George Houser, my shipmate and now close friend, who was the Executive Director of the American Committee on Africa. George dealt with 'The Urgency of American Action'. During the next two days, other participants presented papers and led discussion groups concentrating on countries bordering South Africa. What is striking in retrospect was the number and calibre of people invited to speak and lead the discussions. There were representatives of liberation movements, academics with a focus on Africa, lawyers, the clergy, businesspeople, students, and others who were concerned about US foreign policy in African countries. Nathan Shamuyarira, who was a graduate student at Princeton University, spoke on the 'Crisis in Rhodesia'. He was a former editor of a newspaper in Salisbury (now Harare). Robert Resha, an ANC representative, dealt with 'How the African Views Apartheid'. Tom Mboya, who was then Minister for Economic Planning and Development in Kenya, delivered the closing address at a public meeting and rally. It was a pleasure and an honour to reconnect with Tom, because he had been one of my benefactors during my stay in Kenya and the man who arranged my journey from Nairobi to Cairo.

~

Shortly after this meeting in 1966, however, I informed Nana Mahomo that I was leaving the PAC. I told him this when we were on a train between Delaware and New York City, returning from some or other meeting. My primary reason, I explained, was that I was tired of watching the fighting taking place over the lack of funds among the organisation's overseas representatives. What I did not say was that the source of a good part of this endless infighting over money was him. He was collecting large sums of money from all sorts of sources, some quite dubious, others transparent and legitimate, but was not reporting and sharing these funds with other PAC representatives located in various African countries. He was simply not accountable to anyone when it came to collecting money on behalf of the PAC. And being in London was ideal for this purpose. It was the centre of the anti-apartheid movement and, therefore, of its finances. I still get upset and saddened when I recall what was happening in the PAC offices in London, Accra, and Dar es Salaam at that time.

When the train reached New York, Nana and I went our separate ways, and as things turned out, I didn't have much to do with him after that. Aside from one occasion when, to my initial surprise, he asked me if I could find out what would be involved in securing and operating a Daphne submarine. I said I would look into it. Through a friend who had worked in France, I was introduced to someone in New York who knew quite a bit about this type of submarine. He was a French man and had something to do with the French Consulate. Naturally, he was curious about why I had an interest in a submarine. I told him that a friend who represented a liberation movement in London was interested in knowing what was involved in getting one and what was required to operate it. Two meetings with this man were sufficient. It was clear that Nana and I were on a fishing expedition. I could see that the examination of the yacht at the Port of Southampton in 1964 and this inquiry about the submarine were related. Both were good ideas but needed more serious analysis, knowledge, and financial resources. These searches were fuelled by understandable desperation, the same desperation that made me want to train as a fighter pilot in the UAR in 1961. This is what resistance is all about: the urgent need to find ways of fighting back.

A Meeting and a Departure

At the Washington Square campus, in late March 1967, the Organisation of African Students, which I had founded with other African students, decided to hold a conference on liberation movements in Southern Africa. Our Executive Committee, of which I was president, reached out to some of the leading Permanent Representatives of the few African countries at the United Nations and invited them to come and speak at and participate in the workshops. The UN representatives of Cameroon, Sudan, and Zambia all attended. The main address was delivered by Nathan Shamuyarira, whom I had met at the seminar I had opened the year before. We convened and led several workshops to examine the politics, education, economy, and armed struggle for independence, as well as its psychological impact on both black and white Rhodesians.

Without reproducing the proceedings of this conference, I have selected a few observations that stand out from each workshop. A major observation about the politics of the country was that constitutional politics in Rhodesia was out of the question given the intransigence of the white minority regime which was supported by the South African government. The unity of the liberation organisations was vital in order to overthrow the Southern Rhodesian regime. Economic sanctions were ineffective unless they were comprehensive and included South Africa, which was propping up Southern Rhodesia in multifarious ways. The educational system for disadvantaged blacks in the country was inadequate and not empowering the black population, even though it was better than Bantu Education in South Africa. Consequently, it was proposed that independent African countries should be asked to admit Southern Rhodesian Africans to their tertiary institutions while the liberation struggle was being waged. Militarily, confronting the Southern Rhodesian state was inevitable but required a united front between ZAPU and ZANU as well as support from African states. Psychology focused on the need for the Southern Rhodesian black population, or a good part of it, to take ownership of the struggle for independence by participating in it and gaining confidence that the white minority government could be overthrown despite the support it was receiving internally from South Africa and beyond. A mass uprising was impossible without this confidence and without Africans' taking ownership of the revolution. The conference was very successful. One of the people taking notes of the discussions was Joanna Karvonides, who compiled a full report of the proceedings. By this stage we were very involved in each other's work.

By this time, I had already been informed by the AAI that the scholarship I had been on since my arrival in the US in 1962 had come to an end. I was graduating with a B.Sc. in Economics and apparently there were no scholarships available for graduate studies. The only help the AAI could offer was to refer me to a consulting firm of civil engineers and development economists in East Orange, New Jersey. Austin Brown at the AAI told me that this firm was interested in me joining its development economics division. But first, he said, I had to go for an interview.

7

Louis Berger

Louis Berger International was founded in 1940 by Dr Louis Berger, a former engineering professor at Penn State University. By the 1960s, it had already become one of the largest and most experienced consulting firms in the world.[16] The company specialised in technical and economic feasibility studies and evaluations, construction supervision, and technical assistance in a variety of areas. Its main vocation was to help with the study, implementation, and management of development programmes and projects worldwide, and it had been very active on the African continent since 1960.

I called to set up an appointment to be interviewed. When I got to their offices on Halsted Street, close to the East Orange train station, I met with Dr Berger himself and his nephew, Derish Wolff, a graduate of the Harvard Business School, who was the organisation's CEO. They took me to lunch at the Howard Johnson restaurant, a short walk from their office. The food was good and the conversation very relaxed. We talked mostly about my experiences since leaving South Africa. Very little was said about the job I was being interviewed for, and I was a little surprised to find that I was hired on the spot.

So it was, late in 1967, that I started as a trainee at Louis Berger Inc. in their Development Economic Group (DEG) under the mentorship of Derish Wolff and a handful of other senior economists. They taught me how to search for and respond to requests for proposals (RFPs), especially those that came from the USAID and state and local governments. My first small success was in spotting an RFP from the state of Alaska, which was looking

---

16 Louis Berger International was ranked as the best development economics consulting firm in 1984, 1985, and 1987 by the United States Agency for International Development (USAID), and it continued to be one of the leading consulting firms in this arena into the 1990s and beyond. By 2011, it had nearly 6 000 employees in more than 50 countries around the world.

to refurbish its major airport. I contributed to the background research and did some writing for the response to this RFP. And we won the contract. After this early boost to my confidence, I soon began moving up the ladder in the firm, and in 1968 was designated the Director of Training Programmes for African student interns who came from various countries for training as development economists. Work like this felt particularly meaningful and gave me a feeling of connection to the continent.

Louis Berger Inc. took pride in hiring MBA graduates from the Harvard Business School for the DEG division and engineers of one kind or another, depending on the jobs in progress or expected, from the Massachusetts Institute of Technology. The company recruited mostly from these two institutions. When these recruits arrived at the firm, they tended to take the attitude of being superior to anyone who did not have an MBA from an Ivy League university. Some would even ask where I had obtained my MBA, assuming I had one because I was now the director of training programmes. I realised that without an MBA, as a black person at that time, I would too easily be relegated to the ranks of a low-level employee. I therefore decided that, at some point, I would need to pursue that goal.

While my work at Louis Berger was going well, and the training of African interns felt particularly meaningful, this was also a very difficult time for me personally, as it was for Joanna, as we were experiencing challenges in our relationship at the time. We had reached a bit of an impasse. She wanted to know where the relationship was going, and I was unsure how to answer her. While I had no doubts about her as a person, the idea of marrying a white woman was causing me great unease. I can't put this hesitation into precise words, but suffice it to say that I felt like the worlds we came from were simply too different, and it wouldn't work out between us. She felt my hesitation and retreated. We began seeing less and less of each other, focusing more intently on our respective political and academic projects and moving in separate social orbits. Joanna was doing a lot of organising work for Demokratia in the movement against the dictatorship in Greece, as well as the anti-Vietnam War movement. By this time, I had moved to East Orange in New Jersey to be closer to my new work, while Joanna remained in Manhattan. I remember that she went to Greece for the summer, to meet her Greek family for the first time. During these months we barely communicated, and our separation only deepened the following year. It is a period I look back on with some discomfort.

~

I had been working at Louis Berger for more than half the year when, in mid-1968, I decided that it was now the right time to take the leap with the MBA, and I enrolled at the Graduate Business School of Rutgers University's Newark campus. The duration of the MBA programme I signed up for was one year, halving the usual time people took to do the course. Classes would take place during the day and sometimes the evenings, and I tried to manage it alongside the work I was doing at Louis Berger.

It turned out that I was one of the Business School's first intakes of five black students. The majority of the white administration staff members and professors did not think black students would survive, let alone do well, and it was at the end of the first semester that two of the only five black students in the entire business school were called into a meeting in the Student Advisor's office. The two students were Hayford Tony Alile (we called him Tony) from Nigeria and me. The head of the office and chief recruiter congratulated us on our grades and high overall performance in the programme. The remaining three black students had dropped out before the year was over, despite the study group that Tony and I had organised for us to help one another. Now it was just me and Tony making our way in a sea of white faces. Doing the MBA as a one-year course meant that the load was even more demanding than usual, and between my coursework and my responsibilities at Louis Berger, I was working all the time. In this pressurised atmosphere, Tony and I had to rely on each other. Tony was very good at mathematics, so he could help me with economics, while I helped him with the social science aspect of business. We tutored each other and spent most of our downtime together, sharing meals and going for swims in a friend's pool in the Oranges, New Jersey. Joanna and I talked only once in a while, but she was much more of an absence than a presence in my life at this time.

When we were about to graduate from the Business School towards the end of 1969, a number of firms came to interview students and select possible candidates to invite for further interviews at their offices. Tony was recruited and offered a management position at American Airlines. I was being recruited by International Business Machines (IBM). I was still working with Louis Berger at the time, but a position with IBM was a powerful draw. When I went for further interviews, I spent a good part of the day being interrogated at three of its different offices from nine in the morning until around three in the afternoon. When the third and last interview ended, I was told that I had the job and should choose the division I preferred to join. I chose the International Corporate Headquarters Office on First Avenue, located opposite the United Nations Headquarters. I was then informed that I would soon be sent to the IBM offices in Rio de Janeiro, Brazil – which presented an insurmountable and painful obstacle. I was a refugee and stateless person, still without a passport. While the US had been a port of safety for me and was increasingly feeling like home, it was distressing to realise that I was, at least for the time being, stuck here. I had to turn down the job.

~

It was thus a relief when, right around that time, the Dean of the Business School, Horace De Podwin, approached me and Tony and asked us to help the Business School establish a small business development centre that would work alongside the Regional Offices of the Small Business Administration offices in Newark. This initiative was designed to rebuild small businesses that had either been burned down or simply closed during and after the Newark riots of July 1967.

Because of how relevant they still feel, I would like to take a moment to discuss these riots, which led to this work being necessary in the first place. The riots were sparked by a display of police brutality in which Mr John Smith, an African-American taxi driver, was arrested when he drove his taxi around and ahead of a police car and double parked it on 15th Avenue in Newark. Mr

Smith was stopped by the police and beaten so badly that he had to be taken to the Beth Israel Hospital in the city. Following that incident until July 17, Newark and New Jersey experienced some of the worst civil disorder in its history. When order was finally restored, 26 people, mostly African-Americans were reported killed; another 730 were injured and over 1400 people had been arrested. The destruction of property, especially businesses, was extensive. In the aftermath of these riots many small businesses, particularly those owned by white people, closed or moved from Newark to the white suburbs. Newark was left to die a slow economic death. The African-American community leaders felt that they had remained largely disempowered in Newark despite the city being one of the first big cities in America, next to Washington, DC, with a large black population. What was more upsetting was that the Newark Police Department was dominated by white officers who routinely stopped and questioned black youth for no apparent reason and often arrested them.

Dean De Podwin had been part of the discussions that had been taking place intermittently on campus about what role the Business School could play in helping to rebuild the city and its economy. It was around the same period that corporations like the International Telephone & Telegraph (IT&T) and Ford Foundation were examining what was being done across the country in the field of entrepreneurship among minorities. These minorities were mostly African-Americans and Hispanic-Americans. A couple of years after the riots, the Business School established the Rutgers Minority Business Enterprise Programme, which was designed to ensure that minority groups had an opportunity to enter and participate in the mainstream of America's economic life. This programme developed rapidly under the leadership of Professor Louis T. German of the Accounting Department and his assistant Mr Russell Mass. From the outset, they dispensed with using textbooks and instead assigned MBA students, including Tony and me, to working as consultants with individual clients who wanted to get into business or were already operating but needed help. Student consultants used their knowledge and expertise of every field of business that they were studying. They helped craft business plans, marketing and sales strategies, production plans, and so forth based on their collective analysis and discussions of individual cases in class sessions conducted by Professor German. The sharing of information gathered by student consultants was very useful and instructive. The resulting collective knowledge about small businesses was both revealing and empowering. Tony and I excelled in this class, and our ability to relate to the black clients we dealt with was helpful.

The Minority Enterprise Small Business Investment Company (MESBIC), which Tony and I helped create, worked alongside the Regional Office of the Small Business Administration (SBA) in Newark in screening, processing, funding, and providing free consulting services to applicants. The Business School created a vetting process for applicants, which Tony and I oversaw. We also served on the Loans Committee, working with regional officials to make our decisions.

It is interesting to note that it was in 1969 that the US Congress passed the *Minority Enterprise and Small Business Investment Act* (MESBIC). It is unsurprising that President Nixon recognised the Rutgers initiative by presenting the head of the programme, Professor Lou German, with an Achievement Award for breaking new ground in the field of small business development. This recognition was given to all who had contributed to what was really a unique programme at that time.

This was the situation for me when I finished my MBA at Rutgers in late 1969. I felt a new respect from my colleagues at Louis Berger and, even more importantly, a sense of personal accomplishment. All in all, the world looked more promising to me. There was something I needed to do, however; someone I need to see.

8

The Zulu and the Greek

Joanna remembers that it was snowing the day I came to see her at her apartment on West 10th Street, between Bleecker and Hudson Streets, deep in the West Village. I do not remember that, but I take her word for it. It was the winter of February 1970. We had seen each other only a few times in the past couple of years. We had both been superficially involved with other people. But these other relationships had only given me added clarity that the current situation was not how I wanted things to be. I hoped she would be open to what I wanted to say.

Arriving at her apartment unannounced, I told her I had come to say I loved her, and I wanted us to get married. She asked me if I was sure. It was abrupt, I admitted, but I was sure. She said she was sure, too. And then things happened quite quickly from there. We spoke about the idea of her taking a trip to the continent because, as she knew, I wanted us to move there eventually, and I wanted her to know what it was like. She was happy to do that; she was adventurous and liked to travel. I was apprehensive about how she would react to the poverty she would find. Her response was that I should go to Greece to see the levels of poverty among white people there. Her parents were born in Ordu, a small city in Turkey along the Black Sea. They were among the many ethnically Greek people who were forced out by the Atatürk regime. Her parents had ended up in Greece, as refugees, before continuing to the US and settling in Saco, Maine. Back in Greece, many of her community were still living in difficult circumstances.

Joanna asked two of her friends, both African-American students, if they wanted to come with her. One was a colleague from the City College campus in Harlem, Gerrie Pemberton; the other was a fellow graduate student from NYU, Yolanda 'Cookie' Ratcliff. They would accompany her to Mauritania, Guinea, Ivory Coast, and Ghana. Apartheid South Africa she would have to visit alone, without her friends, who as black people would not have been given visas.

We both put some money together and off she went. The thought of Joanna going to South Africa was very appealing to me. It was exciting that someone so close to me would be visiting my family. Together, we came up with a plan for how she would locate and see them, and she executed it meticulously.

Upon her arrival in Johannesburg, from her hotel room, she consulted the telephone directory and tried to figure out how to make phone calls and, in particular, how to call Soweto. She finally tried the switchboard and asked the operator to assist her in calling the number I'd gotten earlier of a 'Reverend David Nkosi in Orlando West Extension, Soweto'. Calling a township was not an easy thing for her to do alone, but the switchboard managed to locate the number and connected her to my father's home.

A woman answered: my stepmother, Mrs Dlamini. Joanna introduced herself as an American student doing research about the African clergy, and asked if her husband, David Nkosi, would be willing to meet for an interview. We knew that people listened in on calls that went into the township, so she was very careful about how she put things on the phone. My stepmother, whom I have only ever known as Mrs Dlamini, asked her to hold the line. A minute later she came back and said he had agreed. Next, Joanna got in touch with the Institute of Race Relations, at that time a more progressive organisation than it is now, and repeated her story about being an American student doing research into the black clergy. She said she needed to interview an African clergyman, and had been referred to Reverend Nkosi, but since she couldn't go to Soweto, asked if they could meet at the institute. The woman at the institute was amenable, and they arranged the time and date.

My father and stepmother were in the room before she got there. As she tells the story, she went in and uBaba was sitting there: a very tall, very dignified man in a black suit. Circumspect. Without smiling, he just nodded to her. Mrs Dlamini was very friendly and open and smiling. She was a plump woman dressed up nicely and wearing a 'doek'. So they all sat together, and Joanna started telling them the truth, explaining that she was from the US, that she knew their son, Morley, and that Morley had asked her to meet with them. The hard part, she said, was explaining why she really wanted to meet them, which was that we were planning to get married. That's why she was there. My father's response, she said, was very subdued, while Mrs Dlamini was very jovial about it. She told Joanna about her own son, and said she hoped she would see him at some point. My father, meanwhile, was concerned but quiet. After that they parted ways. She spoke to them by telephone almost every day before she left South Africa. But that was the only time she saw them.

During her time in South Africa, she also cautiously met some prominent anti-apartheid activists in Johannesburg; Fatima Meer was one of them. She then left for Durban, where she tried to meet my brother, Stanley, and his family. She had written to Stanley at a post office box number that my stepmother had given her, informing him of the hotel where she would be staying, but the letter arrived on the day she was due to leave, and by the time Stanley got to the hotel it was too late. My stepmother, who could have alerted Stanley to the fact that Joanna was coming, had not done so; and it seems, in fact, that Mrs Dlamini deliberately sabotaged Joanna's meeting with my brother, with whom she had a contentious relationship. (Relating this unfortunate near-miss, I am relieved that this was not the only chance Joanna would ever get to meet my brother.)

After spending about ten days in South Africa, Joanna managed to reconnect with Gerrie and Cookie in Tanzania. From there they visited Kenya and Egypt before going to the United Kingdom and then returning to the US.

When they returned to the US, I asked Joanna which African country she had liked the most. I thought she would say the Ivory Coast, but instead she chose Guinea. I was surprised at Joanna's choice and wanted to know why she had chosen a country that was so beleaguered, as it was at that time.[17] She said she respected

---

17 Guinea at that time was being punished and sabotaged by the French government of Charles de Gaulle because President Sekou Touré did not want Guinea to be part of the of the French-African connection, which, among other obligations, required the country to use the CFA currency,

the resolve and determination of its people to be independent despite the sabotage inflicted and sanctions imposed by France, its former colonial master. She characterised the Ivory Coast as a playground for young French expatriates and an extension of the French Republic politically, socially, and economically. For me, that only strengthened my feeling that we were a good match for each other. I realised that she would be open to experiencing life anywhere on the continent. Both of us intended, at some point, to live and work somewhere in Africa. We realised, however, that pursuing our academic work and earning doctorates would be a wise investment while we were still in the United States. With such credentials, finding work in many other countries would be easier. Before leaving for her trip, Joanna had applied to and been accepted by the doctoral programme in History at the Graduate Centre of the City University of New York. Meanwhile, I had applied to the Ford Foundation for funding for doctoral studies in economics, and they had granted me a scholarship. I had also applied for admission to the Economics programme at the New School for Social Research, also in New York City, where I was accepted. We would both now be pursuing our doctoral studies, and Joanna would continue teaching while I would, at least at first, be a fulltime student.

My father, meanwhile, had gone on to approve our marriage. Since Joanna had gotten his phone number, I was finally able to call him. The telephone call was conducted in IsiZulu and monitored by an African security officer who listened to all phone calls going into and out of Soweto. To hear my father's soft voice, after so many years, was deeply moving. His question was: 'Mtanami, ngiyibonile lentombi obuyi thumele lapha . . . Abekho yini abantu lapho?' Translated literally, he was asking in a concerned voice: 'My child, I've seen this young woman you sent here . . . (But) are there no (black) people there?' My response was: there are many (black) people here, but Joanna

---

which was underpinned by the French franc. Not only did Touré refuse to be a member of the French-African community, he went on to introduce the Guinean franc, which was not tied to the French franc. This was the tipping point for the French government. It quickly and aggressively undermined both the currency and the country. France was determined to impoverish Guinea and remove Touré from power.

and I are compatible and have similar interests. I said that we complemented each other, that she was reliable, and that I loved her. He then gave us his blessing. My father always gave me ample space and responsibility to make decisions about what I wanted to do, as long as I presented a convincing case.

~

The questions of where to get married and who would marry us were a little daunting. Part of the challenge was that I was intending to marry a white woman whose parents (mother, in particular) could not figure out why she would choose a black man from Africa when there were so many eligible young Greek men in Maine. Joanna's elder brother, Constantine, who lived in New York, offered to go up to Maine to tell their mother in person about our plan to marry. The news, delivered in a restaurant, did not meet with a good response. Her mother, Chresoula, was very upset and in fact would not speak to Joanna. Aside from the racial aspect, which was certainly a part of it, she was also worried that her daughter would eventually go with me to South Africa and leave them, her parents, just as she, Chresoula, had left her own mother and father behind in Greece, where they had lived after escaping from Turkey. She was against the marriage. Her father, Nicholas, who was a cobbler and had a gentler nature, was more understanding. Later, when we sent them an invitation to the wedding, Nicholas responded and said he couldn't come because his wife wouldn't come, but he asked Joanna, in more detail, about me: What kind of person was I? Why was I in the United States? They had had only cursory discussions about these things before. She explained again that I was a political exile. 'Do you know anything about his family?' he asked her. Yes, she said, she knew some things. She said she had been to South Africa and had met my father, and he had been an impressive person. That's when he said, 'Okay, have your wedding, and then afterwards please, please come and see us.'

~

For the wedding itself I went for counsel to an important advisor of mine, Frank Montero. Since meeting Frank in January, 1961 in Nairobi, where he helped me to get to Cairo, and meeting him again in November 1962 in the US, he had become a close friend and even a sort of surrogate father. I wanted him to know and meet the person I intended to marry. Joanna and I went to visit the Montero family – Frank, Anne, and their two daughters, Marion and Laurie – at their home in Riverdale, New York. The Monteros liked Joanna and wished us the best of luck going forward.

Frank had himself married a white woman, his wife Anne, in 1950. I never asked him or Anne how their folks reacted to their marriage. I found out later that *The New York Times* headline report of their marriage was that Frank, a Negro, was marrying a wealthy and socially prominent Boston woman who was a descendent of the Puritan preacher, Cotton Mather. The newspaper headline read: MISS ANNE MATHER MARRIED TO A NEGRO. Frank was active and well known both in the black and white communities. He had won his spurs in the National Urban League where he had met Anne, who then brought him to the Bronx. Living in Riverdale opened some new doors for Frank and put him on the radar screens of some big political names like the Roosevelts and the Kennedys. He worked on the victorious campaign that saw John F. Kennedy be elected president in 1960.[18]

After I'd taken Joanna to meet the Monteros, it was logical for us to carry on getting advice and help from Anne and Frank, who were essentially my surrogate parents. Joanna's parents had, for all intents and purposes, gone on strike and would not come to the wedding. But her elder brother, Constantine, said he would come with his wife, Beverly, and their three children, Chrisi, Nicholas, and Mia. Tony Alile[19] and I had remained close

---

18 A foundation Frank headed had approached the US State Department with a request for a $100 000 grant to bring to the US Africans, who for political, social, or other reasons wanted to study there. The State Department turned down the request, but the Kennedy family foundation happily provided the money instead. I was one of the many African students that Frank helped through the Kennedy family foundation. Another colleague of Frank's, William X. Scheinman, an entrepreneur, worked on the same project which focused on airlifting students from Kenya to study in the United States. These airlifts were called 'the Kennedy airlifts'. The major driver in Kenya behind these scholarship airlifts to the United States was Tom Mboya in his capacity as the Secretary General of KANU.

19 Around this time, Tony and I saw an advertisement in *The Economist* in which the International Labour Organisation, the United Nations

friends since our days at Rutgers, and I asked him if he would do me the honour of being my best man. His wife, Patience, was to be Joanna's bridesmaid. Preparations for the marriage included who was going to officiate, where the ceremony would be conducted and by whom, who would be invited, what Joanna and I would wear, and so forth. Frank and Anne came to our rescue again: they said we could get married at their house in Riverdale. As to the question of who would conduct the marriage ceremony, they proposed that we pay Algernon D. Black a visit. He was the Leader Emeritus of the New York Society for Ethical Culture and a member of the Fraternity of Leaders of the American Ethical Union. For more than forty years, he had been a teacher in the Ethical Culture Schools. Joanna and I visited him, introduced ourselves, and explained how I had got to know Frank and that he had recommended that we ask him to marry us. This visit was very reassuring and made us look forward to the wedding day.

Later, when he wrote about our visit in his book called *Without Burnt Offerings: Ceremonies of Humanism* in the part titled 'The Zulu and the Greek', Black notes that when we went to see him to talk about our wedding plans, we were both dressed conventionally. Because neither Joanna nor I were traditionally religious, it was easy to agree on a simple ceremony that would emphasize our common ground of faith in human values and human potentiality. His description of the wedding is flattering but, I think, true. He writes: 'On the afternoon of the wedding on the 24th of October 1970, approximately one hundred people, members of families, fellow students and friends drawn from various national and cultural backgrounds, gathered in the garden. The variety of costumes and friendliness of the people evidenced a spirit and created an atmosphere that made one think of the United Nations. When the wedding was about to begin, the

---

Development Programme, and Nigeria's Planning and Development Agency were looking for a candidate with experience in developing small businesses. We realised that we had a good chance of being interviewed because of the experience we had gained in Newark. Tony applied and got the job. I did not apply. The prospects of working in Nigeria alongside Tony and his colleagues was appealing, but the hot and wet climate was forbidding for me and Joanna. The idea of being inside and running an air conditioner for most of the year was not attractive to either of us.

ushers brought out two white ribbons and held them together so that the wedding procession might have a lane through the guests gathered in the garden. He led the way through the lane with a small dark-haired Greek child, a nephew of the Greek bride, gripping my hand tightly while his free hand held two precious gold wedding rings. Behind us came the groom. He walked proudly, naked except for a loincloth made of zebra hide. His handsome body shone golden bronze in the afternoon sun. His head was topped by a turban of zebra hide, and on his left arm was a shield of the same zebra design. In his right hand he held a spear.' (This was me, I think.)

He continues: 'Behind the groom came the bride. She wore a long plum-colored gown reaching the ground. Her lovely face was framed by a long brown tress and around her neck hung a brilliant blue turquoise necklace sent especially by her brother (in-law) in honour of the occasion. Behind her walked two of her nieces dressed in green velvet dresses and scattering rose petals over her. When the wedding procession arrived at the end of the garden, the ushers removed the two white ribbons. The guests gathered round the bride and groom.'

After we had made our vows and commitments to each other, Zulu drums, songs, and dances filled the air. The Zulu dancers provided the traditional backdrop and entertainment that made our wedding unique. We had been lucky that Paul Makgoba and a troupe of Zulu dancers were in town for some engagements, and he offered to come with his group to perform at our wedding. We are still very grateful and honoured to have had the entire group make our wedding truly memorable. Our wedding pictures captured the electric Zulu dancers in the Bronx on the afternoon of the 24th of October 1970. Coincidentally, this date is also celebrated as United Nations Day.

Black writes that 'in the midst of the toast and the mixing of the guests of many nations, one man said, "I've seen many brides that were underdressed, but I've never seen such a naked groom."' Yes. But this person did not focus on the male Zulu dancers, who were as naked as I was. Algernon adds that because the newlyweds honoured their traditions, it added beauty and taste.

'They shared a profound spiritual experience of commitment to each other and their respective families and ethnic backgrounds and cultural values. They were part of a world which is coming into being, a world of pluralism, human understanding, and cultural enrichment.' What I find interesting is that Black said I was wearing only a loincloth, and the other man said I was naked, while I thought I was fully dressed in traditional Zulu attire.

9

Maine

Now that we were married, two questions remained. The first was, where would we live? I was still in East Orange, New Jersey, and Joanna was still in the West Village, Manhattan. We needed to find a place that suited both of us. The second, equally pressing, question was, what we were going to do about Joanna's parents? While she was not eager to seek any sort of reconciliation just yet, I believed it was crucial to try and persuade her that we should go up to Maine for Thanksgiving. There were two reasons: one, her father had encouraged us to come, and I did not want us to ignore that overture; two, the idea of family has always been important to me, maybe because I had been forced to leave my own. If anything ever happened to Joanna, I remember saying, the first people who would scramble to help would be her family. I thought we might as well go and visit them to see whether we could get along or not. I wasn't afraid of what would happen there. I say that because, for me, dealing with white people who might have assumptions about me was not an unfamiliar experience. I had done it as a young man in South Africa, I had done it in London, and I was doing it every day in the United States. So what was the difference here?

Something else that put my mind at ease to some extent was the fact that Joanna's aunt, Rodi, had already met me in New York when she had been on her way from Greece to visit Joanna's mother in Maine. We had picked her up at the airport when she arrived, and she had stayed with us for a few days at our apartment. Rodi was a very jovial, funny, and loving person and had sat there and watched very carefully how we related to each other. From what we heard later, she was impressed when she noticed that we helped each other around the place, cooking and doing things together. I think what impressed her most was how neat I was. She had laid the groundwork for me with my mother-in-law by saying that 'he's not a slob, he's a good person,' and so on. So, Rodi acted as a kind of ice-breaker, and it was a relief to see her on the night we walked into the Shaw residence in Biddeford, Maine.

Joanna's sister, Mary, had married a man by the name of David Shaw, who came from an established Scottish-American family in Biddeford. She and David lived in a large, two-storey house made of wood on South Street. It stood on a little hill facing an expansive, neatly manicured lawn. Mary had just had her second child, a boy, Jere, and Joanna's mother was living at the house to help with the baby. I remember there had been a huge snowstorm, and we arrived late because it took us longer than usual to get up to Maine. When we walked into the house, I recall David and Mary being very warm and welcoming but Joanna's mother being ice cold, really ice cold. While Mary took our coats and guided us into the sitting room, Chresoula watched me like a hawk and continued to do so for the whole evening. Joanna's father, Nicholas, could look at me, at least; he even talked to me a little; but I could still sense that he was sizing me up. One interesting thing about Nicholas, however, which is worth noting, is what happened at the end of the evening. Rodi and Chresoula were staying to help Mary at the Shaw's, but Nicholas was staying alone at his house, the house Joanna had grown up in. At the end of the evening, when it was clear that people were tired, he said to us, 'Please, I want you to come home and stay with me.' So we went with him, and when we arrived back at the house, a stone house on a winding road that led to the ocean, he offered us his bed to sleep in. Joanna and I were surprised. We thanked him, but said it was unnecessary, and we slept in Joanna's old bedroom upstairs.

This was the first time I had spent time with Joanna's people. Every day we would go between her childhood home and her sister's house. At Thanksgiving dinner, Chresoula was very reserved and sat back, observing. After dinner, we showed them some slides from our wedding and she sat far away and didn't want to engage. But Rodi told her, 'Your daughter is happily married. Your son-in-law is great.' Rodi really loved me, apparently, and this helped. However, it took a few visits to Maine before Joanna's mother began to relax a little. During one of these visits, I also began to notice the family dynamic, the tempestuous, loving, often abrupt way in which they talked to one another. I remember one occasion distinctly, when they were all in her sister's kitchen trying to fix lunch, and the way they were talking to one another distressed me so much that I walked out of the room. And I'm told that they then started asking questions – what's the matter with him? and so on. Joanna said I was not used to people talking to each other like that, and somebody said, 'Well, he's got to get used to screaming.'

~

Having now reconciled with Joanna's family, Joanna and I had to address the question of where to live. Her apartment in Manhattan and my apartment in New Jersey were about an hour apart. We had to find a place to live together somewhere between the two. And so we chose a neighbourhood called Greenwich Village. We scrounged around for places and found a place on Christopher Street, which we took but which ended up being a disaster. It turned out to be on the corner of the last and first bus stop going across town, so there was a lot of noise from the buses. It was also across from a restaurant, the Silver Dollar Cafe, and the trucks delivering food would stop there very early in the morning. We went as far as fitting out the apartment with soundproof windows, but this turned the apartment into a tomb. It was eerily quiet, and we realised this was not the place for us.

Luckily, the landlord was agreeable to us leaving and returning our deposit. Perhaps it was because we had paid for the new windows. We then went hunting for a place and ended up on 13th Street between 5th and 6th Avenues. I remember distinctly the day that I found it. Joanna had come back downtown to her apartment from her teaching job at City College in Harlem, and I called her to say that she needed to come and see this place. When she walked in, she was dressed in a white suit, and looked the part as she entered this beautiful apartment. She was startled because this would be a big change for both of us – this was far fancier than either of our current apartments. It was on the top floor in a low-rise building and had a skylight and all. It was also conveniently located close to the New School and to City University's Graduate

Centre, and just a short walk from a station where Joanna could catch the subway uptown. We decided that with her salary and my salary combined, we could manage it.

~

For Joanna's birthday in May of 1971, I organised a party for her at her brother's apartment on First Avenue and 33rd Street, at the Kipps Bay Plaza. Some members of her family came down from Maine for this occasion. Her friend from NYU, Eleanor, invited someone she was dating, Ambassador Nicol, who in turn came with three other people he had met and had some dealings with. One of them was Mangosuthu Gatsha Buthelezi, the South African politician and traditional prime minister to the Zulu royal family. The other was Alfred 'Alf' Khumalo, a prominent photographer, also from South Africa. The third I don't remember. Of these individuals, there was one that bothered me and Joanna. It was Alf, the photographer, who was taking pictures of everyone but seemed to be concentrating on me and Joanna. I got quite agitated but kept my feelings to myself.

My anxiety came from, firstly, trying to figure out how the South African government had given Alf a passport that allowed him to travel and return to South Africa when most of us had left without any documents and, had we returned, would have been sent to prison. Secondly, I was anxious about what was going to happen to all the pictures he had taken, particularly those of the political exiles, when he returned to South Africa. I was sure that the Bureau of State Security (BOSS) would confiscate some, if not all, of them. The security apparatus at home did not have a single picture of me. In virtually all the political gatherings I had attended, I had made sure to avoid the cameras. The only picture I knew of in which I was visible was one taken when we were on our way to the Orlando Police Station on the morning of the Sharpeville massacre, Monday the 21st of March 1960. The police who arrested my brother early on the morning of the 9th of September 1960, and who were also looking for me, did not know what I looked like. Now, eleven years later, would they be getting photos of me from Alf? Something had to be done.

For some weeks Alf went round the United States taking more and more pictures of South African exiles wherever he went (he even took pictures of Muhammad Ali fighting on the West Coast). I alerted the small community of refugees in New York City that we were all exposing ourselves by allowing Alf to take pictures of us, pictures that might have to be surrendered to State Security upon his return to South Africa. People began to realise the danger. Alf had already amassed a good collection of images in all sorts of settings. So with two very smart South African exiles, we organised a way of retrieving the reels of film from where he was staying. The mission was almost compromised because one of the two men who carried it out, for some damned reason, went to use the bathroom there to wash his hands, took off his wristwatch, left it on the side of the basin, and forgot it there. (He had to collect it the next time he went to Alf's place, this time as an invited guest.) What was peculiar was that Alf never said a word about the disappearance of his films. We could only wonder why. In any case, we felt relieved that the apartheid state was not about to get a whole pile of pictures to stick up on their walls as wanted enemies of the state. Collective security was essential.

~

During those early years that we lived in our beloved 13th Street apartment, we spent a lot of time with Joanna's nieces and nephew, Mia, Chrisi, and Nicholas. We would go to the park with them, visit the zoo, have them sleep over – but only one or two of them at a time. And we'd make them elaborate breakfasts. They adored us and we adored them. But at some point I started to feel tired of playing with other people's children and thought, why don't we have a baby of our own?

By this time, I had obtained permanent residency in the United States. (I obtained it in 1972, and this permanent residency soon led to my becoming naturalised in the US and acquiring a passport for the first time ever.) Starting our own family would be the next chapter of our lives, but before we could embark on it, there were still some difficult experiences to face, experiences that would connect me with my life back home, only not in the way I might have foreseen or wanted.

10

Death and Birth

The first death I heard of back home was that of my older sister, Beauty, in 1969. That was very painful for me. I was close to Beauty and loved her very much. I was told that there had been an accident but was not given many details. I would later learn, to my dismay, that it seemed she had been poisoned by someone in her social circle.

Joanna and I heard about the passing of my sister, Thoko, early in 1974. My brother, Stanley, called to tell us. We didn't receive a lot of phone calls. It was difficult for Stanley to be in touch, considering how closely surveilled phone calls from the townships were, but this time he phoned us to say that Thoko had passed away. Joanna was already a few months pregnant by this time, and although I was again gutted by the news, we had something hopeful to buoy us up. But then, about three weeks later, on the 28th of June 1974, Stanley called again to say that our father had passed away. I think he, my father, was heartbroken at the loss of his beloved daughter, and I believe he died, in part, from a broken heart. Thoko had always lived with him and my stepmother. She never had her own family.

The news came at a time when I was not feeling well. I was having some serious gastrointestinal issues, which turned out to be related to a severe dairy intolerance and probably stress. When I heard the news about Thoko, it hit me very hard, but compounded with the news of my father, I completely lost it. I kept saying to Joanna, 'I want to go home. I must go home.' But Joanna was adamant. 'How can you go home? Look how pregnant I am, and you may never come back.' Slowly the reality sank in that not only was my dad gone, but I would not be able to bury him. I would never see him again.

That I couldn't be there at such a significant moment was deeply frustrating and painful. The truth is that I had never considered that my father might die while I was gone. I had not thought about it – or perhaps I had not allowed myself to think about it. But now I had to adjust. I recognised again that even though I wanted to go home, I would not be able to go home – and not for an indefinite period.

~

I was still sick and processing the loss of my father, but during this period of grief I became preoccupied with my healing, our baby's arrival, and the work and political responsibilities that Joanna and I both had. I carried the mourning with me, but I knew that I would have to bear the grief as I built my new life.

I think being involved politically was a constant reminder that one has to keep struggling, no matter what life throws at you. Whether I would be able to get back home or not, I had no idea. When I would see people from home, other exiles who hadn't had a chance to go home dropping dead in the United States, it only made me more determined to survive and find a way of going home someday.

Our first child, Mandla, was born on the 7th of August 1974 at the New York Hospital in Manhattan. His first name is Zulu and means strength or power. We chose it because we felt that to overcome the experiences I had as a refugee and exile, he would have to be strong and endure many trials. In fact, Joanna and I thought that he should have a name that gave him the power to overcome whatever adversities he met with, wherever he lived. Enduring was not enough; as the child of an exile, he had to struggle to survive. We then gave him a second name, Ares, after a Greek resistance leader during the Nazi occupation of Greece. I have watched him over the years living up to both of his names.

Joanna laboured for many hours giving birth to Mandla. I was there in the room with her, dressed up like an assistant to the doctor and very curious about the whole process. And when Mandla finally came out, I followed the doctor to make sure that he did the right things that I'd read about, like using the little pump to clear his nostrils and so on. I was so relieved that both Joanna and Mandla were fine after such a long labour.

Mandla went everywhere with us as a small baby. Joanna would carry him in a wrap against her chest, and we had fun with him right from the beginning. Then, of course, he started to grow and develop quickly, wanting to get out of his playpen and crib and walk around holding the furniture. And before we knew it, he would go to the front door. Then we knew that he wanted to go outside and around the city with us. We didn't have a family support system to help us. We were, to a large extent, on our own. But raising Mandla was not a difficult or a new job for me, because when I lived with my parents, I was the one who often stayed with and took care of my older sisters' children. I knew how to look after babies and children; it felt natural to me.

I think people at home knew Mandla had been born, but at that point I was quite disconnected. It's not that I had deliberately made up my mind to start a new life, but home was emotionally and physically too far away.

~

During that period in our lives, I was teaching at Rutgers University Graduate Business School in Newark and still working for Louis Berger. It was in 1975 that something happened that made me reconsider my involvement with this organisation – and with business consulting in general.

During my tenure as Director of Training Programmes at the company, one of the trainees was a Bene M'Poko from the Democratic Republic of the Congo. Later, in 1975, Bene unwittingly got me into an uncomfortable and serious confrontation with City Bank officials on Park Avenue in New York City. Apparently, he had found a job with City Bank and was working in their Head Office on Park Avenue. The bank officials learned from him that there was a black South African at Louis Berger International where he had interned. Bene then called Dr Berger and asked him to tell me that City Bank wanted to meet and talk to me. Dr Berger persuaded me to go and hear what they wanted but did not tell me that this request had come through Bene. I felt a little awkward visiting the bank's offices on Monday when two days earlier on Friday, I was part of a large demonstration outside the same building holding placards and chanting slogans against the bank's involvement in extending loans to the South African government.

When I showed up for the appointment on Monday, there was Bene. I immediately suspected that he had something to do with organising this visit. I was quickly ushered into an office where I met two white American men who oversaw the bank's operations in Southern Africa and other places overseas. They had collected intelligence on where I had gone to university and whom I was working for in the US. After a few, brief pleasantries the conversation turned to the housing needs of black South Africans, especially in the township of Orlando. The two officials thought that the South African government should provide long-term leases to Africans who needed houses in the townships. I differed with them on this issue and said that the residents who lived in these houses had lived there and paid rent for a very long time. They should be allowed, I argued, to buy the houses at discounted prices, own them, and be given title deeds. This ended the argument.

During this argument about Africans leasing or owning township houses, three international phone calls came in one after the other at very short intervals. From listening to what was being said in response, it was evident that they were speaking to someone or other in South Africa. I could not resist asking them why their South African branch seemed to rely on them here in New York City to make decisions about operations on the ground in South Africa? I asked this question innocently but from a practical point of view. They then told me that that is what they wanted to talk to me about.

In short, they wanted an African who could handle their Barloworld account in South Africa. I asked them why they could not find an African there, and they replied that they could not find one who was unafraid of dealing with whites. Because I had worked with white people previously, was currently working with white people, and even went to university in the US with whites, they figured that I wouldn't be intimidated by white South Africans. Interesting, I thought. I decided to push the envelope a little further by asking how they would deal with the fact that

South African state security officials were still looking for me? They told me with incredible confidence that they had sorted out that problem and that I would not be arrested if I returned. In short, I was made to believe that I could return home under the protection of City Bank! I could not believe what I had just heard. I was shocked and angry at the audacity they showed in playing such a dangerous game with my life. To this day, I cannot get over their scheme. I don't recall exactly how our conversation ended, but it was abrupt. It was an awful experience. An embarrassed Bene was summoned in and told to escort me out of the building. Bene and I left the offices of the bank and went out of the building to a nearby coffee shop where I vented my anger at his bosses and the organisation he was working for.

11

The New School for Social Research

Jacob Wayne Fredericks was a businessman and diplomat who served as the Deputy Assistant Secretary of State for African Affairs in the 1960s, and he is the person that I am indebted to for funding my doctoral studies. Wayne, as we called him, first went to South Africa in the 1940s as an engineer responsible for building a Kellogg cereal plant. He worked for the Kellogg company until 1956 and then went on to direct various domestic and foreign projects for the Ford Foundation. In the 1960s, he worked for the State Department under President John F. Kennedy and Lyndon B. Johnson. He also helped develop United States relations with emerging African countries. From 1961 until 1967, he established contacts with liberation movements in Southern Africa and worked with an Anglo-American-Canadian parliamentary group engaged with postcolonial Africa. He is credited with fostering links between the United States and Africa. During my years of exile in the United States, Wayne was a personal friend, and his relationship with the Ford Foundation was how a substantial part of my graduate studies were funded.

Some background about the New School for Social Research will help to show how this institution had such a profound impact on my intellectual development. It was founded in 1919, and its graduate school began in 1933 as the University in Exile. It was an emergency rescue programme for Jewish scholars who had been dismissed from teaching positions by the Italian fascists or who had to flee Nazi Germany. In 1934, it was chartered by the New York Board of Regents and changed its name to the Graduate Faculty of Political and Social Science and was later renamed the New School for Social Research. Its economics department offered a broad and critical approach to the subject covering a wide range of the history of economic thought. This range included classical political economists from Adam Smith to John Stuart Mill to David Ricardo to Karl Marx to John Maynard Keynes and post-Keynesian economists. Both institutional and structural approaches to the study of economics were taught. The courses emphasized the historical roots of economic ideas and their application to contemporary economic policy debates. It is these approaches and orientations that I found attractive in the New School. Little did I know that I would soon be engaged with other academics and students in agitating for the expansion of course offerings to include Political Economy and Marxian Economics.

In the Economics Department I met and befriended four 'hot-headed' colleagues. Two were American, Nina and Richard; one Puerto Rican, Rosando; and one Brazilian, Edmondo. Together, we motivated for the introduction of a course titled Marxian Economics at both the Masters and doctoral levels. To get the faculty to entertain or consider our proposal, we needed the support of a majority of the students taking traditional courses in the department. Canvassing for this broad support meant endless meetings just before evening classes began at six from Monday to Friday for several weeks. We worked tirelessly trying to persuade our colleagues to endorse our proposal. Students who were working on Wall Street during the day gave us a hard time but eventually came round to supporting our proposal. Their interest was more in understanding how the capitalist system functioned so that they could make their way up the corporate ladder. Ultimately, their focus was on accumulating capital. We seemed to be questioning their aspirations. But we convinced most of them to help us introduce this course, develop a radical economics programme in the Graduate Centre, and attract radical students from other universities to come to the New School's Economics Department. Once we had the majority support required, we went to the office of the Chairperson of the Department, the venerable Professor Robert L. Heilbroner. He said it was fine but asked who would teach this new course? We said the faculty already had Professor Stephen (Steve) Herbert Hymer who was teaching a popular course called Political Economy.

Steve was a graduate of McGill University in Canada and MIT in the US, where he received his doctoral degree in economics. His supervisor was Professor Charles P. Kindleberger, who suggested that Steve integrate two fields of study: large corporations and government. His thesis was titled *The International Operations of National Firms, A Study of Direct Foreign Investment.* Steve was the first person in the United States to investigate the overseas expansion of US multinational firms and explain the economic forces behind their investments outside the United States. His work was seminal and an enduring contribution to the theory of transnational corporations, foreign direct investment, and the international political economy.[20]

At the New School, Steve was the first tenured faculty member assigned the task and responsibility of shaping a student-motivated programme in political economy. This gave him the freedom to teach courses on Marx and develop his critiques of prevailing economic theories. He continued to pursue his research on multinational corporations while incorporating much of what he had learned as a practising economist in Canada, the United States, Western Europe, and West Africa. These experiences deepened his intellectual analysis as a political economist. He saw the multinational corporation as a particular vehicle of capitalist development and no longer an organisation that could be explained by theories of oligopoly and dynamic growth. The courses that he developed on political economy encouraged students and activists to come together to study, debate, and share ideas and experiences as they interrogated and reflected on the dominant economic theories and paradigms that underpinned the study of large firms and multinational corporations. His courses increased the students' enrolment in the Economics Department

---

20 Steve had spent a year in Ghana where he and a colleague, Reginald H. Green, traced the relationship between government practice and economic development by documenting the colonial government's virtual disruption of Ghana's cocoa industry. When he returned to the United States, he taught at MIT and Yale University. It was at Yale that he began to develop an alternative framework and approach to traditional mainstream economics. His research, visits, and collaborative academic works with intellectuals at Cambridge University in England, the University of the West Indies in Trinidad, and the International Studies program at the University of Chile radicalised him. So did the mass movements of the 1960s. He joined the Union of Radical Political Economics and in the spring of 1970 taught his first course on Marx at Yale University. In 1969, he and a colleague, Stephen Resnick, publicly announced that they were Marxists. Yale responded by denying them promotions and tenure. In the fall of 1970, the New School for Social Research in New York offered Steve a position.

considerably. Then followed another demand from the radical students, a course on Marxian economics. Steve was again asked to teach this course. It meant more work for him but a welcome challenge for one in search of a different and more democratic paradigm in economics and international trade theory. He agreed to develop the course content and teach the course.

It was Steve's courses on political economy and Marxian economics that gave students a critical understanding of the dominant economic theories. These theories were researched, interrogated, and in some cases promoted as policy frameworks. Both developed and developing countries tended not only to adopt these policy frameworks but to implement them as well.[21]

The knowledge gained in this arduous academic journey guided by an accomplished professor like Steve has provided me with an informed understanding of the changes that have occurred in the fields of theoretical and applied economics. The irony is that, concurrently with my graduate studies at the New School, where I was deeply engaged in learning about Marxian economics, I was an assistant professor of economics at the Rutgers University Graduate Business School, where I taught mainstream courses on micro- and macro-economics to aspiring captains of industry without becoming an intellectual schizophrenic. In fact, this apparent bifurcation helped deepen my understanding of the field referred to as political economy.

That semester, a member of the faculty at the Business School had invited an eminent economics professor from Romania to lecture as a visiting professor. I asked the visiting professor to give a lecture in my economics classes on central planning in Romania. His country had an economic system similar to the

---

21 This is reflected in the General Introduction of a book titled *The Multinational Corporation: A Radical Approach: Papers by Stephen Herbert Hymer*, which was published by Cambridge University Press in 1979. I co-edited this book together with four other fellow students who were also Steve's students and the leaders of the radicals in the Economics Department. Robert Cohen and I contributed quite a lot to the book. Both of us spent months researching and writing the introduction. This introduction and some of Steve's seminal papers in this book reflect, in a way, the long academic journey that I have travelled in the field of economics at the New School's Graduate Department of Economics.

one in the Soviet Union but more centralised. He explained how local communities systematically determined and prioritised their needs, taking into account what resources were available at the local and regional levels in order to meet those needs. The results of such extensive plans would then be submitted to higher authorities who would examine them in the larger context of the state's obligations to allocate the needed resources to different areas. Planned targets included financial requirements, material inputs, production outputs, sales, exports, and imports. Pricing the required resources would involve consultations and participation at all levels so as to maintain a consultative and democratic process that did not short-change other communities. This kind of local planning was elaborate, country-wide, and centrally controlled. The state played a pivotal role in that it established the prices at which the required resources would be exchanged, unlike in the capitalist system under which prices are essentially determined by supply and demand or the 'invisible hand'. My graduate students found this lecture interesting but very distant from their own experience and what they were learning. From their facial expressions and the few questions they asked, I got the impression that they were listening to a story being told by someone from another world. All they knew was that Romania was a communist country and operated a command economy. Perhaps some benefitted from this exposure. I can only hope they did.

12

Hoboken

When Mandla was a year old, Joanna and I left our apartment in the Village and moved to Hoboken, a city just across the Hudson river. We bought a three-storey brownstone at the corner of Garden and 11th Streets. At that time Hoboken had a stock of old row houses being sold by second- and third-generation immigrants. The younger generation was attracted to the more tree-lined suburbs of New Jersey, so the houses left by the older generation became quite popular with young professionals like us who wanted to be near Manhattan but did not want to move to the suburbs. The selling prices for these row houses were relatively low and affordable for people renting in New York City. The advice and persuasion to buy in Hoboken came from a friend's mother, Edith I. Spivack. Her advice helped us stop paying rent and instead invest in what would later become valuable real estate in a place that was effectively an extension of the Village across the Hudson River. And it was in Hoboken that we met and developed what has turned out to be a lasting friendship with Edith's daughter, Amy, and her husband Geoff Bass, who were also living there.[22]

The political activities that I was involved in during the 1960s continued into and through the 1970s and 1980s. Two of them stand out. To relate the first, I will have to jump ahead a little. Sometime in the early 1970s when I had begun my doctoral studies, I was approached by Randall M. Robinson, the founder of the TransAfrica Forum, the oldest African-American foreign policy organisation in the United States. Its stated mission was to serve as a major research, education and organising institution for the African-American community, offering constructive

---

22 When she died in 2005 at the age of 95, *The New York Times* called Edith the ' "brains" of [the] city's law office'. She was a tireless lawyer who worked for the New York City Law Department from 1934, when few women were government lawyers, until 2004, when she reluctantly stopped showing up four days a week. She had initially been appointed by the well-known and progressive mayor Fiorello LaGuardia.

analysis of US policy as it affected the African diaspora. Randall invited me to debate one John Chattel from the South Africa Foundation (SAF). This debate was to be on live television during the early evening when many viewers were watching. WETA TV in Washington, DC had organised this debate for the evening of 11 April 1984. It was to cover events in and outside of South Africa but focused on US policy in South Africa. US policy at that time was called 'Constructive Engagement', which was designed by Chester Crocker, the Assistant Secretary of State for African Affairs during the Ronald Reagan Administration. This policy mirrored Britain's policy towards South Africa under Margaret Thatcher's government. Both the US and British governments secretly providing the South African government with incentives to motivate it to gradually move away from apartheid.

When I accepted Randall's invitation to debate John Chattel, I didn't know who Chattel was. I also knew almost nothing about the SAF and its role in the UK and the US. When the live debate started, it was clear that he had lots of access to information on South Africa which I did not have. He was very familiar with the politics and economy of South Africa from the perspective of a white man. His advantage was that I had been away from South Africa for 24 years and the conditions there had changed quite a bit since my departure in September 1960. As an example of how things had changed, he described the extensive highway infrastructure developments around Johannesburg, a sign of how the city had become a modern metropolis like any other in the developed world. He said nothing about the political, social, and economic conditions of black people in Johannesburg or the country. That was the opportunity I needed, and I therefore exploited it to the hilt during the television debate. We were face to face, and our anger and disdain for each other was palpable. It was prime time on television in the early evening. This confrontation is not easy to forget.[23]

---

23 Little did I realise that I would later, in the 1990s, actually meet some of the major leaders of the SAF in South Africa in their organisation's Parktown offices in Johannesburg under changed conditions created by the imminent democratic dispensation. Given the changes that were to take place, SAF members in South Africa were attempting to find common ground and form a single organisation with black business

When I was writing this book, I decided to find out who John Chattel was and what the SAF was all about. I discovered that his organisation was established in December 1959 as a direct response to the formation of the Boycott South Africa Movement, which was a precursor to the Anti-Apartheid Movement in England. Its primary job was to act as a public relations unit for the South African government. It focused its public relations initiative on keeping South Africa's international lines of communications open without being seen to defend apartheid. Its work was supported and funded by the South African government, which at that time was desperately looking for foreign investments to grow the economy. To promote this initiative, the government approved a plan by which P. W. Botha's secret Defence Special Account supplied funding that would not be declared in Parliament. The SAF was financed through this secret account.

It is also reported that from its inception the SAF was to function as a shadow of South Africa's Department of Information. Dr Eschel Mostert Rhoodie, a civil servant, public relations person, and spin doctor (sometimes referred to as Apartheid's Goebbels), was the head of this department. The SAF was also described as trying to do on a private basis what the Department of Information was doing publicly. Dr Rhoodie served as Secretary of the Department from 1972 to 1977. During this period, South Africa had two propaganda agencies, the SAF and the Department of Information. Both were handled by the Bureau of State Security (BOSS), which was directly in charge of representing the country internationally. BOSS was very powerful during the 1970s. Its head was the ruthless General Hendrik van den Bergh, and by the

---

organisations like NAFCOC and FABCOS. NAFCOC took the position that SAF should submit a proposal to the black business organisations on how it thought black and white business could work together. This position was based on my previous experience of meetings that Bax Nomvete and I had in Lusaka and Harare with delegations representing the black and white chambers of commerce and industry, where it was evident that black chambers were gravely disadvantaged. Before this submission could be tabled at the next meeting, members of the SAF had covertly lobbied prominent black business members and convinced them that NAFCOC's position was unnecessary. This effort failed because of the duplicity of the SAF and the naivety of the black business organisations that were represented. I represented NAFCOC and witnessed how my own kind left me standing alone.

early 1970s, it had proved itself to be one of the most effective propaganda organisations in the Western world. All economic centres of power in South Africa participated in the SAF.

Also during the 1970s, the foundation began to develop a scholarly veneer to hide its propagandistic purpose. John Chattel, the SAF representative in the US, took a very aggressive approach in developing this strategy. In a publication titled *South Africa and the International Media 1972–1979: A Struggle*, Chattel is quoted as saying, 'We [the SAF] did some research into the extent to which the US media was concentrating on South Africa, as opposed to the Soviet Union . . . [We] gave it to Accuracy in Media and they made quite a bit of it.' Beyond conducting this kind of research, Chattel's other duties on behalf of the SAF included testifying at the Africa Sub-committee of the Senate Committee on Foreign Relations, speaking on South African issues throughout North America, and keeping in close contact with Donald deKieffer, the lobbyist for South Africa's Department of Information based in Washington, DC. While this propaganda onslaught was raging in the countries that supported the apartheid regime, South Africa's *dirigisme* was on the decline. Something had to be done.

The approach to growing the economy was largely influenced by Hendrik Johannes van der Bijl, a South African electrical engineer and industrialist. His thinking and primary goal was to industrialise the country and create employment opportunities for Afrikaners, a goal aligned with the Nationalist Party objectives. The investments for this initiative were to come first from domestic sources then from foreign direct sources. Van der Bijl's plan was to operate these state-owned enterprises along commercial lines with the public interest in mind. This model had been germinating in his mind while he was teaching in Germany and working for Western Electric, an electrical engineering and manufacturing company, in the United States.[24] When Dr Hendrick Verwoerd became Prime Minister, he adopted the industrialisation model developed by van der Bijl. This was after the Transvaal wing of the National Party took over from the Cape Province wing. Van der Bijl's plan suited the grand design of apartheid

---

24 Western Electric was later incorporated into the Bell Telephone Company.

which placed foreign direct investment in a secondary position to domestic investment and thus threatened British private capital's interest and investment space in the South African economy. The SAF was formed as a countervailing strategy to van der Bijl's, which threatened foreign investment interests from countries like Britain.

Dr van der Bijl was the founding chairman of the Electricity Supply Commission (ESCOM, later ESKOM) in 1923. In 1927, he was elected president of the South African Institute of Electrical Engineers (SAIEE). He also established the Iron and Steel Corporation (ISCOR) and was its chairman for many years. The city of Vanderbijlpark, where ISCOR's major steel works was built, is named after him. This area was established to allow black workers direct access to workplaces without them having to go through white residential areas. He was also chancellor of the University of Pretoria from 1934 until 1948 when he died at the age of 61. In South Africa, he was a central figure in shaping its economy during the World War II years when he was the Director General of War Supplies. He was a family friend of General Louis Botha, General Jan C. Smuts, J. B. Hertzog, and Sammy Marks, the Lithuanian-born industrialist and financier who worked closely with Paul Kruger in the old South African republic. The foregoing background on Dr van der Bijl is instructive for understanding the influence he exerted on shaping the growth of the country's state-owned enterprises, which drove the economy and provided job opportunities for Afrikaners. His approach was an earlier version of state capitalism, which preceded the recent Chinese type in which state-owned enterprises are the leading drivers of economic growth ahead of foreign direct investment.

There was a significant political incident that occurred towards the end of the 1970s. It had to do with a meeting in New York City between myself and Johnstone 'Jonny' Mfanafuthi Makhathini, who became the head of the ANC Mission to the United Nations. Two of the first people who met him a day or so after his arrival at the Beaux Arts Hotel, located a block from the United Nations, were me and Joanna. We presented him with a comprehensive brief on what the United States' position was towards South Africa but, more importantly, with information on the different solidarity organisations engaged in the anti-apartheid movement. Later, out of concern for how the ANC could be more effective in its representation in the US, I drew up an agenda of matters for us to discuss. This agenda is dated May 5, 1977. The first item on it was US representation both at the United Nations and throughout the US and the organisational efforts that were required. The second item dealt with the proposed ANC guidelines that were to govern the committees that would be formed to carry out various tasks. The third item advanced reasons why a strong US representation and organisation were vital. The reasons were that the US is the heart of capitalism and the new imperialism and also influenced the West's policies on Southern Africa. The fourth item dealt with the attempt to develop an efficient communications network among all ANC offices and its head office in Lusaka, Zambia. Added to this agenda was the critical roles of the United Nations, the Universities across the US, the Communist Party of the US, the African-American and Hispanic populations, Liberal Democrats, churches, and individuals not associated with political organisations.

In sharing this agenda with Jonny, I thought the issues raised, and hopefully discussed, would assist in integrating all operational centres; keep selective but vital information flowing through these centres; increasingly ensure that people in and outside the ANC were informed; cultivate an image of an efficient and effective organisation deserving support in its struggle to liberate South Africa; attract and recruit into the ANC 'healthy' South Africans who were not engaged in the struggle for whatever reasons; demonstrate the capacity and strength of the ANC internationally; and pre-empt the opportunism of some individuals and organisations who were known to disseminate false information about South Africa and the liberation movements. The last item was a proposal that the ANC began developing as a database on 'human resources and skills' that were available and necessary, particularly for non-military assignments during the different phases of the struggle and beyond.

The database idea came from having retrieved a list of all South African students who were studying in the United States at that time. I used this list to send out invitations to a meeting at which we would launch the ANC branch in New York City. This was in 1979. Some of the people who were there were the late Fred Dube, Barbara Masekela, and Moeletsi Mbeki, to name a few. The election of office holders was very interesting because Fred Dube was hoping to be elected as chairperson. He wasn't. Instead, Barbara got the overwhelming vote. I was nominated for the position of political commissar and supported by a majority because of the work I had been doing in the ANC since 1966. Fred vehemently opposed this nomination on the grounds that I was a former PAC leader at home, so I withdrew for the sake of avoiding divisions before the branch even started to function. Most of the people who were there felt very bad about what Fred had said. I took it in my stride because I had achieved my objective which was to establish a branch. Besides, Fred did not know how long I had been working on ANC initiatives in the United States since I left the PAC in 1966.

~

At the New School, I worked with determination, taking doctoral courses, writing examinations, searching for a dissertation topic, submitting it for approval, and then writing the dissertation under the supervision of three professors in the Economics Department. Working on my doctoral studies was very demanding, so much so that almost every alternate Saturday, Stanley Mahlahla and I would leave our homes in the morning and meet at the university to study and keep up with the workload of our economics courses. Stanley was from Southern Rhodesia. There were Saturdays when he would leave for Geneva where he would join thirteen other Southern Rhodesians, mostly Africans, who were engaged in research and attempting to understand the Southern Rhodesian economy and develop a national plan as they prepared for their country to achieve independence. This research project was initiated and led by Bernard Chidzero, an economist also from Southern Rhodesia who was then serving as Deputy Secretary General of the United Nations Conference on Trade and Development (UNCTAD). On one of the many days that Joanna and I spent in the Wertheim Study Room of the New York Public Library, I stumbled across a book on the economy of Southern

Rhodesia authored by Colin Stoneman. I took the details of this book and shared them with Stanley on the following Saturday when we met to study together. He was stunned and furious because Colin was part of the team working with him and others in Geneva but would often show up just to see what was happening, looking over his colleagues' shoulders, and leave. He never told any of his colleagues that he had already done some work on what they were busy researching nor did he contribute anything in the process. It was then that I asked Stanley to explain exactly what they were doing in Geneva. I took notes of what he said.

The colleagues working out of Geneva in 1978 were Bernard Chidzero, Kombo Moyana, Leonard Tsumba, Stanley Mahlahla, Daniel Ndlela, Ibbo Mandaza, and eight others. In 1976, the Zimbabwe African Peoples' Union (ZAPU) had begun working along similar lines as the Chidzero team. In 1977, the Zimbabwe African National Union (ZANU) approached ZAPU and proposed that this exercise be a joint venture. The combined group of fourteen people came largely from the two major parties, ZAPU and ZANU, from in and outside Southern Rhodesia. It included three whites, one of them the aforementioned Colin Stoneman, a British citizen. Some members of this group worked full-time on the project while others were part-time because of other job commitments and obligations, such as Chidzero and Moyana at the UN in Geneva and New York respectively and Stanley who was working on his doctorate at the New School. The UN had provided financial assistance for the project amounting to between $500 000 and $750 000.

What was striking to me was the method this team had developed and decided to use. First, they studied the past ten to twenty years of socio-economic history of the country, since past trends help to explain the present. Second, in the process of investigating the past, they focused on developing an understanding and grasp of the economy of the country. Third, with a better understanding and appreciation of the economy, they examined in depth and detail the individual sectors and industries within this economy. Fourth, when investigating these sectors and industries, they identified the inequities faced by black people in order to correct them. Fifth, they analysed these inequities and designed solutions to ameliorate them. These solutions were the basis of future realistic government policies. The solutions ranged from outright nationalisation (with or without compensation) through to buying shares in strategic or key firms with the objective of privatisation. They were also mindful and careful about choosing realistic solutions by not 'throwing out the baby with the bath water' in appeasing the prevailing African Nationalist political rhetoric. I think the dictum was 'take what you find (or get) and gradually but deliberately transform it'. The project took about one year.

From being familiar with the origins of this initiative, the participants, and how they designed a simple but revealing method that would help inform their country's development plan, I came away with the following observations. First, the method laid out was like a 'war plan'; therefore, it had to be accorded the security and urgency that go with such a plan. Second, some of the glaring inequities were found in the agriculture and mining sectors. Several primary issues that were identified were the ownership and distribution of land, investment in the economy and manufacturing, employment patterns, and wage and profit rates. When it was clear that independence was around the corner, large multinational firms began moving out their assets in order to reduce their exposure in case they were 'taken over'. Smaller firms did not follow suit. In fact, they developed adversarial attitudes towards the large multinationals and consequently acted as allies to the liberation movements that took over in 1980.

The report of this project is titled *Zimbabwe: Towards a New Order: An Economic and Social Survey: Working Papers, Volumes 1 and 2* (UN, 1980). Of the range of realistic policies adopted by the Zimbabwean government in addressing economic issues, nationalisation was dropped. Building state-owned and state-operated firms that would compete with existing firms in the private sector was contemplated, but quietly buying into existing key and strategic companies was adopted as the best immediate to medium-term strategy. My wishful observation was that both the ANC and PAC as well as their respective affiliates would follow the example of their Zimbabwean colleagues to some extent.

13

A Changing Family

Our second child was born on the 30th of July 1980 at New York hospital in Manhattan, like our first. We named her Thenjiwe, which in Zulu means 'the one who is trusted'. Her middle name, Niki, is from the ancient Greek goddess of victory, Nike. Again, it is a marvel that she, like her brother, has also lived up to the names we gave her. As I look back, I see that getting married and having a wedding was a celebratory event which we enjoyed with a few members of our family and many friends and colleagues from teaching institutions. But raising a family was a serious and very personal journey into the unknown.

The children both grew up playing in the streets of Hoboken but going to school in Manhattan. Joanna drove back and forth through the Lincoln Tunnel for several years with Mandla and Thenjiwe and our friends Amy and Geoff's two children, Jonathan and Susanna Bass, who were about the same age. She would drop the kids in lower Manhattan and dash along the East Side Highway up to Harlem where she taught at City College, then pick them up on her way back. When Joanna needed to travel to conduct research for her doctoral thesis, I would be left to look after the children with the aid of very capable and loving helpers and a couple of neighbours. Then when I travelled to London and Oxford for my doctoral thesis, she would manage the kids in similar ways. In both cases, as difficult as these times apart were, we both enjoyed the one-on-one time with the children when one of us was away. I still remember the fun times I had with Mandla in Central Park. These were filled with pretzels, hotdogs, ice cream, and bagels with different spreads, which we ate when we weren't going on the kids' rides.

But the greatest treat was during the summer recess when both Joanna and I had summer breaks and weren't teaching. These were times for holidays, rest, family get-togethers, some research, and writing our dissertations. Almost every summer break after our marriage involved driving to the twin towns of Biddeford and Saco in Maine to see Joanna's family. Once the children were born, Chresoula's attitude softened significantly, and her feelings towards me became much warmer. Thanksgivings, Christmases, and summer holidays were pilgrimages that we all looked forward to. In our case, the long distance from Hoboken to Maine was filled with adventure and excitement. It took us five to six hours to drive there. The drive was generally quite scenic for Joanna and me but not for Mandla and Thenjiwe, who always wanted to know whether we had reached our destination, even though we had hardly left New York and still had go through Connecticut, Massachusetts, and New Hampshire before crossing the bridge into Maine. The nagging would often be distracted by the many provisions Joanna had bought at different Jewish and Greek delis and packed for the trip. We all looked forward to spending quality time with the family, outdoor activities, and Greek cuisine and treats made by the best chef the families had, Chresoula.

Apart from spending time holidaying in Maine during our summer breaks, I got involved in what was a useful experience as a consultant to the Pepperell Trust Company, a local bank that was started by the family of my brother-in-law, David Shaw, and was co-owned by David and Mary, Joanna's sister. Given my experience in teaching at a graduate business school and engaging in some consulting work, I offered to assist Mary and David in any way I could to improve and modernise their bank. They accepted my offer without reservations.

As an example of what I did, an entry in my diary lists the following files, which were well-developed and ready to be used in writing up the pertinent projects to be executed. These were the loan policy, the officer call program, pricing selective bank services, adjustable mortgage rates, student loan program, micro-computer uses in the bank, a teller training program, review resumés for four prospective employees, an organogram for the bank, job descriptions for all the employees, the strategic plan, and budget. The last two were critical for the state and federal governments' regulatory agencies. Because what I was working on was very critical, at some point I organised a seminar hosted by the bank and invited a former colleague from

A Changing Family

Rutgers Graduate Business School, Professor Paul Nadler, to lead the discussions. Paul was a renowned and widely respected authority on community banks. The seminar was very successful and the advice he gave was invaluable. It also helped to confirm my initiatives.

In reflecting on these times with family, both resting with them and working with them, I doubt whether I would have managed in exile without Joanna and her family. Although it was rocky in the beginning, they eventually took me in as one of their own. Even though I was still, at the time, classified as a stateless person by the US Department of Immigration, because of them, I did not really feel like a fugitive anymore.

14

Hofstra

In the second half of 1981, I accepted a teaching position at Hofstra University in Hempstead on Long Island. From Hoboken, the commute was long and hard. My first class began at nine in the morning. I had to leave home quite early to catch a PATH subway going to 33rd Street and 6th Avenue in Manhattan. I would then walk quickly across 33rd Street to the main station of the Long Island Rail Road below Madison Square Garden to catch a train to Hempstead. This was during peak travel times in the morning when Long Islanders were coming to the city to work. My daily struggle was navigating my way through the hordes of passengers who were disgorged out of the trains and were competing to get onto the escalators or run up the stairs to exit the station and head for work. I learned to coast along the walls of the shops in order to avoid being crashed into and trampled by the stampede. As I coasted, I had to look out for the homeless people who sought refuge by huddling against the walls of the shops out of the way of the stampede. The numbers of homeless people were at their largest during the winters, and this scene highlighted the desperate economic and social difficulties faced by very poor people in New York City.

Despite the gruelling commute and the teaching schedule, I enjoyed Hofstra University. This university is the largest private and not-for-profit, non-sectarian institution of higher learning located on Long Island in the Village of Hempstead. It was established in 1935 as an extension of New York University (NYU) but in 1937, it severed its connection with NYU. Its students came from fairly diverse racial, ethnic, cultural, religious, and socio-economic backgrounds. During my time there, I was teaching at the undergraduate level, and students tended to come with open minds and were curious to experience what it was like being in college. Many of them found the transition from high school to college very challenging. Most were uncertain about what they wanted to study and why. Some were there simply because after graduating high school, the next destination was college. Others were there because their parents told them to go to college. There were others who came for all sorts of reasons, including drifting with the go-to-college tide. At Rutgers Graduate Business School, however, students knew exactly what they had signed up for: it was to graduate with MBAs. This degree opened up the prospects of being able to climb the corporate ladder wherever they were employed.

I was appointed as an assistant professor in the Economics Department. Subjects that I taught were macro- and micro-economics, government and business, and economic development in Third World countries. There was a sizable number of black students, mostly from the West Indies, who organised themselves and motivated the university to establish an Africana Studies Programme, and they succeeded. I was asked to be the director of the programme, a position I accepted with great enthusiasm even though I had a heavy teaching load. One of the first university-wide lectures this programme organised was delivered by the late Professor Herbert G. Gutman, a distinguished social and labour historian at the Graduate Centre of the City University of New York, who also happened to be Joanna's doctoral supervisor. His topic was the 'Black Family and Growth in Slavery and Freedom.' The lecture was held at the Student Centre Theatre of the university. Black students on the main campus were politically conscious and very sensitive to issues affecting black people both in the US and in underdeveloped countries, especially those in Africa and the Caribbean. Issues that touched on slavery, the conditions facing black families, and civil rights were frequently discussed given their currency in the country. This lecture enhanced the stature of the programme and attracted more students to the courses I taught.

~

On the 1st of January 1983, I made the following entries in my diary (I think they were my New Year's resolutions). The first was to spend more time with my family, including going on vacations. The second was to help Joanna work on her doctoral dissertation by taking on more of the family and domestic chores. Third, fix both the major and minor things in our three-storey home. Fourth, reorganise the Africana Studies Programme at Hofstra by designing new courses, producing a new brochure, planning events, and writing a proposal for the programme to have its own budget. At the New School Graduate Centre, I was involved in establishing a Political Economy Track Alumni Association with the help of some of my radical classmates, Frank Roosevelt, Phil Harvey, and Nadine Felton, among others. On the South African political front, I planned to organise a group of South African activists to work on tracking US investments and trade with South Africa, cutting out business sections of the international edition of *The Star* for analysis, and extracting from the same newspaper all articles on labour in South Africa. This newspaper was available at a shop on 42nd Street between 6th Avenue and Broadway. The last diary entry stated that I needed to select fields that I wanted to spend the rest of my life engaged in. South Africa was number one. Number two was labour, in South Africa and Internationally. Third, was the study of multinational corporations; last, but not least, was economic development. I had set myself rather ambitious and daunting goals.

I decided to follow through on the first of these resolutions – to spend more time with the family – by initiating a trip to Nova Scotia in Canada. The adventure was a success, and I think it might be worth relating it here in some detail, since it was one of the few trips I had taken for leisure in my life up to that point.

On the 4th of July, Independence Day, Mary and Chresoula drove four of us and Jere, our nephew, to Portland to board the MS Scotia Prince bound for Yarmouth in Nova Scotia. This ship left Portland at 9 p.m. All five of us were in a small, tight room, cabin 569. There was a section on the ship where gambling took place, and at 10:30 p.m. people descended like a mob upon the machines. It was a sight we had never seen before. Naturally, the kids wanted to play some games, and Joanna and I tried our luck on the slot machines (we lost). We left shortly thereafter for our tiny cabin. The ship arrived in Yarmouth the next morning at 8 a.m., and we went through Canadian customs (astoundingly, to me) simply on our word, without having to produce any documents. It was a wet, misty day. We picked up a rented car from Avis, a Pontiac Parisienne, and checked in to the Grand Hotel, where we had some breakfast before driving up the Evangeline Trail going north. This drive gave us a good look at rural underdevelopment, which brought home the crucial importance of the basic infrastructure necessary for developing fishing, subsistence agricultural, pastoral farming, cottage industries, and social cohesion in rural communities. Later, in the afternoon, we returned to Yarmouth where we visited the Yarmouth Historical Society. The curator showed us around both floors, which were studded with maritime historical collections of pictures of ships, soldiers and settlements, artefacts, and other memorabilia, all beautifully arranged.

We then decided to include Halifax in our itinerary and thus extend our stay in Nova Scotia. This required making some changes to the car rental, the boat we were sailing on, hotel reservations, and of course alerting the Greek tribal chiefs in Maine. After re-arranging our itinerary, we had dinner at Forchu's on Maine Street in Yarmouth. We left Yarmouth and the Grand Hotel the next day after breakfast. Halifax was about 300 km from Yarmouth. We drove through Yarmouth county, which was relatively well populated and quite pretty. Shelburne County was very interesting because of its United Empire Loyalists history and dominance dating back to 1783. The other counties we drove through had very rocky terrains with sparse vegetation and trees. But the closer we got to Halifax, the more beautiful the scenery became. Once we got there, we checked in at the Holiday Inn on the corner of Robie and Quinpool streets, and were given a room with a terrific view of the city and its surrounds.

After dinner at a nearby restaurant, we drove around a little and soon spotted Dalhousie University, about which Joanna and I had heard very complimentary things. It was good to see it even if we did not enter the campus. Altogether this was a very promising start to our short visit to Halifax, and we were all quite happy with how we had spent the day. The next day was also eventful. We visited the Citadel, a historical fort, which was fun and instructive. It included a staged scene of the Canadian Mounted Rifles wearing Stetson hats in the South African Anglo-Boer War of 1899 to 1902. From the Citadel we drove to Dartmouth. It was quite distressing to visit the community of African Nova Scotians because of the abject poverty we saw there, especially considering that the first black person in Nova Scotia is recorded as being one of the founders of Port Royal in 1604. The black community of Nova Scotia grew out of slavery during the 17th and 18th centuries.

We returned to Halifax's Maritime Museum of the Atlantic, another high point and an educational experience for all of us, as we learned the basic principles of steam power and observed working engines that illustrated these principles. From there we drove to Point Pleasant, where we took a walk while many young people jogged past us in both directions. That evening we sampled another restaurant, then checked out early the next morning. At the rotary on our way out, we saw reflections of houses in the lake. It was a magnificent sight on a cool, clean, sunny morning. The rest of the trip back to Yarmouth was one of great natural beauty, with mist hanging over lakes and valleys. It took us three hours to get back to Yarmouth. The next morning, after breakfast, we returned the car to Avis and went to the port, where we lined up to board the MS Scotia Prince. Luckily, this time we got a larger cabin. We arrived back in Portland a few minutes after 9 p.m., and the summer holiday of 1983 was over. We went back home to Hoboken and I got down to the work of finishing my dissertation.

~

The fall of 1983 was a crucial time for me because I was in the process of putting the final touches on my dissertation and getting ready to defend it. On Wednesday the 16th of November, my advisor, the late Professor David Gordon, in consultation with four other professors from the Graduate Faculty in the Political Science, Sociology, and Economics Departments, had set Wednesday the 1st of February 1984 as the date of my defence. I had the rest of November, December, and January to prepare myself for the unknown under the scrutiny of five professors, three from the Economics Department and two from the Political Science and Sociology departments. I worked hard to get ready. I remember well when the day and hour came. Walking down Washington Street to catch the PATH subway from Hoboken to Manhattan on 14th Street and 6th Avenue, and walking to the corner of 14th Street and 5th Avenue where part of the New School was located, was weird. Even though there were people on the streets and in the subway and I saw them, I was totally wrapped up in my own anxieties and thoughts about my defence. Once in the school building, a little before the set time, I waited outside a large classroom where five of my 'inquisitors' were caucusing and interrogating my work before inviting me to come in and defend it.

When David Gordon opened the door to the classroom, my heart went into overdrive out of anxiety and fear. Luckily, the seats were arranged round an oval table and thus the atmosphere was less intimidating. The questions were deliberate and to the point. They had to do with my sources (given the fact that I could not go to South Africa), and with the methodology and the fact that some comparative studies were limited. Days before this defence I kept repeating to myself that no one in the examination committee knew my work as well as I did. This gave me strength and courage and fortified my resolve to defend my thesis successfully. I don't remember how long this gruelling interrogation lasted. When I was finally asked to leave the room and wait outside, one request was that, if possible, I should find some figures to add to a section that dealt with wages of black and white miners in the mines. I walked out and waited. I lost track of how long I sat and waited outside with my eyes fixed on the door to the room in which I had just been tortured. When it finally opened, and David appeared smiling and said, 'Come in, Dr Nkosi', I was dumbfounded. Once inside, all five professors stood up to shake my hand and congratulate me. My response was a rapid series of exuberant thank yous because I honestly did not know how else to react. Afterwards I walked across Fifth Avenue, on to 13th Street, and passed our old apartment, almost oblivious of the traffic and people along the way. My head was in the clouds all the way home to Hoboken.

15

Manley

My students at Hofstra who were taking courses on economic development in African and Caribbean countries wanted more than just textbook exposure. One of them, their spokesperson, Rhoan Cassells, asked me to invite the former Prime Minister of Jamaica, Honourable Michael Manley, to come and give a lecture on international trade and its impact on economic development in the Caribbean. They assisted me in getting in touch with him when he was in New York City, and I introduced myself and explained the origins of the request. He was very understanding and agreed to come and give a lecture. We arranged a date, time, and place at which I would pick him up in New York City and drive with him to Hempstead. I collected him on the set day and time. We were in a car on our way to the campus when he asked me to remind him what he was expected to talk about. I couldn't believe it. I was a little stunned, scared, and worried but stayed calm and contained my feelings. I carefully went over the Africana Studies Programme, its students, and the courses I taught, including the one on international trade. I reminded him that the students' request was for him to speak on how international trade affected developing Caribbean countries such as Jamaica. Unfazed, he said that that was fine. The campus had been blanketed with leaflets announcing this important lecture to be given by Michael Manley.

The auditorium was packed to capacity with students and faculty members from different departments. I had put together a short and impressive resumé about our guest speaker which I used to introduce him. Michael Manley was the son of the father of Jamaica's independence. He was a graduate of the London School of Economics, a fighter pilot in the Canadian Air Force, a trade union negotiator, a civil rights activist, and a member of the People's National Party. He rose through the party ranks to become the party's leader in 1968 and Prime Minister of Jamaica from 1972 until 1980. It is said that during his tenure as Prime Minister, he attempted to establish a democratic welfare state in the northern American periphery, steering a course between the Cuban revolution and the Puerto Rican model of total dependence on the United States.

His lecture focused on what is called 'triangular trade', an historical term which refers to trade among three regions or ports. The classical model depicting this type of trade shows how slaves were shipped from Africa to the Americas where they were sold and worked on plantations growing sugar cane, tobacco, and cotton. These raw commodities were then shipped to the northeast of America and Europe where they were processed into sugar, rum, tobacco, textiles, and other manufactured goods. The final products were then shipped and sold in African countries at much higher prices than they were sourced for in their raw state. Using this model, the former Prime Minister chose three regions, West Africa (Ghana and the Ivory Coast in particular), the Caribbean, and Britain. Cocoa grown in West Africa was harvested, sold, and then shipped to Britain. Sugar cane grown in the West Indies was harvested, also sold, and then shipped to Britain. In Britain, both the imported cocoa and sugar cane were processed in the manufacture of chocolates, rum, and other goodies which were then shipped to West Africa, including Ghana and the Ivory Coast, where they were sold at prices that were multiples of what was paid for them as raw sugar cane and cocoa. The prices Britain had paid when sourcing these raw commodities were much lower than the prices it charged for the manufactured products that it sold to West Africa, the Caribbean, and other markets. The resulting terms of trade favoured Britain much more than West Africa and the Caribbean. This imbalance retards the development and growth of the economies of Ghana, the Ivory Coast, and Jamaica.

Manley's lecture was riveting, in part because he spoke without any notes. It was clear that he had first-hand experience of what international trade meant and how the terms of trade affected countries at the same level of development as Jamaica. Even when it came to answering questions, it was evident that he had extensive practical experience in issues associated with international trade. His academic tenure at the London School of Economics and experience in the trade union activities and premiership of the country were all evident. The lecture was very successful. It was exactly the information and knowledge my students were curious about. It also helped my students and those who attended better understand and appreciate what was called triangular trade. It gave them a better grasp and understanding of the practical implications of the contents of the textbooks that I had prescribed for the course dealing with international trade and economic development in less developed countries.

Long after Manley's lecture, I discovered one of the earliest versions of the expression 'triangular trade' when I read a book authored by Noel Rae titled *The Great Stain: Witnessing American Slavery*. Noel Rae credits Sir John Hawkins as having coined this term. It seems that in the sixteenth century Hawkins left England with three ships on an adventure funded by several wealthy English investors who, Rae writes, 'burst upon the African slave trade in the usual vigorous and self-righteous manner – a drawn sword on one hand, a Bible on the other'. It was as early as 1562 when Hawkins sailed into the West Indies. When he gave up trading slaves in favour of other adventures, he wrote a short book called *An Alliance to Raid for Slaves*. In this alliance, he advocated for joint operations with African rulers who would be expected to deliver slaves to him and his fellow slavers. By buying goods in England, exchanging them for slaves in Africa, bartering the slaves in the West Indies for gold, sugar, hides, ginger, pearls, and other local products, then selling these on his return to England, he would earn a large profit at each corner of the triangular trade, says Noel Rae. And this was in the 1560s while Michael Manley's lecture was in the 1984. Triangular trade had evolved over four hundred years on the backs of black human beings.

The economics department at Hofstra University established another creative and challenging programme, which was based in Manhattan at 13 Astor Place, the head offices of District Council 65, located on the east side of the Village. The Economics Department itself was located on the main campus in Hempstead and consisted of several male professors, most of them Jewish and progressive, one white woman who was not Jewish, and me. One of the men, Bertram Silverman, had worked as a trade union economist. He approached the leadership of District Council 65 with a proposal offering evening college courses to its union members. The trade union accepted. He then used this consent to motivate the university's main campus administration to approve this proposal and agree to award a joint university-trade union college bachelor's degree for working adults who would be taking courses in the evening programme taught by members of the economics department from the main campus. The university agreed. This programme was called the District Council 37/Hofstra Labor Institute. I was drafted to teach a couple of economics courses at the Institute in the evenings.

The District Council 65 traces its origins back to 1933 when a group of workers in the dry goods warehouses on the New York Lower East Side formed the Wholesale Dry Goods Workers Union. Through a series of mergers, it grew to over 15 000 members in the early 1940s. During the post-war years, the union expanded its reach and eventually represented workers in such diverse fields as publishing, museums, and university administrations. It was known for its participation in social issues of the day, including the women's movement, the civil rights movement, and efforts to end the Vietnam War. A book written by Lisa Phillips titled *Renegade Unionism: A History of District 65* (University of Illinois Press, 2012) chronicles most of these activities. These and other social issues of the time resonated with the ideological and political views of all the faculty members of the Economics Department.

Teaching college courses in the evenings to adults who had graduated from high schools several years ago and were all employed during the day was a daunting task. What was taught during the day at the main campus in Hempstead was what we had to teach in the evenings at District Council 65 in Manhattan. The evening students were enrolled with the goal of graduating with the same degrees as the day students on the main campus, so the course contents had to be the same for both the day and evenings students. Professor Paul Samuelson's tome of a textbook on economics had to be used creatively by simplifying and pitching it to the level of adult evening students. They came to classes after a full day's work and were already tired by then. But they were determined to get the education and qualifications that came with it. This would improve their prospects of promotion at work. Paul Samuelson's *Economics: An Introductory Analysis* (1948) and Leonard Silk's *Economics in Plain English: All you need to know about economics – in a language anyone can understand* (1978), were the two basic textbooks that I chose to use.

Paul Samuelson was a professor at the Massachusetts Institute of Technology. *The New York Times* considered him the foremost academic of the 20th century. Leonard Silk was an economic columnist for *The New York Times*, a former Senior Fellow of the Brookings Institution, and also taught as Ford Foundation Distinguished Professor at Carnegie-Mellon University. My students, in both the evening and day classes, benefitted from the creative pedagogy of using the two books together. I myself also learned quite a bit through using these two books. I became increasingly aware that one of the hallmarks of a good teacher was to take what appeared to be complex textbook formulations and to recraft, distil these, and present them in simple and understandable English. This ability went a long way in demystifying the subject for my students as well as for me. The pass rate of my students in the evening classes was as good as that of the day students, and the fact that both groups graduated with the same degrees was the high point of my teaching career at Hofstra University. Altogether this university helped me grow as a person through my responsibilities in the Economics Department and in the Africana Studies and District Council 65 programmes.

Mandla and Thenjiwe Nkosi in school uniforms from St George's and Chisipite, Harare, Zimbabwe 1989.

Mandla, Morley and Thenjiwe with family pets, Kim and Aslan, outside home in Harare, Zimbabwe, 1990.

16

USA For Africa

Sometime at the beginning of 1983 while I was still teaching at Hofstra, I was invited by Michael Manley to the launch of his book, *Jamaica: Struggle in the Periphery*. We had kept in touch after Michael's lecture at Hofstra. The event was to be held at the Community Church of New York on East 35th Street. The Community Church was a Unitarian Universalist parish whose congregation was actively engaged in issues of social and political justice in the United States and beyond, including in South Africa.

When I arrived at the church, I immediately noticed, amid the crowd, three tall men chatting. I recognised one of them to be Michael, but at first I couldn't place the other two, even though their faces were familiar. It turned out that one was Harry Belafonte and the other was Sidney Poitier. Michael must have told Harry about me, because that's when Harry turned around with his inimitable smile, standing tall, and said to me: 'I'll be damned. We are running this thing called USA for Africa, but we don't have an African in there. I'd like you to come and join us.' I had a vague idea of what USA for Africa was all about, but it was hard for me to concentrate; I was simply overwhelmed to find myself in this company. To this day it seems fantastic that I met all three of them like that at the same time. Harry, who began to tell me more about the project, was very easy to talk to; in fact, none of them had pretensions of any kind, despite their accomplishments.

Later, when we made time to talk properly, Harry explained how he and Ken Kragen had formed the United Support of Artists for Africa (USA for Africa) after Harry's visit to Ethiopia in 1984, where he witnessed first-hand the ravages of the famine. I gladly accepted Harry's invitation and served on its Africa Review Board. The board's task was to read and assess hundreds of applications received by the organisation for funds for a variety of projects in different countries of sub-Saharan Africa. On this board I met Maurice Strong, the Canadian diplomat who had served as Under

Secretary of the United Nations. Another prominent member of this board was John Gerhart, who was with the Ford Foundation and would later serve as the foundation's representative in South Africa before moving on to be president of the American University in Cairo. John was married to Gail whom I had met in the mid-1960s when I had gone to speak on South Africa at Harvard University. Several decades later, Professor Gail Gerhart was awarded the Order of Companions of O. R. Tambo by the Presidency of South Africa for her significant research, writing, and publishing detailing the liberation struggle and African resistance to apartheid.

USA for Africa is best remembered for its recording of the song 'We are the World' on the 28th of January 1985 and the 'Hands Across America' event in 1986. In the 30 years of USA for Africa's existence, it raised more than $100 million that went to help ease the pain and ravages of poverty and starvation in parts of Africa and the United States. It accomplished its goal of creating opportunities to make a difference in the lives of affected people. 'Hands Across America' was a consciousness-raising, fundraising, and grant-making project that funded poverty programmes in the United States only. I remember attending 'The Fourth Annual World Hunger Media Awards' organised by Kenny and Marianne Rogers and hosted by Walter Cronkite at the United Nations on the 26th of November 1985, where I watched a clip showing a poor white family somewhere in the southern part of the United States surviving on harvesting, cooking, and eating cactus plants almost every day. This short film highlighted the existence of poverty in the United States, something that not a lot of people know exists in the 'land of plenty'.

Apart from serving on the Africa Review Board, I was also assigned the job of visiting some of the organisations shortlisted for possible funding by the board and evaluating their viability. This was the important thing about my involvement in USA for Africa: it really gave me the experience a development economist needs to have, the practical experience of economic development, and not only the theoretical knowledge gained in graduate programmes. When I think back to what Tony Alile[25] and I had in mind when we were students – our determination to make contributions to changing our countries and the continent – I see that USA for Africa gave me the opportunity, years later, to do exactly that.

My return to the continent felt very significant, not least because West Africa and the DRC were both new to me. Overall, I was happy to be there for work and to be able to use my knowledge and experience to help African countries make needed changes. For this reason, I felt driven, and went about my work there with determination and focus. I enjoyed meeting people, listening to their stories, and sharing my expertise. But on an emotional level, it was strangely underwhelming. Although it was an African context, it still felt far away from South Africa: it didn't feel like home.

On my first visits to West and East Africa, a second generation of umbrella NGOs were being established. One of these was the Forum of Voluntary Development Organisations (FAVDO), which was formed in 1986 when I happened to be in Senegal. Its founder and executive officer was Mazide Ndiaye, a charismatic and very capable nationalist who was fluent in French, English, and, of course, the local dialects. Ndiaye was also a founding member of the Forum of African Voluntary Development Organizations (FAVDO). He was very well respected in the NGO communities in both the north and south. I had the privilege and honour of working alongside him while on missions for USA for Africa. Through this organisation, I was able to meet

---

25 Upon his return to Nigeria, Tony became the head of the Management Consulting Department at the Centre for Management Development in Nigeria in 1973. Its primary role was to promote the development of indigenous small to medium-sized businesses. In 1976 he became the head of the Nigerian Stock Exchange where he served for 24 years. He was also a close confidant of Chief Mashood Abiola. He and Chief Abiola persistently tried to persuade me to come and live in Nigeria, seeing that I could not go home to South Africa. Tony also served as a board member of several major companies in Nigeria, including the Central Bank of Nigeria and the Security Printing and Minting Company. In 2001, he was ordained as an Apostle in a church that was founded by his parents, the St Joseph's Chosen Church of God. Sadly, after celebrating his 80th birthday in grand style, which Joanna and I attended, he passed away in October 2018.

and vet some of the organisations and people in Senegal who had applied for funding. I visited the sites that had requested funding to assess their needs and further process their applications. These and other site visits and assessments of projects in different countries deepened my understanding of what was expected of a development economist. The experience I gained gave me a lot of confidence in my assignment, and I remain indebted to Harry Belafonte for this development and growth in my professional career. He was later recognised for his significant contribution to the liberation struggle against apartheid when he received the Order of Companions of O. R. Tambo from the Presidency of South Africa. Harry and I remained close friends, keeping in touch even after I left the US. His death in 2023 left a hole in my life.

~

During this period, I was still teaching at Hofstra University. Reflecting on my happy years teaching there, I feel compelled to relate three memorable stories. The first has to do with the composition of the Economics Department. This department was much smaller than the one at the Graduate Business School at Rutgers University. Its chairperson, Jacob Wiseman, was, true to his name, a wise, venerable, and progressive intellectual. On the day that he called me into his office to inform me that the University had granted me tenure, he relayed some interesting stories that had been circulating about me for some time. The department had two 'minority persons', Helen Updike, a white woman, and me. During registration periods when students were choosing subjects they wanted to register for, word was that if you were really and truly committed to studying economics, you would sign up for Professor Nkosi's classes. 'But be careful,' Professor Wiseman related with a smile, 'he is very demanding.' The latter was true. Unacceptable work in my classes meant getting a 'D' grade, which stood for poor, or an 'F', which meant failure. Not all students appreciated this. It turned out that when I gave out such grades, some students went home and complained to their parents, who would come and speak to Professor Wiseman. He told me that he would simply listen to the unhappy and sometimes angry parents and respond by saying that Professor Nkosi knew what he was doing and was a good teacher. What they actually said

Professor Wiseman would not tell me. He just chuckled. What he found interesting, though, was the response to twenty-five letters sent to a randomly selected group of students who had taken my courses over the four years, asking whether they thought I should be granted tenure. All had said yes. When he told me this part of the story, we both had a good laugh, considering the complaints he had been fielding on my behalf for the past four years.

The second story has to do with a very smart white student in one of my classes. She was the best in her class, and from time to time I would ask her to proctor my class if I had to go to my office or the administration offices. She liked working with me. It seems that she had picked up on some of the complaints that certain students had voiced about me, and one day she told me that she had told her father about me. I don't know what she told her father. But she came back to tell me that if I had any problems with some of the white students, I should let her know – her father would take care of them. She hinted that he was a leading member of the Italian brotherhood on Long Island. I was a little surprised and taken aback because I quickly remembered that Hoboken, where I lived, had the same brotherhood, which provided me and my family with some protection merely by having accepted us into the community. Here I was on Long Island now being offered protection again.

The third incident was also an eye-opener for me. A few very smart and curious students, including my proctoring assistant, persuaded me to arrange a visit to the Federal Reserve Bank of New York. The motivation for this arose from one of the economics courses I was teaching, which dealt with international trade and how at some period gold was used to settle payments between trading countries when their foreign reserves were insufficient to settle accounts. In the course of interrogating this financial aspect of international trade and the use of gold, a question arose about which country was holding what amount of gold and where. My response was that some of the largest reserves of gold were in the United States at Fort Knox, the International Monetary Fund, and the Federal Reserve Bank of New York. I had aroused too much curiosity and was then asked whether the class could visit the Federal Reserve Bank in New York, since it was a short train ride from Hempstead on Long Island to downtown New York City. They wanted to see the gold themselves, and I agreed.

I called the Federal Reserve Bank and told them who I was and what my students had asked me to arrange. My request was promptly and very efficiently processed. I had twenty or so of my students meet me in front of the Bank, which was on Wall Street, because I was coming from Hoboken, which is in the opposite direction from Hempstead. Once we were all assembled in front of the Bank, we walked in and had to sign the daily register. We were briefed on the procedures to be followed, which included not taking any pictures. It was not long before a white, stocky officer dressed in a white, long-sleeved shirt and a black tie, black pants, and well-polished black shoes separated us into two groups to avoid cramming us into one elevator. When both groups had reached rock bottom of the building and were ready for what we thought was going to be a tour, the officer escorting us said there would be no walking around. He pointed to a massive, shiny, circular steel door with a diameter of about six feet. That, he said, was the entry to the vaults containing the gold we had come to see.

Only two officials had the code to open this huge steel door. One knew only half the code; the other knew the rest. The second officer had not arrived. We were waiting for him when I suddenly spotted an impressive drawing on the wall directly facing the gold vault. This was a very skilful drawing of the Witwatersrand Gold Fields in South Africa. I was surprised and amazed. I was at that stage making the final touches to my doctoral dissertation, which was titled *Determinants of the Labor Structure on the Witwatersrand Gold Fields, 1902–10*. I drew my students' attention to this map but did not indicate what it meant to me. When the second official arrived, the first official went and entered his code then stepped back to allow the other one to do the same. Then both approached the heavy door and swung it open. When it swung open, we saw many cages stacked with gold bars though we were not allowed to enter the vault. Some cages had more gold than others, but there were no empty cages. We had never before seen so many gold bars. That was the end of the tour, but it was very instructive for all of us. For me, it confirmed my interest in the thesis topic I had chosen and urged me to complete my dissertation and defend it. I did defend it, as I have related, and was awarded my doctorate in 1984. I left Hofstra University in 1986 after being granted tenure. This was a major milestone in my academic career.

The commute between Hoboken in New Jersey and Hempstead on Long Island was gruelling, but moving to Long Island was out of the question for my family. I found a teaching position at Upsala College which was in East Orange, closer to home. Its name was chosen in honour of both the historic Uppsala University in Sweden and the Meeting of Uppsala, which firmly established Lutheran Orthodoxy in Sweden in 1593. Upsala College in the United States was originally founded in 1893 in Brooklyn, New York City. It later moved first to Kenilworth and then to East Orange in New Jersey in 1924. It was a private college affiliated with the Swedish-American Augustana Synod. I was appointed as an associate professor of economics and chairperson of the Departments of Accounting, Business Administration, and Economics. Being the chairperson of three departments and teaching economics courses was onerous, but I did not mind it because the college was small and so were the three departments I was responsible for. However, marking handwritten examination papers was taxing, and deciphering illegible handwriting and often trying to reconstruct strange English sentences in order to understand the intended meaning was torture. The teaching load was quite heavy, too, though the classes were small, and the teaching itself was enjoyable. And the fact that home was no more than an hour away on the Erie Lackawanna Railway from the East Orange station to Hoboken, which was the end of the rail line, made a huge difference. When I got off the train at the Hoboken station, I often walked home.

~

Sometime towards the end of 1985 I received a phone call from my brother, Stanley, to say that he was coming to the United States. By then, Stanley was a well-known music producer, and, as he explained, he would be travelling to the US with a colleague of his, a musician, producer, and songwriter by the name of Koloi Lebona. They were coming to have a meeting with EMI, an international record company. Stan was also trying to find a way of promoting a record company he had co-founded called Soul Brothers with the eponymous music group that he produced. By this time, black South Africans could travel more freely, and Stanley used this work trip as an opportunity to find me.

When I picked him and Koloi up at the airport, I couldn't recognise him. I was looking for a younger version of my brother, and standing there was a man with a prominent moustache. After a moment I realised that this was him. He immediately recognized me. He looked older, of course, because it had already been 25 years. He resembled our father because he too was tall and his moustache was like Stanley's. He had a camel-coloured coat on and was leading Koloi, who was blind, by the arm. The two of them stayed with us in Hoboken before travelling out to California for their work.

It was a wonderful visit. I heard the news of family and home in great detail, and how things were in South Africa. We ate a delicious rib dinner together one night that the two of them wouldn't stop talking about and that I, to this day, still happily remember. Having Stanley there made me feel hopeful that if I went back, there would still be people there whom I would know.

The next year, Stanley returned with his wife, Ruby, whom I had not seen since the morning I went into exile. We took them all over New York City and Maine with the children, who loved being with them. They stayed a few weeks, and it felt like my family of origin was finally getting to know the family I had made and raised in the US.

~

Around the same period, when I was teaching at Upsala College, I had a meeting with one John de St Jorre. Moeletsi Mbeki, son of ANC leader, Govan Mbeki, who was based in Harare, Zimbabwe, had suggested that I get in touch with John, as he was looking for South Africans to contribute to a project he was working on. John had a Ford Foundation assignment. He was a freelance writer who worked as a journalist, author, lecturer, and editor for a number of organisations such as the United Nations, the Carnegie Endowment, the Catholic Relief Services, and the Rockefeller and Ford Foundations. When I met him, his assignment was to edit the

South Africa Update, which consisted of five books on the critical years that led to the end of apartheid. He had been the senior writer of *South Africa: Time Running Out*, which was an acclaimed two-year study on US policy towards South Africa.

When John and I first met at the Ford Foundation offices opposite the United Nations Headquarters on First Avenue and 43rd Street, he was frustrated by his inability to identify a single black South African economist who could contribute to the update. For a moment I wasn't sure that I understood what he was talking about. I processed his frustration in my mind and wondered where he was looking. I responded by saying that he was looking at one. He could not believe me; his facial expression said it all. As a university professor who taught many white undergraduates and graduate students, I had ample experiences watching and interpreting white facial expressions of disbelief. John slowly came to believe his eyes, I think. But proof was still to come. In order to give him some assurance, which he obviously wanted, I proposed that the piece he wanted written could be co-authored by Moeletsi Mbeki, who was then working as a journalist for *The Herald* newspaper in Harare, and myself. Moeletsi was on the ground and based in one of the frontline states of the struggle and I was in Hoboken which was very close to New York City with its well-resourced libraries where I could conduct the necessary research. He was comfortable with this approach and the division of labour.

Little did I realise that I would spend the better part of eight months in the United Nations' Dag Hammarskjold Library working on the assignment John had given us. This library was dedicated to serving the information needs of United Nations Member States' delegates and their secretarial staff, but because I was working on a Ford Foundation project, I was granted access to the library and other United Nations facilities, including its cafeteria. This meant I did not have to leave the building in search of something to eat during my lunchbreak. A brief history about this library is valuable. It was originally called the United Nations Library and later the United Nations International Library. In the late 1950s, the Ford Foundation gave the United Nations a grant to build the new library. Dr Dag Hammarskjold was instrumental in securing this grant. He was an economist, author, and Swedish diplomate. Unfortunately, he was killed on the 17th of September 1961 when he was on a peace mission to Rhodesia to negotiate a ceasefire between Moise Kapenda, leader of the Katanga Province of the Democratic Republic of the Congo (DRC), and Patrice Lumumba, who was the national leader of the DRC. Hammarskjold's plane was shot down in Zambia's air space. The new library in the United Nations building was dedicated on the 16th of November 1961, shortly after his death and named after him. To this day, conspiracy theories abound about who was responsible for the downing of his plane.

The fact that I was conducting research for the Ford Foundation allowed me unfettered access to this valuable repository of international information. The product of this research is reflected in the piece 'Economic Rivalry and Interdependence in Southern Africa' in the volume titled *Update South Africa: Time Running Out – Changing Fortunes: War, Diplomacy, and Economics in Southern Africa*. This book was co-published by the Ford Foundation and the Foreign Policy Association. The piece we wrote focused on the rival strategies pursued by the Southern African Development Co-ordinating Conference (SADCC) and South Africa's Constellation of Southern African States (CONSAS). The latter was to comprise four 'independent homelands' – Transkei, Venda, Bophuthatswana, and Ciskei. SADCC membership consisted of Angola, Botswana, Lesotho, Malawi, Mozambique, Swaziland, Tanzania, Zambia, Zimbabwe, and Namibia, which joined on the 1st of April 1990. The economic and political struggles between SADCC and South Africa had to do with transportation routes, trade patterns, investments, and migrant labour. These factors bound the rival groupings firmly together even as the black independent states preserved their real or sometimes nominal independence. These and other related issues were explored and analysed in our paper, which was very well received by the Foundation. I was pleasantly surprised when, a few months later, the foundation offered me an independent study grant to conduct further research on economic integration in Harare, Zimbabwe. I jumped at the opportunity. I was getting closer to home.

17

Zimbabwe

It was in our bedroom one morning that Joanna and I informed the children that we would be moving to Zimbabwe. They had lots of questions, of course. Though we had often spoken with them about the possibility of such a move, the reality of it must have been quite unsettling. What was foremost in my mind was that Zimbabwe was an important frontline state. From a political engagement point of view, Joanna and I had already spent a great deal of time working on liberation issues to do with South Africa and Zimbabwe. And now, after independence, it was a politically friendly environment that had taken the position of trying to help liberate South Africa, and that was critical for me. In addition, of course, the prospect of moving there was exciting because it was so close to home.

The Ford Foundation grant provided us with the financial resources we needed to relocate to Zimbabwe. The only obstacle to moving there was getting a residence permit. But we had had many Zimbabwean friends in New York, and several of them had returned to Zimbabwe in the mid-1980s, so now we had people who were officials in that country who could assist us, and we turned to them for help. Notably, it was through the intervention of our family friend, Nathan Shamuyarira, Zimbabwe's first foreign minister, that we were able to quickly settle in Zimbabwe. We finally secured the permit with help from the University of Zimbabwe, which sponsored me.

I had no doubts about us moving to Zimbabwe. It was clear that we could continue to fight from there to get home to South Africa. Joanna seemed quite resolute as well. However, one challenge as a family, I clearly recall, was that Mandla was not keen on coming. He was thirteen, just entering his teenage years, and didn't want to leave his friends in New York and New Jersey. I felt (incorrectly, as it turned out) that he would eventually come round. What I was concerned about was that his schooling would be badly affected, though we would do our best to help him settle into a new school.

The next question was where we were going to stay. The way this question was resolved was fortuitous, to say the least. Our friends Moeletsi Mbeki and Miriam Patsanza had been living in Harare; some months earlier, Moeletsi had received a Niemann Fellowship from Harvard University to study journalism there. He and Miriam were preparing to leave for Cambridge, Massachusetts, and when they learned that we were coming to Zimbabwe, Miriam graciously offered her house in Marlborough, a suburb in Harare, for us to stay in while they were away. So it was that the question of where we would land, at least, was resolved.

Now the only issue became the logistics of getting our belongings across the Atlantic Ocean and down to Zimbabwe. Our things would take some months to come by ship, so when we arrived, we only had a few suitcases with us. Joanna immediately began sorting out our daily life there, and the children started getting to know the neighbourhood. Thenjiwe learned to climb the guava tree we shared with our neighbor, and we would often find her sitting in its branches, eating the fruit happily with the children from next door. The car we had was a Citroen and it would only start with a push. Joanna or I would have to push the car with one of the children, and the other child would have to steer and attempt to start it. When it started, Joanna or I would jump in and take over. It was an amusing daily ordeal in hindsight. We stayed in that house for some months before moving to Greendale and subsequently to Selous Street in Highlands.

The children were both enrolled in schools quite quickly, Mandla at St George's College and Thenjiwe at Chisipite Junior School. After living in New Jersey and New York, it was a change of pace for all of us. The city of Harare was much smaller and slower, and the children had more space to roam and play. But despite the change in pace, I was working harder than I had worked in the US. I was driven now to make change in South Africa from this base in Zimbabwe, and interestingly, because I knew so many people there, it was somehow less stressful than the life we were living in the US. It felt as if we were in a very supportive environment and part of a community, and life was a lot gentler there than in the US.

Being so close to South Africa now, we were able to see my family. We decided that Joanna should be the first one to visit. She went first, in April 1989, to pick up the car we had bought, and stayed with my brother, Stan, and his wife, Ruby, in Soweto. We had bought a Peugeot, which was shipped from France to Durban. She went to Durban first, picked it up, and drove it back to Johannesburg, and for a day or so she stayed in a hotel in Hillbrow. My brother, his wife, their daughter, Phindi, and young grandchild, Noluthando, came to visit her. She then spent a few days with Stan and Ruby at their home in Pimville, Soweto. She also did some shopping for things we couldn't get in Harare and returned.

Mandla was the next to visit in December of 1989 and also stayed with Stan and Ruby in Pimville. We were happy that he saw not only Stan and Ruby and their children but the whole extended family. Mandla also had the experience of slaughtering a sheep as a thank offering to welcome him. Everybody was there, all the relatives, and he had a good time.

But mostly, Mandla was not happy living in Zimbabwe at that time. The change was too drastic for him. He longed for his life as a young person in New York City. He wanted to go back and finish his high-schooling there, and eventually we agreed to his wishes. This was not an easy decision for us, but we made it hoping that it would be the best for him.

~

In mid-1989, I was recruited by Bax Nomvete, a South African who was the Secretary General of the Preferential Trade Area for Eastern and Southern African States (PTA), which is now called the Common Market for Eastern and Southern Africa (COMESA), based in Lusaka, Zambia. I joined the PTA as a private sector development specialist, seconded by the United Nations Development Agency (UNDP) office in New York.

My assignment was to find out why trade among PTA member states was a meagre 4% and the remaining 96%

was with European countries, mostly former colonisers. This project was commissioned by the Sixth Session of the General Assembly of the PTA Federation of Chambers of Commerce and Industry (PTA/FCCI) held in Nairobi, Kenya in November 1989. The PTA/FCCI had thirty members, and its programmes for upgrading the capabilities of its members' enterprises in agriculture, industry, trade, transport, communications, and the monetary sectors were adopted by its General Assembly held in Nairobi. The General Assembly recommended that the PTA/FCCI launch a comprehensive programme for the identification and development of local enterprises in the PTA region. To this end, it directed that an Emergency Operational Plan be launched. It was in compliance with this directive that the PTA Secretariat recruited me to lead this project with finance from the UNDP.

The prospect of making changes made me work harder than ever and with extreme focus. Not that I thought things would change overnight, but I knew there would be a difference now that I was working from a frontline state. I had to immerse myself in work, as the job I was given at the PTA was quite daunting. Thus I don't have many memories of our life in Zimbabwe aside from my work.

Working for the PTA, I was constantly on the move, visiting chambers of commerce and industry in neighbouring countries. I travelled almost every week. For a while, I even worked out of Lusaka, from where I visited PTA member states and conducted research while the family remained in Harare. Something I recall from those flights was the feeling I used to get in the plane when we were coming down to land at Harare International Airport. It was a very peaceful feeling; I would feel very calm and relaxed. I knew I was coming to a place where I didn't have to hustle anybody, and nobody would hassle me. It is a feeling I have never forgotten, even though many years have passed since then.

~

At the beginning of the new decade, in early 1990, Joanna returned for a month or so the US to defend her doctoral dissertation. She stayed in our old house in Hoboken, which was still in the process of being sold. Thenji had made friends quite quickly, so even though it was a challenging experience to be a solo parent again, I had support and managed quite well. It was mostly a relaxed time for the three of us.

Something I remember well from that time was how one afternoon – it must have been late January or early February in 1990 – Joanna telephoned from Hoboken. She had called to speak about Mandela's imminent release and the implications of this momentous event for our family. We were both very excited, and I urged her to hurry up and finish her work and come home so that we could start planning our first visit to South Africa. We didn't know when we would be able to go home for good, but we knew that things were changing, quickly and substantially.

A month after Mandela was released, on the 11th of February 1990, Namibia declared independence. This too was a momentous moment, and I was determined to be at the inauguration of Sam Nujoma, whom I had met in Cairo in 1961. It felt particularly important for me to be there because Theo-Ben Gurirab, who was at the UN in New York for many years and had been a family friend since 1963, was to become the first foreign minister. There were many other Namibians whom I knew and wanted to celebrate with. I had a network there, many of whom I had worked with over the years, and I flew to Windhoek a day or so ahead of the inauguration. The inauguration was a huge event on the parliament grounds, where, among other things, they unveiled the new Namibian flag. I marveled at seeing some of my old friends becoming ministers and being put in other powerful positions and, of course, at witnessing Sam Nujoma being inaugurated as president. Thinking back on it, this event gave me a lot of strength and reassurance. White South Africans had been given the mandate by the League of Nations at the end of the First World War to run what they called South West Africa. They had ruled for more than seventy years. Now, as the Namibians finally declared independence, it was clear that other changes were on the horizon.

18

The Way Home

Joanna and I realised that the time was drawing near when we would able to go home. Even though she had grown up in Maine, this was how we spoke about it together: *we would be going home.* It was a time of exiles returning, and we knew – I knew – that before long I would be one of them. It occurred to Joanna and me that we would need to do a sort of reconnaissance mission to start setting up our new life in South Africa. As things stood, there were too many uncertainties awaiting us. So, at the time that I went to Namibia, Joanna, Mandla, and Thenjiwe came to South Africa with the idea that Joanna would see if she could get a sense of where we might live, what schools Thenji would go to – in short, how we would be able to make it work.

In the meantime, my work continued, and perhaps to take my mind off our imminent return, I began work on the PTA/FCCI project with great focus. I spent the months of April and May consulting and having discussions with the PTA Secretary General and directors of different sectoral departments, from whom I solicited ideas to develop an approach and method for capturing critical data on the location of each enterprise, the nature of its business, its export potential, its size and capitalisation, as well as the constraints it faced in the marketplace internally and across the border. In May and June, I spent five weeks in Mauritius, where I successfully tested the method, then in Swaziland where it was first implemented. There, too, it worked quite well.

All the work done from the beginning of April until the end of June was funded from the meagre financial resources of the PTA Secretariat. By the end of June, these funds were depleted, so additional funds were solicited from various international organisations. The UNDP OPS office in New York responded with a five-month grant for the period 1 August to 31 December 1990. Between these two dates, I travelled on field visits to Zimbabwe, Lesotho, Malawi, the Comoros, Mozambique, and Angola collecting data. During one of these visits, the Secretary General of the PTA requested that I attend the PTA/FCCI General Assembly in Harare in August, the PTA trade fair in Mauritius in October, and finally a PTA summit in Swaziland, which he was planning to stage in November.

For the PTA summit, I was tasked by the organisation's secretary general with negotiating for it to be held in Swaziland. This mission was a secret between the two of us, and as for the negotiations involved, I was on my own. He was not to be seen as having anything to do with it because he was a South African and South Africa was not a member of the PTA. For him to be seen organising a summit so close to South Africa and then inviting the leadership of the ANC to attend would have resulted in an unpleasant political fallout. I accepted this risky assignment, even though I too was a South African and still a political exile. I did it even though I was being put at obvious risk. If I were able to convince the Swaziland government to host the summit, the PTA would surface and lend its full support. If I failed, I would have been personally responsible for this failure, and the secretary general of the PTA would have distanced himself from the initiative.

Through the intervention of a prominent member of the Swazi Upper House, the Senate, I managed to secure a meeting with the Prime Minister, the Honourable Obed Dlamini. My surname, Nkosi, is generally associated with two lineages. One is Dlangamandla and the other is Dlamini. The origins of the former can be traced back to the northeast part of KwaZulu Natal; the latter clan left Zululand due to King Shaka's ambition to build a large and powerful Zulu kingdom. The Dlaminis seem to have been those Zulus who distanced themselves from King Shaka's forays and fled into what is now called eSwatini (formerly Swaziland).

The Dlangamandlas are more numerous, tend to be quite bellicose, and think of themselves as senior to the Dlaminis, who are less numerous and said to be generally very gentle, humble, and peaceful. When I introduced myself to the Prime Minister, he immediately wanted to know whether I was a Dlamini. I replied that I belonged to the Dlangamandla clan and that the Dlaminis were our smaller relatives. He burst out laughing, and his laugh was contagious. I also couldn't help laughing. This broke the ice, and we could now talk like clansmen. He accepted my proposal. He had been in the process of getting in touch with the secretary general of the PTA. The Ninth PTA Summit and the Sixteenth Council of Ministers' meetings started on the 15th of November, 1990 in Swaziland, with the ANC leadership in attendance. I left Swaziland on that day bound for Angola. Bax was very pleased. His plan of sending me out on a limb had paid off.

The background of the plan to host the Summit in Swaziland had to do with some concerns of the ANC's Department of International Affairs in Lusaka during the 1980s. The question raised at the summit was: What was the role of black business during the struggle for liberation and what would its role be after that? The Department of International Affairs had also facilitated the meetings between NAFCOC and the PTA/FCCI in addition to consultations between the ANC and NAFCOC. These meetings had essentially two objectives. First, they were to inform NAFCOC, particularly the leadership of black business in South Africa, about the role that indigenous businesses were expected to play in contributing to the development of their country. Second, they were intended to expose NAFCOC to the types of problems black businesses would face once democracy had been achieved.

Bax Nomvete invited and hosted the leadership of both NAFCOC and their counterparts, the white officials of the South African Chambers of Commerce and Industry of South Africa (SACCI), for meetings. The first meeting was held in Lusaka and the second one in Harare. Bax and I were curious about the imminent political transition in South Africa and wondered if and how these two bodies might work together in a democratic South Africa. Having met each delegation separately on both visits, what was obvious to us was that the white chamber was far more developed than the black chamber, which had obviously been disadvantaged for historical reasons. The outcomes of these two meetings left us feeling quite frustrated, angry, and sad.

My experiences in visiting the PTA/FCCI Chambers of Commerce and Industry exacerbated my feelings about NAFCOC's weakness. In terms of its development, NAFCOC was way behind the Mauritian and Zimbabwean Chambers of Commerce and Industry, which stood out from the rest in the PTA/FCCI. The Mauritius Chamber of Commerce was the most developed, efficient, and effective, and I would claim that it could easily have held its own even when compared with the white SACCI in South Africa at that time.

My final report was submitted to the New York office of the UNDP just before the 31st of December 1990 and was well received, to the extent that I was offered to head up the UNDP office in Dar es Salaam, Tanzania. I graciously declined. Harare was a stone's throw from Johannesburg; to move to Dar es Salaam would take me away from where I was heading.

Towards the end of my short tenure at the PTA/FCCI, I was approached by a bright young Zimbabwean woman, Mercy Zinyoma, a director-designate of the Indigenous Business Development Council (IBDC). She was a banker and had been sent by her black business colleagues to find me. She tracked me down in Mbabane, Swaziland and said that she had been sent to ask me to help advise the IBDC in organising a national conference of black indigenous businesses in Zimbabwe. Mercy and her colleagues were planning to invite as many black businesspersons as they could from all over the country's nine provinces. The purpose of this conference was to interrogate the reasons why black businesses in Zimbabwe were still on the margins of the economy after a decade of independence. Their organisational efforts, which included consultations and meetings with black businesses and professional people, had reached a stage where they were planning to meet with the President of the country, Robert Mugabe, to present their findings, grievances, and ideas. I agreed to help them organise a national conference of small businesspeople, but because I was a South African and not a citizen of Zimbabwe, I declined to be part of the delegation that met with the president.

Joanna and I were asked to get involved in organising and launching the Indigenous Business Development Council

(IBDC).[26] We agreed and took on very active roles in organising and arranging the launch. The keynote speech of the launch was written by Tony Alile, my close friend and former MBA colleague, who was then Head of the Nigerian Stock Exchange. He could not come himself but sent a senior researcher to deliver the address. It was exactly what I had asked him to write. His contribution was a resounding success and reflected Tony's extensive experience in developing small and medium-sized black businesses, both in the state of New Jersey in the US and in Nigeria. Hearing what big brother Nigeria was succeeding in doing had a great impact on little brother Zimbabwe. The speech was very well received and helped to launch the IBDC successfully.

Once my PTA/FCCI assignment was over, I was recruited to join the African Capacity Foundation (ACBF) by the late Jonathan Frimpong-Ansah, the first Executive Director of the ACBF. The founding of this organisation was preceded by extensive discussions, consultations, and negotiations among officials of the World Bank, the International Monetary Fund (IMF), the UNDP, the African Development Bank (AfDB), International Aid Organisations, and a few foundations and numerous other experts in economics, finance, and development. ACBF was established in 1991 in response to the desperate need for human and institutional

---

26 The IBDC was established in December 1990. Its founding members included Chemist Siziba, who was its chairperson; Strive Masiyiwa, who was secretary general; John Mapondera; and others. They argued that promoting black small and medium-sized businesses was critical for growing the economy, creating job opportunities, and improving the lives of Zimbabweans. IBDC's first demand was that government should remove all laws and procedures that hindered black businesses. Second was to legislate reforms that would allow state resources to be allocated to black businesses on preferential terms. Third was to persuade financial institutions to extend loans to black businesses at interest rates which were below prevailing market interest rates. Other demands included distributing land in a way that would help build a strong black commercial class in the agricultural sector and anti-trust laws that would limit the power of white monopoly capital. By 1994, the IBDC's membership stood at 8 000 people. It received funds from the government, Barclays Bank, and the World Council of Churches' Development Fund.

capacity in the areas of policy research and development on the African continent.[27]

The ACBF offices were in the Cabbs Building on Jason Moyo Street in Harare. I facilitated the submission of its credentials and secured authorisation for it to operate in the country through the good offices of Nathan Shamuyarira, whom I had first met in 1966 at a New York University conference on Southern Rhodesia. I was the first person to be employed by the ACBF as a consultant. Dr Jonathan Frimpong-Ansah and I were responsible for setting up the office. Frimpong-Ansah was in charge of executive tasks while I performed the administrative work and later developed the research agenda with him. Our first research initiative led us to two strategic public institutions that we thought were critical for Zimbabwe's economic development. These were the Zimbabwe Electricity Supply Association (ZESA) and the Zimbabwe Iron and Steel Corporation (ZISCO). Both were indispensable for the country's industrial and economic development. However, I had barely started working on how to approach the research to be undertaken and propose the method I would use to Dr Frimpong-Ansah when I received an offer from NAFCOC in South Africa to take up a position as the director of its recently built Management and Leadership Development Centre (MLDC) in Soshanguve, a township just north of Pretoria.

~

This offer was initially mooted when a NAFCOC delegation, led by Sam Motsuenyane, attended the launch of the IBDC. But then a formal letter was sent to me to make the offer official. My family had moved to Zimbabwe with the intent of going back home when an opportunity was available, and this was that opportunity. I felt some sadness at giving up a chance to contribute to the development of Zimbabwe, the country that had been a safe haven

---

27 The late Dunstan Wei, then a senior advisor to Edward Kim Jaycox, the Vice President of the Africa Region of the World Bank, summarised the objectives of the organisation as follows: 'to produce on a long-term basis a critical mass of professional Africans in policy analysis and development management; ensure effective utilisation of existing trained and skilled man-power; and strengthen, rehabilitate existing institutions or establish new ones but where possible focus on strengthening existing ones'.

for me and my family and had also contributed immensely to the struggle against apartheid. But returning home after thirty-one years of exile was paramount. The opportunity to contribute to the rebuilding of South Africa, by helping an organisation like NAFCOC, was a wonderful opportunity for me. Since the early 1960s, I had known that the way in which I wanted to contribute to the development of the African continent was in the economic and business domain, rather than the political. That was what had motivated my switch from Columbia to the business school at NYU; that was what had driven me as I worked on my dissertation and as a teacher, expanding my knowledge and expertise and sharing it with students. Now there would be an opportunity to work with a federation of chambers whose members comprised shop owners, taxi drivers, hawkers, small-scale farmers, and small industrialists. It was a weak organisation that needed help. I was elated to be joining them and to be coming home at last.

~

It was in January in the year of 1991 that I finally returned to South Africa after an absence of more than thirty years. I have to make a strange admission, however. Joanna has told me this date, but I do not recall having made this first journey at all. The memory of returning to South Africa that I do have, and which I will describe, was in fact my second trip home. Here's what Joanna has described about the first trip. She says that she, Thenjiwe, and I took a flight from Harare to Johannesburg. My brother, Stanley, met us at the airport and took us back to their house in Bramley. We apparently went into Johannesburg's city centre and walked around, looking at how much the city had changed. It was a short trip, less than a week, which, Joanna says, we used primarily to reconnect with family. We then returned to Harare and spent a few weeks finalising our preparations to leave. I am not clear about why the first time I went back has completely faded from memory. Perhaps the overwhelming emotions at returning after being away for so long made it difficult for my mind to hold on to that experience.

My second trip to South Africa in November 1991 is the one I do remember. It was not in fact a trip; I was returning to stay.

When I flew out of Harare International Airport bound for Jan Smuts International Airport in Johannesburg, I was going to begin a new life in my old home. Joanna and Thenji had stayed behind for a few months to finish packing up the house. I remember the flight, and come to think of it, my memories from that flight must have mingled over time with the memories of the first flight, because I recall sitting at the window, looking out and thinking about how someone had told me I wouldn't recognise Johannesburg because of the extensive infrastructure changes, the highways, and so on. I was looking to see whether those things really existed. And I did see them, and I realised how much Johannesburg had indeed changed. I also remember that Jan Smuts Airport, as it was called then, was much larger and busier than the Harare Airport, or any of the other airports in the African countries I had worked in during my stint with the PTA.

Going through immigration and customs control had always been an anxious experience for me. Even when I had a US passport and was legally travelling in and out of the US, I would feel my anxiety rising when going through immigration. My experience as a stateless person had made me susceptible to it. But now I had the necessary documents that allowed exiles back into the country, and I was dealing with more welcoming immigration officers, who were my country people. I sailed through without any hassles.

My brother, Stanley, was waiting for me and greeted me with great jubilation. We hugged and laughed before heading out of the airport building to find his car. I recall looking around at the buildings and the sky. We drove in his car to Bramley where he and his family lived. I was a little afraid at the speed at which we and the other cars were driving, tearing down the dual-carriage highways which were completely new to me in this context. I had gotten used to smaller single lane roads and fewer cars on Enterprise Road, the main road in Harare, and other smaller roads in the region. Stanley was amused and laughed as he reassured me that the speed he and the other drivers were going was normal.

It was almost overwhelming to get to his house, which was going to be the temporary home for me, Joanna, and Thenji, who were to follow me later. It was a four-bedroom house with a sizeable garden and swimming pool. He was living there with Ruby, his daughter, Phindi, and her small children, Noluthando and Lungile. It would be a little tight, but the children would all sleep together and we would make it work until we found our own house. I slept well that night.

The next morning, I asked Stanley to take me to see a few places that I was curious about, and he was very keen to show me around. The first place I wanted to visit was the graves of our parents. I knew they were both buried in the Croesus Cemetery in Newclare just to the south of the city centre. I recall driving through the suburbs until we reached the M1 highway, and then heading south, my face pressed to the window, soaking in impressions of a world that was at once deeply familiar and entirely strange.

Croesus Cemetery is ringed by mine dumps and split in two by a large road. Stanley parked his car and we got out and walked in together. I remember the day as being clear and cloudless. We did not speak much. We had gone to pay homage and show our respect to our parents. A rich, sad silence had fallen between us. We found my father's grave first. I stood at the head of it and read the name on the headstone. I had spoken to my father on the phone a few times, but I had not seen him since I'd escaped into exile some thirty years before. Stan waited for me, and then he pointed to my mother's grave next to my father's. My sister Beauty's child, Khetiwe, had died in childhood and was buried with my mother. Again, we simply stood and looked. Being there was a heavy experience I cannot put into words. Before we left, we went around looking at the tombstones of other relatives and neighbours from the ENT whom we remembered. My brother and I felt thankful to our ancestors and to our parents that we had survived.

Postscript

The excitement of coming home in 1991 was coupled with uncertainty, anxiety, and trepidation about what was going to happen next. I had returned to a country that was different in so many ways from the one I had left in 1960. From the moment I arrived, I began the complex process of reconnecting with the country, with the people I'd known, and with the spaces I used to know. It was a difficult process of reorientating myself within what was, in large part, a new landscape.

During those first days of arriving back and staying at Stanley's house, I wanted to see all the old sights. I wanted to see the area where our neighbourhood, George Goch, used to be, and Stanley was more than happy to show me around.

What was home where I had grown up had been razed to the ground after the area was declared a place for whites only. Our house, which had been situated several hundreds of metres from the main entrance to the Eastern Native Township, had been demolished when all the African residents of the township had been removed by the apartheid government following the enactment of the *Native (Urban Areas) Act* of 1923. This township was the last of the old 'native locations' in Johannesburg to be removed, following the recommendation of a government committee in October 1962.

In an article in *Revue d'Histoire Contemporaine de l'Afrique*,[28] historian Alan Gregory Cobley says that ENT was re-designated for African hostel accommodation only, while the permanent residents were moved and relocated to parts of what was referred to as the South Western Townships, or Soweto. The townships in Soweto were given euphemistic names indicating the ethnicity of their new residents. This was in keeping with the grand design of separate development in the urban areas that blacks were deposited in once they were moved out of white areas. Some

---

28 '"The Vuka Africa" Store: African shopkeepers and urban cultural practices in South Africa under segregation and apartheid, 1880s–1960s', *Revue d'Histoire Contemporaine de l'Afrique*, no. 2, 66–68 (2021).

examples of these names are Emdeni, which is isiZulu; Molapo, which is Sesotho; Senaoane, also Sotho; and Chiawelo, which is Xitsonga. Once these zones were full, they built what were referred to as extensions.

Nothing was left of the Dutch Reformed Church in George Goch which was my father's parish and home, and the three other churches around it, the Anglican, Methodist, and Coloureds' Church (called Broer en Sister Kerk), were all gone. All that remained of the ENT was an old, huge, drab African men's hostel surrounded by a massive number of informal shacks, a dilapidated stadium with broken seats and no roof, and a soccer field circumscribed by a running track, both overgrown with tall grass and weeds. This is what we saw when Joanna, Mrs Tuge, and on another occasion Sis Adelaide Tambo and I went to see what was left of where we had grown up. What had replaced the township and other building structures were a few businesses and on- and off-ramps linking the area via the M1 highway to the Central Business District of Johannesburg.

There was no evidence left to show that this area was once a thriving black community which produced the likes of John Mavimbela, one of the founders of the Black Chamber of Commerce in Soweto in the early 1950s, a precursor to NAFCOC; his wife, Julia Mavimbela, who started the Kindergarten Class at the Albert Street Methodist School where I started my schooling; Jacob Moeketsi, the pianist of the popular jazz band called the Merry Black Birds and of other bands, who was also the elder brother of Jeremiah 'Kippie' Morolong Moeketsi, the famous musician and renowned alto saxophonist; General Jabulani Duze, a jazz guitarist, singer of indigenous music, and television star; and Adelaide Tshukudu (later Mrs O. R. Tambo), a respected nursing sister at the Johannesburg General Hospital. There are numerous other notable individuals who were born and lived in the ENT of George Goch. By the time I came back home most had died and some had moved or simply disappeared, like my closest friend Shadrack 'Shada' Mabuza, with whom I had started the Pan Africanist Congress (PAC) branch in George Goch in 1958.

Postscript

On the same day, we went to Vicars Road where our old house once stood. Then Stanley took me to George Goch Station and its surrounds. I remember that I specifically wanted to see a man by the name of Desai, an Indian tailor who had a shop just a few metres from the station. As a young man, I used to stop there every afternoon to have a chat with him about all sorts of things. He was no longer alive, but we found his relatives there. It was his son who told us that after I had disappeared, the police had harassed his father because they thought he knew where I was.

I had lost contact with many other friends, acquaintances, and political comrades. One of them, Cyprian Mahlaba, who was my best friend at the Albert Street Methodist Church Primary School, was still around, employed and engaged in other pursuits. Shadrack Mabuza, whom I grew up with in George Goch, had disappeared from the face of the earth without a trace. His sister, Connie Nkosi, had searched far and wide for him and even visited numerous morgues in and around Johannesburg, but nothing came of it. He has never been found. Another old friend of Shadrack's and mine, Vela Mabuza, I managed to track down in one of Soweto's neighborhoods where he owned and operated a hardware store. I visited his shop twice, but he would not come out of his back office to meet me for reasons I cannot fathom. Both Vela and Shadrack were the two friends and comrades who helped me and travelled with me distributing leaflets on the Witwatersrand on the Saturday evening and Sunday morning before the fateful day of Monday the 21st of March 1960.

What dawned on me in those early days of being back, and what became clearer as time passed, was that it was going to take a while for me to understand this new landscape and my place in it. For example, I had never heard of Soshanguve, where NAFOC was located and where I would be working, nor did I know where it was. It turned out that it was a township beyond Pretoria and had been established after I had gone into exile. Soshanguve was named after the ethnic groups and languages that were spoken in that area, Sotho, Tsonga, Nguni, and Venda, and people were divided according to their groups when they were resettled there.

I had left the country a young single man and was now returning married and with two children. During the 1990s and even after, our interracial family attracted a lot of attention and raised eyebrows among both black and white people in the United States and at home in South Africa. Generally, here at home, black people would discretely take a quick glance at us then look away without any expression of shock, disapproval, or hate. If anything, they seemed surprised because my spouse and I looked older, as if the question was, how had this happened in South Africa? White people generally tended to stare at us without blinking. And in many instances, they looked flabbergasted and sometimes quite hateful. We would often catch a few making remarks of one sort or another about us. We did not bother about these remarks: we had survived this strange curiosity in the US, and we would survive it here.

Post-Apartheid South Africa was now in the throes of change, hopefully for the better. But the emergence of a new society and political order was shrouded in the tumultuous and, in many cases, deadly contestations that were taking place during the transition from apartheid to democracy. The struggles were fought overtly and covertly for political, economic, and social control by both the outgoing regime and the liberation movement that was on its way to power. In many instances, the consequences of these contestations were violent and deadly. For any exile trying to find his or her place in the midst of such turmoil was extremely complicated. But I was driven to do so – to find my place and to understand in order to be able to contribute to uplifting and empowering our people. The story of the last thirty years since 1991, which I have been writing about since finishing this book, has been the story of how I tried to actualise that lofty desire. South Africa is a country still fraught with unresolved challenges inherited from colonial rule and apartheid, and the way in which the current political leadership has addressed, or failed to address, these challenges is disheartening. This is an important story, but one for another time, and I will now put this postscript aside and get back to writing that story. I am 89 years old, and although I have reached an advanced age, I am healthy, energetic, and, most of all, still determined to contribute to building economic and social justice in South Africa.

Acknowledgements

It was in July 2014, in Dar es Salaam, that I first seriously considered turning certain ideas I had for a story about my years in exile – ideas that had been floating around in my head for years – into a book. At a dialogue there, organised by the *Mandela Institute for Development Studies*, I gave a talk on pan-African solidarity and was afterwards approached by several people who urged me to write my story. To all those people, whose names I do not recall, I give my thanks for that all-important nudge.

Then my thanks to all my family members and friends who regularly asked me when I would be finished with the manuscript. The late Professor Selma Browde was perhaps the most persistent of the lot. Also keenly interested, and prodding, were Amy and Geoff Bass, dear friends from the US. My great thanks too to Kassahun Checole, president and publisher of *Africa World Press*, who has been a supporter of this project throughout.

I could not have asked for more helpful and constructive critics than Dr Joanna Nkosi, my life partner, and our daughter Thenjiwe Niki Nkosi and her husband Daniel Browde. The arrangement and flow of the narrative were enhanced by all three. Our son Mandla in Boston, far from the coalface, might not realise how much he contributed to the development of this book by helping me keep mind and body aligned. We could always count on him. Our granddaughter, Lumuka, took an interest in reading parts of the draft and gave me inspiration to continue.

I am indebted to Professor Tshilidzi Marwala, former Vice-Chancellor of the University of Johannesburg and now Rector of the United Nations University and Under-Secretary-General of the United Nations, for urging me to write this story. Professor Marwala's interest has been taken up by Professor Letlhokwa George Mpedi, the current Vice-Chancellor and Principal of the University of Johannesburg. I am especially grateful to have received this embrace and encouragement from a university that is located in the city where I grew up, and to which I am consequently emotionally attached.

The manager of UJ Press, Wikus van Zyl, was accommodating and helpful in navigating the process from manuscript review all the way through to printing. He was always professional and easy to work with. The copy editor, David Oldert, did his job with care and seriousness. To him, and to everyone else who helped me complete this part of my story, thank you.

www.ingramcontent.com/pod-product-compliance
Lightning Source LLC
Chambersburg PA
CBHW070835160426
43192CB00012B/2201